Job Creation
and Destruction

Steven J. Davis

John C. Haltiwanger

Scott Schuh

The MIT Press
Cambridge, Massachusetts
London, England

This book was set in Palatino by Windfall Software using ZzT$_E$X and was printed and bound in the United States of America.

Library of Congress Cataloging-in-Publication Data

Davis, Steven J.
  Job creation and destruction / by Steven J. Davis, John C.
  Haltiwanger, Scott Schuh.
      p.   cm.
  Includes bibliographical references (p.) and index.
  ISBN 0-262-04152-9 (hard : alk. paper)
  1. Job creation—United States. 2. Business cycles—United
States. 3. Occupational mobility—United States. 4. Labor market—
United States. 5. Business enterprises—Longitudinal studies—
United States. I. Haltiwanger, John C. II. Schuh, Scott.
HD5717.5.U6D38   1996
331.12'0973—dc20   95-46260
                                                            CIP

Dedicated to Frank, Charlene, Rita, Jeanne, and Susan.

Contents

Tables

Figures

Foreword

Official statistics—the facts that frame the nation's discourse and inform the policies and practices it adopts—depend on the quality of the research and analysis that guide their creation and development. *Job Creation and Destruction* by Steve Davis, John Haltiwanger, and Scott Schuh is an example of the kind of research and analysis that the U.S. Bureau of the Census hoped to encourage when it supported development of the Longitudinal Research Database (LRD) and the Center for Economic Studies (Center).

The Center maintains and develops the database from information collected from business establishments by surveys and censuses conducted by the Census Bureau. It also administers programs that allow outstanding scholars from academia and government to use these microdata in an environment that ensures that the data remain confidential. *Job Creation and Destruction* was written by Davis, Haltiwanger, and Schuh while they were research associates at the Center.

This is a detailed and original look at the process of job creation and destruction. The authors have created important new time series for job creation, job destruction, and total job reallocation—gross job flow statistics—in U.S. manufacturing industries from 1972 through 1988. The data series will be of great use to researchers and analysts for many years and, we hope, the beginning of a new product line for the Census Bureau. For now, the annual and quarterly statistics that Davis, Haltiwanger, and Schuh developed for the book are available directly from the Center.

But the authors do much more than simply develop new data series. They also provide us with important methodological tools and a measurement framework that helps fill a major gap in literature dealing with reallocation of workers in a market economy—the demand or job side of the labor market. While most studies examine the worker's side of the reallocation process, these authors focus on the establishments where workers are employed. This enables them to describe in great detail the characteristics of establishments

that create and destroy jobs. With this approach, they are able to describe the relationships between job creation and destruction and establishment characteristics such as size, industry, geographical location, capital intensity, age, extent of international competition, productivity performance, and level of wages.

The picture that emerges from this careful analysis is one of an incredibly dynamic economy in which restructuring and change are the rule, not the exception. Whether the economy is expanding or contracting, job flows are large, persistent, and highly concentrated. The book also presents evidence showing that the large-scale job destruction and creation characterizes virtually every sector of the U.S. economy and extends to other market economies.

This work has broad implications for economic research and policymaking in many areas. The issues dealt with are fundamental and cut across a wide variety of fields in both macro- and microeconomics. For example, the high rates of job destruction documented in virtually every sector of the economy argue strongly that workers need the flexibility to adapt to changes in the location and skill requirements of jobs. The authors also show that the job reallocation rate is countercyclical because job destruction exhibits greater cyclical variability than the job creation rate in the U.S. manufacturing sector. This fact runs counter to many business cycle theories. Perhaps most important from the perspective of policymaking, the authors document the importance of idiosyncratic factors in the determination of job creation and destruction. This means that easily observable factors such as industry, employer size, region, wages, and extent of foreign competition provide little in the way of systematic guidance about job creation and destruction. Thus, for example, knowing the industry to which an establishment belongs provides very little information about its job creation or destruction.

The work of Davis, Haltiwanger, and Schuh already is having a major impact on the development of official statistics and economic research at the Center and beyond. A large number of projects now under way around the world are developing longitudinal microdata panels for the purpose of creating job creation and destruction statistics. These statistics are being compared country by country and linked to a wide variety of data in large-scale efforts to understand how jobs are created and lost. A long list of research papers, both theoretical and empirical, have already been motivated by the material in this book.

An early version of this book inspired the call for further research on job creation and loss emanating from the G-7 Jobs Conference in Detroit, Michigan, in early 1994. These recommendations have spawned many studies and conferences by the Organization for Economic Co-operation and Develop-

ment (OECD) and its member countries. Included in these activities was a major international conference—The Effects of Technology and Innovation on Firm Performance and Employment—that took place in Washington, D.C., in May 1995. This conference brought together scholars, policymakers, and members of official statistical agencies to explore the usefulness of longitudinal microdata and to consider how they can be developed and accessed. The deliberations in this conference and many others throughout the world have resoundingly demonstrated the importance and usefulness of the data and analysis produced by the authors.

Job Creation and Destruction is an important new book, with information of critical importance to policymakers and to statistical programs trying to maintain up-to-date and vital statistics for the twenty-first century. We are hopeful that the Census Bureau will make these data products available in a timely and accessible form as part of our regular statistical programs. We are also hopeful that these analyses will soon be extended to the entire economy. To this end, the Census Bureau has begun a project to extend the LRD to the entire economy. This project, like the earlier one that spawned this book, represents successful collaboration with the academic community and the National Science Foundation, which originally provided funds for the development of the LRD and supports numerous research projects at the Center. The Census Bureau is extremely pleased to have been a part of this important new book.

Martha Farnsworth Riche   Lewis Alexander
Director   Chief Economist, Department of Commerce
Bureau of the Census   Economics and Statistics Administration

Robert H. McGuckin
Chief, Center for Economic Studies
Bureau of the Census

Acknowledgments

This book is the product of a long and ongoing research program at the Center for Economic Studies (CES) on the development and analysis of new measures of job creation and destruction. Over the course of the past five years, we have received help from many quarters in both our research and writing.

We thank Robert McGuckin, head of the CES, and his entire staff (past and present) for providing a stimulating research environment and for their assistance during this time. Bob McGuckin has been a constant source of support and encouragement over the course of this project. Special thanks also go to Robert Bechtold, Mark Doms, Tim Dunne, Kathy Friedman, Cyr Linonis, Jim Monahan, Al Nucci, Arnie Reznek, Ken Troske, and Rebecca Turner.

We also thank many other Census Bureau and Commerce Department employees (past and present) for support and assistance: Lewis Alexander, Jane Callen, Stacey Cole, Michael Darby, Everett Ehrlich, Easley Hoy, Paul London, Thomas Mesenbourg, Mark Plant, Ruth Runyan, and Charles Waite.

The final versions of the tables and figures for the book were produced by the staff of the Administrative and Publication Services Division at the Census Bureau. They have demonstrated considerable care, professionalism, and patience in working with us in the development of this book. We thank Linda Ambill, David Coontz, Bernadette Gayle, Gary Lauffer, Walter Odom, Neeland Queen, and Jan Sweeney for their substantial contribution to this book.

Numerous friends and colleagues read portions of the book in draft form and provided valuable criticism and suggestions. In addition to many of the persons listed above, we thank David Altig, Joseph Beaulieu, Olivier Blanchard, Danny Blanchflower, Ricardo Caballero, Robert Hall, Alec Levenson, Prakash Loungani, Gisele Marino, Bruce Meyer, Dale Mortensen, Ariel Pakes,

Richard Rogerson, Lew Solmon, Mahlon Straszheim, Steve Strongin, and Janice Weiss. In addition, we thank the participants in the many seminars and conferences at which this work has been presented for their input.

Without the continued support of the National Science Foundation over the last eight years, this project would not have been possible. Davis also thanks the University of Chicago Graduate School of Business. Haltiwanger also thanks the Census Bureau and American Statistical Association for support under their joint fellows program during the 1993–94 program year. Schuh thanks the Federal Reserve Board for providing access to the Census Bureau under contract with the CES.

We thank Laura Power, Catherine Buffington, Lucia Foster, Karen Kalat, and Peter Simon for providing excellent research assistance. Laura Power was the primary research assistant on this project during the period in which the establishment-level data were processed and tabulated to generate the gross job flow statistics.

We thank Francis Pierce for providing excellent editorial services. His assistance was especially helpful in developing a working draft of the book, which was circulated at the G-7 Jobs Summit in March 1994. We also thank Ron Goettler for constructing the index.

The authors are research associates of the Center for Economic Studies, where the work for this book was conducted. The analyses and conclusions set forth in this book are those of the authors and do not necessarily indicate concurrence by the Department of Commerce, Bureau of the Census, Center for Economic Studies, the Board of Governors of the Federal Reserve System, the Federal Reserve Banks, or other members of their staffs.

Introduction

Market-based economies undergo continual creation and destruction of jobs. Existing plants expand or contract, new plants start up, and old plants shut down. As we show in this study, large-scale job creation and destruction turn out to be pervasive among countries, regions, industries, and various types of plants and firms.

A Statistical Portrait of Job Creation and Destruction

Job creation and destruction at the level of individual plants reflect adjustments to the myriad economic events that buffet businesses and workers. As chronicled by journalists and business analysts, these events include the development of new products and production processes, the growth and decline of markets, competition from foreign and domestic rivals, negotiations between employers and labor organizations, corporate restructurings, extensions and denials of credit, regulatory and tax law changes, and changes in the cost or availability of labor and nonlabor inputs. This study develops a statistical portrait of the microeconomic adjustments to these events, as manifested in the creation and destruction of jobs. The study focuses on the U.S. manufacturing sector from 1972 to 1988.

The Impact on Workers

Much of the burden of reallocating jobs across regions, industries, and plants inevitably falls upon workers. The creation and destruction of jobs cause workers to switch employers and shuffle between employment and joblessness. In the process, some workers suffer long spells of unemployment or sharp declines in earnings; some retire early or temporarily leave the labor force to work at home or upgrade their skills; some change residence to secure a new

job, migrating short or long distances, often with considerable disruption in the lives of family and friends.[1]

Matching Workers and Jobs
Job-losing workers differ greatly in the bundles of skills and capabilities they bring to the labor market; likewise, new jobs differ greatly in the skill requirements they demand from workers. Consequently, the matching of displaced workers to new jobs is a complex, often time-consuming, task. The extent to which this matching and rematching process operates smoothly and efficiently determines, in large part, the difference between successful and unsuccessful economic performance.

The Connection between Job Reallocation and Worker Reallocation
Of course, much worker reallocation activity does not stem from the creation and destruction of jobs by businesses. Workers enter and exit the labor force for a variety of reasons related to health, schooling, child rearing, and retirement. Workers switch jobs for reasons related to career advancement, job satisfaction, and family relocation. These factors generate worker reallocation levels over and above those induced by the reallocation of job opportunities. As these remarks suggest, job reallocation and worker reallocation are distinct concepts. The two concepts are intimately related, however, because job reallocation is the driving force behind much of the reallocation activity undertaken by workers. We develop the connections between job reallocation and worker reallocation more fully in chapters 1, 2, and 6.

The Comparative Dearth of Knowledge about Job Reallocation
Although economists know a great deal about employment and worker reallocation, they know comparatively little about the creation, destruction, and reallocation of jobs. The U.S. Departments of Commerce and Labor regularly report statistics on employment levels for regions, industries, and the aggregate economy. Changes in these reported statistics provide estimates of *net* employment change—that is, job creation less job destruction—but these employment statistics cannot be used to cast a spotlight on the underlying behavior of *gross* job creation and destruction.

---

1. Numerous studies investigate the impact of job loss on workers. Recent studies include Hamermesh (1987, 1989), Podgursky and Swaim (1987), Ehrenberg and Jakubson (1988), Addison and Portugal (1989), Kletzer (1989), Topel (1990), Gibbons and Katz (1991), Ruhm (1991), Jacobson, Lalonde, and Sullivan (1993), Carrington (1993), and Farber (1993).

Government statistics derived from household surveys provide information on the number of workers who experience a change in employer or labor market status (employed, unemployed, not in the labor force). These indicators of worker reallocation activity are usefully classified by worker characteristics like age, sex, race, education, and income, and by reasons for change such as layoff, quit, or retirement. Although enormously valuable to researchers and policymakers, these statistics provide highly incomplete information about the reallocation of jobs and very little information about the characteristics of the businesses that create and destroy jobs. The absence of suitable data on job creation and destruction sometimes leads data users to blur the distinction between job and worker reallocation. Often the net or gross flow of workers into employment is mistakenly equated with job creation, and the flow of workers out of employment is mistakenly equated with job destruction.

Filling the Gap in the Statistical Knowledge Base

As our previous remarks make clear, worker reallocation reflects many factors in addition to the creation and destruction of jobs by businesses. This study focuses its statistical spotlight squarely on job creation and destruction. We can thereby better assess the roles they play in the reallocation of workers, in economic growth and cyclical fluctuations, and in the evolution of industries and regions. We anticipate that statistical analyses of job creation and destruction will contribute to more informed economic judgments and better economic policymaking. Throughout much of the book, especially in chapter 7, we explain how job creation and destruction statistics inform our understanding of the economy and provide a more solid empirical foundation for economic policymaking.

The Message from Earlier Studies

In recent years, several other researchers have undertaken studies that measure job creation and destruction from longitudinal data on plants or firms.[2] Like this book, these studies measure job creation and destruction by adding up plant-level (or firm-level) employment changes. Previous studies uniformly find high rates of job creation and destruction, indicating that large-scale job reallocation represents the norm in the U.S. economy. Our analysis confirms this empirical regularity.

---

2. Studies based on U.S. data include Birch (1979, 1987), Leonard (1987), Dunne, Roberts, and Samuelson (1989a, 1989b), Brown et al. (1990), and the Small Business Administration (various years).

The Limitations of Earlier Studies

Unfortunately, previous studies suffer from several limitations imposed by the quality, frequency, and scope of the underlying data. The data limitations vary, but the most important involve unrepresentative samples, infrequent sampling, severe restrictions on geographic scope, an inability to distinguish ownership transfers from births and deaths, and a failure to distinguish between firms and establishments. Although they provide fascinating glimpses into the process of job creation and destruction, previous studies stimulate a desire for closer analysis based on better data.

The Data Underlying Our Statistical Portrait

This study exploits a rich, largely untapped data source to construct detailed measures of job creation, destruction, and reallocation. We construct these measures from the most complete plant-level data source currently available in the United States—the Longitudinal Research Database (LRD), housed at the Center for Economic Studies in the U.S. Bureau of the Census. The LRD contains annual and quarterly plant-level data for the U.S. manufacturing sector from 1972 through 1988. Information in the LRD permits classification of plants by detailed industry, location, size, age, degree of product specialization, energy use, average wage, and other characteristics.

Among U.S. data sets that have been brought to bear on the measurement of job creation and destruction, the LRD contains the most detailed information on plant characteristics, the most careful treatment of the statistical sampling frame, and the best treatment of plant entry and exit. Unlike most other U.S. data sets, it also contains annual and quarterly observations on a major sector of the economy spanning a period of more than fifteen years. We exploit these data to deepen our understanding of job reallocation in the U.S. manufacturing sector and, by extension, the U.S. economy.[3]

Some Uses of Our Statistical Portrait

We believe that the statistical portrait of job creation and destruction developed here can inform economic discourse and policymaking in several areas. Examples include the role of small business in job creation, the wisdom and efficacy of targeted industrial policies, the desirability of trade policies intended to preserve jobs, the economic benefits of a flexible workforce, the consequences of legally mandated employment security provisions, the impact of international

---

3. Studies by Dunne, Robertson, and Samuelson (1989a, 1989b) use the quinquennial Census of Manufactures data, which make up part of the LRD. Unlike this study, they do not exploit the annual and quarterly data available from the Annual Survey of Manufactures.

trade on job security, the relative importance of high-wage and low-wage employers as creators of new jobs during the 1980s, the nature of cyclical downturns and labor market adjustment to these downturns, the effects of aggregate stabilization policies, the nature of industry evolution, and the usefulness of industrial classifications as devices for categorizing the fortunes of firms and plants or targeting government economic policies. We return to these matters in chapter 7.

New Statistics on Job Creation and Destruction Activity

Among academic economists, our research on job creation and destruction has attracted some interest and a growing demand for additional statistics on gross job flows.[4] Accordingly, a machine-readable data release coincides with the publication of this book. Instructions for obtaining the data appear at the end of the technical appendix. The data release contains all job creation and destruction statistics constructed from the LRD for the purposes of this book, including a large number of detailed series that are not reported here. We hope that this statistical release proves valuable to our colleagues in the research and policymaking communities, and we anticipate that updates to it will be issued by the Census Bureau on an ongoing basis.

Better Economic Statistics without Heavier Reporting Burdens

Many prominent economists and advisers have expressed a desire for better economic statistics.[5] Our job creation and destruction measures illustrate how new and useful statistics can be gleaned from data that are already collected by government agencies—without imposing any additional reporting burden on businesses or individuals. The economic surveys exploited by this study are essential to the federal government's construction of the National Income and Product Accounts and to widely used statistics on industrial production,

---

4. Our recent research on job creation and destruction is reported in Davis and Haltiwanger (1990, 1992) and Davis, Haltiwanger, and Schuh (1990). Other academic writings that are motivated by our research, or that rely heavily on job creation and destruction statistics constructed in our research, include Albaek and Sorensen (1995), Anderson and Meyer (1994), Andolfatto (1992), Baldwin, Dunne, and Haltiwanger (1994), Blanchard and Diamond (1990), Blanchflower and Burgess (1993), Boeri (1994), Boeri and Cramer (1992), Borland (1994), Borland and Home (1994), Broersma and Gautier (1995), Burda and Wyplosz (1994), Caballero (1992), Caballero, Engel, and Haltiwanger (1994), Caballero and Hammour (1993, 1994a,b), Contini and Revelli (1992), Contini et al. (1994), Gautier and Broersma (1993), Gavosto and Sestito (1993), Hall (1991), Hopenhayn and Rogerson (1993), Hosios (1994), Klette and Mathiassen (1994), Lagarde, Maurin, and Torelli (1994), Lane, Isaac, and Stevens (1993), Mortensen (1992), Mortensen and Pissarides (1992, 1994), Nocke (1994), Picot, Baldwin, and Dupuy (1994), and Wagner (1994).
5. See, for example, the March 8, 1993, issue of *Fortune* magazine with its discussion of Executive Office of the President, Council of Economic Advisers (1991).

capacity utilization, investment, employment, payroll, and other measures of economic activity.

What distinguishes our calculations from better-known statistics derived from the same economic surveys is our longitudinal perspective on the underlying plant-level data. We exploit the fact that the government's economic surveys and administrative records follow individual plants for several years consecutively. In contrast, the statistics produced by the government from these information sources typically exploit only the cross-sectional aspects of the available data.[6] In the spirit of further enhancing the usefulness and quality of statistical products, we remark that other important databases maintained by federal and state agencies could be used to construct job creation and destruction statistics for nonmanufacturing industries, and to place the calculation of these statistics on a nearly real-time basis. We return to this matter in chapter 8.

An Outline of the Book

The remainder of this book contains eight chapters and a technical appendix. Chapter 1 precisely defines job creation, job destruction, and related concepts. It also provides an overview of the data used to measure the concepts. Chapter 2 describes basic properties of job creation and destruction, stressing aspects that are common across regions, industries, and sectors of the economy. It also quantifies the connection between job reallocation and worker reallocation.

Chapter 3 describes how the main characteristics of job creation and destruction vary across industries, regions, and groups of plants—the latter defined in terms of wage level, capital and energy intensity, degree of product specialization, exposure to international trade, and other observable characteristics. Chapter 4 extends this focus on cross-sectoral differences to consider how job creation and destruction vary by employer size and age.

Chapter 5 investigates how job creation and destruction fluctuate over economywide and industry-level business cycles. The empirical evidence leads us to the conclusion that prevailing views about the nature of business cycles are unsatisfactory and incomplete. This conclusion prompts us to sketch some theoretical elements of a richer view of recessions more in line with the facts on gross job flows. Chapter 6 continues the analysis of economic fluctuations and

---

6. Efforts by ourselves and other researchers at the Center for Economic Studies to exploit the longitudinal character of the underlying data led to many improvements in its quality. Thus, aside from enabling the construction of new statistics, linking the individual plant data over time engenders quality improvements that benefit even cross-sectionally based statistical measures. The technical appendix describes some of the quality improvements that were undertaken in the course of this research.

explores the relationships among job flows, worker flows, and unemployment over the business cycle.

In chapter 7, we draw several economic and policy lessons from the statistical portrait constructed in chapters 2 through 6. This chapter illustrates how the measurement and analysis of gross job flows can inform our thinking about the economy and economic policymaking.

Some limitations of our statistical portrait, especially its focus on the manufacturing sector, prompt us to consider possibilities for developing more comprehensive measures of gross job flow activity. Chapter 8 considers the prospects for constructing more comprehensive, timely, and detailed gross job flow measures from administrative record databases maintained by federal and state agencies.

The technical appendix describes the details of our measurement procedures and explains how we dealt with various obstacles to accurate measurement. It is of interest primarily to researchers and policy analysts who wish to evaluate our measurement procedures, use our gross job flow statistics in their own work, or construct gross job flow statistics from other data sources.

How to Read the Book

In writing this book, we strove to make it accessible to a wide audience of researchers, policymakers, journalists, and business analysts. We also adopted an organizational structure that facilitates a rapid perusal of our main empirical findings, a concentrated focus on just a subset of the book's topics, or a quick path to the most important economic and policy messages. For the many readers who will not wish to proceed studiously from beginning to end, we offer a few remarks on how to read the book profitably.

For readers who are not familiar with our previous work, we recommend beginning with sections 1 and 2 of chapter 1. These short sections introduce a few key concepts and terms that appear repeatedly throughout the rest of the book. With this background, one can quickly glean our main conclusions and empirical findings by reading the bullet points that appear at the openings of chapters 2 through 8. These bullet points also serve as a road map to sections of the book that most powerfully strike the reader's interest, or simply as indicators of whether the book merits a closer examination.

Chapters 2 through 8 are largely self-contained, but most readers will find it helpful to first digest chapter 2, which sketches out the central elements of our statistical portrait. Chapters 3 and 4 are usefully read as a pair, as are chapters 5 and 6. Readers with a keen and impatient interest in the economic and policy lessons that emerge from our statistical portrait should proceed immediately to chapter 7.

1   Concepts, Measurement, and Data

Although the concept of a job is easily understood, meaningful measurement and interpretation of job creation and destruction statistics require careful definitions and assumptions. In this chapter, we explain what we mean by a job and a plant. We explain how to use plant-level employment changes to calculate job creation and destruction, and we spell out the relationship between job reallocation and worker reallocation. We also briefly describe the Longitudinal Research Database (LRD), which is the source of our statistical calculations. Detailed descriptions of our measurement procedures and the LRD appear in the technical appendix.

1.1   Job Creation and Destruction

In this study, a job is an employment position filled by a worker. Our data do not distinguish among part-time, full-time, and overtime employment positions—all count equally as a single job. Except for the breakdown between production workers (e.g., assemblers and machine operatives) and nonproduction workers (e.g., managers and secretaries), our data do not distinguish among different occupations. We do not measure the number of vacancies (i.e., unfilled positions) at a point in time or the change in vacancies over time. Rather, we measure plant-level changes in the number of filled employment positions.

The basic observational unit underlying our job creation and destruction measures is the plant—a physical location where production takes place. As distinguished from a plant, a company or firm is an economic and legal entity that encompasses one or more plants and, possibly, administrative offices that specialize in management functions. Although we provide tabulations broken down by company and plant characteristics, all job creation and destruction measures reported in this study are cumulated from plant-level employment

changes. Except for the breakdown between production and nonproduction workers, the plant represents the finest level of disaggregation available in the LRD for calculating job creation and destruction statistics.

We calculate job creation and destruction from plant-level net employment changes over twelve-month and three-month periods. If, for example, a plant expands by ten employees between March 1987 and March 1988, then, according to our calculations, the plant contributes ten jobs to the 1988 creation count. If another plant contracts by eight employees over the same time interval, it contributes eight jobs to the 1988 destruction count.

Because plants represent the observational units in the LRD, our calculations capture the effects of companies' shifting employment between plants. By the same token, our calculations do not capture the effects of job shifts within plants. For example, if a plant replaces several secretaries with an equal number of computer programmers, no net change in plant-level employment occurs; hence, our calculations record no job creation or destruction associated with this event. Because of the point-in-time nature of LRD employment data, our calculations also do not record plant-level employment changes that are reversed within the sampling interval. For example, if a plant lays off some workers in July 1987 and recalls an equal number in September 1987, there is no net effect on the plant's employment change between March 1987 and March 1988; hence, no contribution to job creation and destruction would be recorded as a result of this episode of layoff and recall. For both reasons—the failure to capture within-plant job shifts and the point-in-time nature of LRD employment data—our job creation and destruction measures understate the true magnitudes.

We interpret measured increases and decreases in plant-level employment as changes in desired employment levels rather than as changes in the stock of unfilled positions. When a vacancy arises as the result of a quit, for example, the position can likely be refilled within three or twelve months, if desired. This intrepretation is buttressed by the fact, reported in chapter 2, that measured job creation and destruction occur primarily at plants that undergo substantial contraction or expansion during the sampling interval.

With these remarks as background, we supply the following definitions:

Definition 1   (Gross) job creation at time t equals employment gains summed over all plants that expand or start up between $t - 1$ and t.

Definition 2   (Gross) job destruction at time t equals employment losses summed over all plants that contract or shut down between $t - 1$ and t.

In line with these definitions, plants with unchanged employment contribute to neither job creation nor job destruction. We shall typically express job creation and destruction figures as rates by dividing through by a measure of the employment level.[1]

Definition 3   The net employment change at time t is the difference between employment at time t and employment at time $t - 1$.

A simple and important relationship links the concepts described by these three definitions: *The net employment growth rate equals the job creation rate minus the job destruction rate.* In other words, job creation and destruction figures decompose the net employment change into a component associated with growing plants and a component associated with shrinking plants.

The job creation and destruction components of the net employment change provide information about employment dynamics that is unavailable from other government statistics. For example, suppose that aggregate employment grew 2 percent during the past year. That growth rate could be supported by 4 percent job creation and 2 percent job destruction rates, or by 22 percent creation and 20 percent destruction rates. Important aspects of economic behavior and performance are likely to vary with rates of job creation and destruction. Higher rates of job creation and destruction mean larger numbers of workers compelled to shuffle between jobs and, most likely, a greater incidence of unemployment. For a given net growth rate, higher rates of job creation make it easier for displaced workers and labor market entrants to find employment, and higher rates of job destruction imply less job security for employed persons. Higher rates of job creation and destruction also imply greater heterogeneity in the behavior of employment growth across plants. Thus, job creation and destruction figures offer a window into the diversity of plant-level employment outcomes masked by aggregate employment statistics.

1.2   Job Reallocation and Worker Reallocation

A useful way to summarize the heterogeneity in plant-level employment outcomes is to count the number of jobs that either disappear from shrinking plants or newly appear at expanding plants. We refer to this job destruction

---

1. To convert time-t job creation and destruction measures to rates, we divide by the average of employment at t and $t - 1$. Similarly, we calculate plant-level growth rates on a base that equals the average of employment in the current and previous periods. The resulting growth rate measure has several technical advantages over more conventional growth rate measures. See the technical appendix for further information.

and creation activity as job reallocation, because it entails the reshuffling of job opportunities across locations.

Definition 4 (Gross) job reallocation at time t is the sum of all plant-level employment gains and losses that occur between $t - 1$ and t.

Note that the job reallocation measure equals the sum of job creation and job destruction.

As employment opportunities shift across locations, workers undertake conformable shifts. Job-losing workers find employment at different plants, become unemployed and search for a new job, or leave the labor force. Newly available jobs are filled by jobless or previously employed workers. Of course, as we stressed earlier, workers often switch employers or change employment status for reasons largely unrelated to the reallocation of jobs.

There are many useful ways to quantify the various aspects of worker reallocation activity, but we focus on a measure that relates most directly to our job reallocation measure:

Definition 5 (Gross) worker reallocation at time t equals the number of persons who change place of employment or employment status between $t - 1$ and t.

A change in employment status means a transition from employment to nonemployment, or vice versa.

There is an important economic link between the job and worker reallocation concepts expressed in definitions 4 and 5: *Job reallocation equals the maximum amount of worker reallocation directly induced by the reshuffling of employment opportunities across locations.* We say the "maximum amount" because some job-losing workers move from a shrinking plant to a new job at an expanding plant within the sampling interval. Such workers are counted twice in the job reallocation measure—once in the job destruction column and once in the job creation column. To eliminate any possibility of double counting in quantifying the link between job and worker reallocation, we take the larger of job creation and job destruction:

Definition 6 Minimum worker reallocation equals the larger of job creation or job destruction. It represents a lower bound on the amount of worker reallocation required to accommodate job reallocation.

Definitions 4–6 suggest a way to quantify the contribution of job reallocation to worker reallocation. First, measure total worker reallocation, using suitable data on individuals. Second, use job creation and destruction measures

to compute upper and lower bounds on the amount of worker reallocation induced by job reallocation. Combining the various measures yields upper and lower bounds on the fraction of worker reallocation induced by shifts in the distribution of job opportunities across locations. Drawing upon Current Population Survey data to measure gross worker reallocation, we carry out these calculations in chapter 2.

An additional measure derived from plant-level employment changes will prove useful for understanding the sources of job reallocation and, in particular, the role played by shifts in the sectoral composition of employment demand.

Definition 7 Excess job reallocation equals the difference between (gross) job reallocation and the absolute value of net employment change.

Excess job reallocation represents that part of job reallocation over and above the amount required to accommodate net employment changes. It is an index of simultaneous job creation and destruction.[2] The usefulness of the excess job reallocation measure stems from the fact that it can be decomposed into two components: one that captures between-sector employment shifts, and one that captures excess job reallocation within sectors. Chapter 3 reports results of this decomposition based on several alternative sectoral classification schemes.

1.3   The LRD: Data and Measurement

The Longitudinal Research Database (LRD), housed at the Census Bureau's Center for Economic Studies, contains data on U.S. manufacturing plants with five or more employees.[3] Two legally mandated Census Bureau economic surveys provide the data for the LRD—the quinquennial Census of Manufactures (CM) and the Annual Survey of Manufactures (ASM). The LRD currently contains CM data for 300,000–400,000 plants in each year 1963, 1967, 1972, 1977, 1982, and 1987, and ASM data for a probability sample of 50,000 to 70,000 plants in each year from 1972 to 1988. LRD employment data are available at annual and quarterly frequencies for each plant. Individual plants are assigned unique, time-invariant identifiers that enable us to calculate plant-level employment changes. Thus, the LRD constitutes a panel data set.

---

2. Gross job reallocation rises with simultaneous job creation and destruction, but—unlike excess job reallocation—it also rises with the absolute value of net employment change. For this reason, excess job reallocation is a more appropriate index of simultaneous creation and destruction than is gross job reallocation.

3. The actual size cutoff is not always based on employment, but the five-employee rule is a good approximation. See the technical appendix for further information.

ASM panels are selected from the manufacturing universe identified by the CM, commence two years after the CM, and continue for five years. An ASM panel contains observations on roughly one-seventh to one-fifth of manufacturing plants and two-thirds of manufacturing employment. Plants with at least 250 employees in the CM are included in the subsequent ASM panel with certainty.[4] Plants with 5–249 employees in the CM are included in the subsequent ASM panel with probabilities that increase with plant size. Using these probabilities, plants are selected randomly for panel inclusion. Thus, the ASM represents a random probability sample, which means that we can accurately estimate job creation, job destruction, and other quantities for the U.S. manufacturing sector.[5]

In the first period of a new panel, we observe employment changes for all certainty plants but only for a subset of the plants included on a random selection basis. This aspect of ASM sampling procedures creates special problems for estimating job creation and destruction during the first period of each panel. As explained in the technical appendix, we have developed procedures that yield useful estimates of job creation and destruction during the first period of each panel. These procedures enable us to report continuous time-series estimates of basic job creation and destruction statistics. Unfortunately, for certain tabulations, cross-panel linkage problems prevent the construction of high-quality statistics in all periods. These cross-panel linkage problems account for the gaps in a few of the time series we report.

As an ASM panel ages, many plants shut down or start up. Some plants start up for the first time, whereas others start up after a period of inactivity. The LRD provides information about plant location, company ownership, plant history, and panel status that enables us to accurately identify births and deaths and to distinguish these events from ownership transfers and from rotation into or out of the panel. Plants that start up after the quinquennial CM are incorporated into the ongoing panel annually to preserve the representative character of the ASM sample.[6]

Two types of plant-level employment data are available in the LRD. Total employment (TE) equals the sum of production worker employment (PW)

---

4. The 250-employee rule approximates the actual, more complicated rules for inclusion with certainty.

5. The small plants (fewer than five employees) excluded from the ASM sampling frame, although large in number, account for about 4 percent of manufacturing employment.

6. Although our ability to distinguish among startups, shutdowns, and panel rotators in the LRD is good, it is not perfect. In addition, the exact timing of plant startups and shutdowns is difficult to pinpoint from LRD information. These problems, which complicate the task of measuring job creation and destruction, are treated at length in the technical appendix.

Table 1.1
Selected LRD Information Variables

Variable	Description (Number of Sectors or Categories in Parentheses)
Age-simple	Plant age defined crudely, all years (3)
Age-detailed	Plant age defined more specifically, certain years (8)
Capital	Plant capital intensity (10)
Size-average	Average plant employment size (9)
Size-current	Current plant employment size (9)
Size-company	Company employment size (12)
Energy	Plant energy intensity (10)
Exports	Export-competing industry (5)
Recent History	Continuing, startup, and shutdown plants (3)
Imports	Import-competing industry (5)
Industry-2	Two-digit SIC industries (20)
Industry-4	Four-digit SIC industries[a]
Ownership Type	Single-plant or multi-plant company (2)
Region	Census geographic regions (9)
Specialization	Plant product specialization intensity (5)
State	U.S. states (50)
Wage	Plant-level mean hourly production-worker wage in $1982 (5)

[a] Our industry series covers 448 industries in 1972-86 and 456 in 1987-88 because of changes in the Standard Industrial Classification. A total of 514 distinct industries appear under at least one of the classification systems.

and nonproduction worker, or other worker, employment (OW). Annual TE and PW data are available for the payroll period covering March 12. Our annual job creation and destruction figures reflect plant-level March-to-March changes in total employment. Quarterly data on PW employment are available for payroll periods covering February 12, May 12, August 12, and November 12. Accordingly, our quarterly job creation and destruction figures reflect plant-level employment changes from the middle month of one quarter to the middle month of the next quarter.[7]

The LRD also contains other information about plants and companies that we use to tabulate job creation and destruction statistics for various sectors and groups of plants. Table 1.1 lists selected variables that pertain to product markets, plant location, plant and firm size, plant age, factor intensity, average plant wages, and exposure to international trade.[8] In addition to providing statistics broken down by these information variables, we also provide

7. In fact, the LRD records PW employment for March, not February, which necessitates certain adjustments to obtain job creation and destruction estimates for equally spaced quarterly intervals. The technical appendix describes these adjustment procedures.
8. Table 1.1 includes information variables from other data sources that we have matched to the LRD at the industry level.

statistics in the data release accompanying this book for selected multi-way breakdowns, such as industry–region.

To sum up, several LRD attributes facilitate the construction of interesting, high-quality statistics related to job creation and destruction behavior. The next several chapters highlight key findings and noteworthy patterns that emerge from the statistics.

2   Basic Facts about Job Creation and Destruction

This chapter documents four key facts about job creation and destruction:

• **Magnitude:** *Job creation and destruction rates are remarkably large. Over a typical twelve-month interval, about one in ten manufacturing jobs disappear, and a comparable number of new manufacturing jobs open up at different locations.*

• **Persistence:** *Most of the job creation and destruction that we observe over twelve-month intervals reflects highly persistent plant-level employment changes. This persistence implies, for example, that most jobs that vanish over a twelve-month interval fail to reopen at the same location within the following two years.*

• **Concentration:** *Job creation and destruction are concentrated at plants that experience large percentage employment changes. Two-thirds of job creation and destruction takes place at plants that expand or contract by 25 percent or more within a twelve-month interval. About one-quarter of job destruction takes place at plants that shut down.*

• **Cyclicality:** *Job destruction rates exhibit greater cyclical variation than job creation rates. In particular, recessions are characterized by a sharp increase in job destruction accompanied by a relatively mild slowdown in job creation.*

The final section of this chapter draws upon these facts to develop and quantify the connection between job reallocation and worker reallocation. We estimate that from a third to half of all worker reallocation represents a direct response to the reallocation of employment opportunities across locations.[1]

---

1. See chapter 1 for the definition of worker reallocation.

2.1 Magnitude

Table 2.1 reports summary statistics for rates of job creation, job destruction, job reallocation, net employment change, excess job reallocation, and the
minimum worker reallocation required to accommodate job reallocation. As
explained in chapter 1, the annual job flow measures reflect March-to-March
plant-level employment changes. The quarterly measures reflect plant-level
employment changes over three-month intervals.

The key message conveyed by table 2.1 is the large magnitude of gross job
flows. On average, 10.3 percent of manufacturing jobs were destroyed over a
twelve-month interval during the 1973–88 period. Twelve-month job creation
rates averaged a slightly lower 9.1 percent, which reflects the net shrinkage
of manufacturing employment between 1973 and 1988. The twelve-month job
destruction rate never fell below 6.1 percent of manufacturing employment,
and it reached as high as 16.5 percent in the recession of 1975.

The quarterly data summarized by table 2.1 provide an even sharper impression of large-scale job creation and destruction, but these data should be
intrepreted with greater caution. As we show below, the difference between
the annual and quarterly job flow rates partly reflects the lower persistence
of plant-level employment changes measured over three-month intervals. In
particular, most of the job creation and destruction captured by the quarterly
figures reflects plant-level employment changes that are reversed within a year.
Hence, the annual job flow measures provide a better indication of permanent
job reallocation activity.

Summing the creation and destruction rates to obtain the job reallocation
rate, table 2.1 reveals that nearly one in five manufacturing jobs are either
destroyed or created over an average twelve-month interval.[2] This simple fact
highlights the remarkable fluidity in the distribution of job opportunities across
locations in the U.S. economy.

The remaining two columns in table 2.1 shed light on the implications of
this large-scale job reallocation activity. Recall that excess job reallocation
equals total job reallocation minus the minimum amount required to accom-

---

2. The available evidence points to similarly high job reallocation rates in other U.S. industry
groups. According to Leonard's (1987, table 6.6) tabulations for Wisconsin, annual job reallocation rates are 28 percent higher in the private, nonmanufacturing sector than in manufacturing.
In contrast, Leonard and Zax (1993) report substantially lower job reallocation rates among local government employment units. Based on a six-state sample that excludes firms with fewer
than fifty employees, Anderson and Meyer (1994, table 11) report nearly identical annual job reallocation rates in manufacturing and in all sectors combined. Because smaller firms have higher
job reallocation rates and account for a larger fraction of employment in nonmanufacturing, their
tabulations overstate manufacturing's relative job reallocation rate.

Table 2.1

Job Flow Rates in Manufacturing: Summary Statistics

	Annual Flows as a Percentage of Employment, 1973-1988				Quarterly Flows as a Percentage of Employment 1972:Q2-1988:Q4			
	Aver-age	Standard Devia-tion	Mini-mum	Maxi-mum	Aver-age	Standard Devia-tion	Mini-mum	Maxi-mum
Job Creation	9.1	2.1	6.2	13.3	5.2	0.9	3.2	7.3
Job Destruction	10.3	3.1	6.1	16.5	5.5	1.7	3.2	11.4
Job Reallocation	19.4	2.1	16.7	23.9	10.7	1.6	7.6	14.7
Net Employment Growth[a]	−1.1	4.8	−10.0	5.7	−0.3	2.1	−8.2	2.6
Excess Job Reallocation	15.4	2.0	12.3	18.8	9.1	1.2	6.5	12.5
Minimum Worker Reallocation Required to Accommodate Job Reallocation (Lower Bound)	11.7	2.3	8.3	16.5	6.2	1.4	4.1	11.4

Annual Job Flow Rates in Manufacturing, 1973-1988

Year	Job Creation	Job Destruc-tion	Job Reallo-cation	Net Employ-ment Growth[a]	Excess Job Reallo-cation	Lower Bound
1973	11.9	6.1	18.0	5.7	12.3	11.9
1974	9.0	9.3	18.3	−0.3	18.0	9.3
1975	6.2	16.5	22.7	−10.3	12.3	16.5
1976	11.2	9.4	20.6	1.8	18.8	11.2
1977	11.0	8.6	19.6	2.3	17.3	11.0
1978	10.9	7.3	18.2	3.6	14.6	10.9
1979	10.3	7.0	17.4	3.3	14.0	10.3
1980	8.0	9.1	17.1	−1.1	16.0	9.1
1981	6.3	11.4	17.7	−5.4	12.6	11.4
1982	6.8	14.5	21.3	−7.7	13.6	14.5
1983	8.4	15.6	23.9	−7.2	16.7	15.6
1984	13.3	7.6	20.9	5.7	15.1	13.3
1985	7.9	11.1	19.0	−3.2	15.8	11.1
1986	7.9	12.1	20.1	−4.2	15.9	12.1
1987	8.4	10.1	18.5	−1.7	16.8	10.1
1988	8.3	8.3	16.7	−0.0	16.6	8.3

[a]The net employment change statistics in this table do not exactly match those obtained from data published in the *Census of Manufactures* and *Annual Survey of Manufactures* because of minor discrepancies between the published data and the LRD data. See the Technical Appendix for details.

modate the net change in manufacturing employment. In other words, excess reallocation measures the extent of simultaneous job creation and destruction. According to table 2.1, excess job reallocation averages 15.4 percent of employment per year.[3] This result indicates that even during years with unchanged total employment, a large fraction of employment opportunities change locations.

How does this reshuffling of employment opportunities across locations affect workers? Table 2.1 provides the beginning of an answer. Recall from chapter 1 that minimum worker reallocation and job reallocation represent lower and upper bounds, respectively, on the fraction of workers who must change place of employment or employment status to accommodate the reshuffling of jobs across locations. In an average year, the amount of worker reallocation induced by job reallocation is bounded between 11.7 percent and 19.4 percent of employment. The 8.3 percent entry for the minimum value of worker reallocation says that *in every year,* more than one in twelve workers switch jobs or employment status as a direct consequence of the reshuffling of employment opportunities across locations. In the recession year of 1975, job reallocation directly affected at least 16.5 percent of manufacturing workers and as many as 22.7 percent.

How does this large-scale job reallocation activity in the United States compare with the experiences of other countries? The United States is widely perceived to operate with a flexible and fluid labor market. The large-scale and continuous reshuffling of employment opportunities across locations summarized by table 2.1 reinforces this view of the U.S. economy. Perhaps surprisingly, it turns out that other market economies exhibit comparable rates of job reallocation activity. Table 2.2 makes the point.[4] Although differences in sectoral coverage and other aspects of the data hamper fine cross-country comparisons, table 2.2 clearly shows that other developed economies exhibit large-scale job reallocation activity. The available data point to even higher rates of job reallocation in developing economies. According to the international evidence, the constant churning of job opportunities that characterizes the U.S. labor market represents the normal state of affairs for both developed and developing market economies.

---

3. To compute this average, we first calculate the excess job reallocation in each year and then take the mean across years. Because net employment growth switches sign, the average excess job reallocation rate is less than the average gross job reallocation rate minus the average absolute net employment growth rate.

4. A summary of available evidence by the Organization for Economic Co-Operation and Development (1994, chap. 3) also reports high job reallocation rates across a number of industrialized economies.

Table 2.2
International Comparison of Net and Gross Job Flow Rates (Annual Averages as Percentages of Employment)

Country	Period	Coverage	Job Creation	Job Destruction	Net Employment Growth	Job Reallocation
USA	1973—88	Manufacturing	9.1	10.2	−1.1	19.4
USA	1976—85	Pennsylvania	13.3	12.5	0.8	25.8
Canada	1979—84	Manufacturing	10.6	10.0	0.6	20.5
Canada	1979—84	Tax-Paying Firms	11.1	9.6	1.5	20.7
France	1978—84	Private, Nonfarm	11.4	12.0	−0.6	23.3
Germany	1978—88	Private	8.3	7.7	0.6	16.0
Sweden	1982—84	All Employees	11.4	12.1	−0.8	23.5
Italy	1984—89	Social Security Employees	9.9	10.0	−0.1	19.9
Australia	1984—85	Manufacturing	16.1	13.2	3.9	29.3
New Zealand	1987—92	Private	15.7	19.8	−4.1	35.5
Denmark	1983—89	Private	16.0	13.8	2.2	29.8
Finland	1986—91	Private	10.4	12.0	−1.6	22.4
Norway	1976—86	Manufacturing	7.1	8.4	−1.2	15.5
Colombia	1977—89	Manufacturing	13.2	13.0	0.2	26.2
Chile	1976—86	Manufacturing	13.0	13.9	−1.0	26.8
Morocco	1984—89	Manufacturing	18.6	12.1	6.5	30.7

Sources: Canada (tax-paying firms)-Organization for Economic Cooperation and Development, OECD *Employment Outlook*, September 1987, Table 4.1; Canada (mfg. plants)-Baldwin, Dunne and Haltiwanger (1994), Table 1; USA (Pennsylvania)-OECD *Employment Outlook*, September 1987, Table 4.1; USA (mfg. plants)-Table 2.1 in this chapter; France-OECD *Employment Outlook*, September 1987, Table 4.1; Germany-Boeri and Cramer (1991), Table 1; Sweden-OECD *Employment Outlook*, September 1987, Table 4.1; Italy-Contini and Revelli (1992), Table 1; Israel-Contini and Revelli (1992), Table 1; Australia-Borland and Home (1994); Norway-Klette and Mathiassen (1994); Denmark-*OECD Employment Outlook*, July 1994, Table 3.1; Finland-*OECD Employment Outlook*, July 1994, Table 3.1; New Zealand-*OECD Employment Outlook*, July 1994, Table 3.1; Chile-Roberts (1994); Colombia-Roberts (1994); Morocco-Roberts (1994).

2.2 Persistence

How persistent are the plant-level employment changes that underlie our job creation and destruction figures? An answer to this question will further our understanding of plant-level employment dynamics. The persistence of plant-level employment changes also bears directly on the character of the worker reallocation associated with job reallocation. To the extent that job creation and destruction represent short-lived employment changes, those changes can be implemented largely through temporary layoffs and recalls. To the extent that plant-level employment changes are persistent, they must be associated with long-term joblessness or worker reallocation across plants.

In thinking about how to measure persistence, we stress that our focus is on the persistence of the typical newly created or newly destroyed job. This focus is distinct from a focus on the persistence of the typical existing job

or the persistence of establishment size. In line with our focus, we measure persistence according to the following definitions:

Definition 8   The N-period persistence of job creation is the percentage of newly created jobs at time t that remain filled at each subsequent sampling date through time $t + N$.

Definition 9   The N-period persistence of job destruction is the percentage of newly destroyed jobs at time t that do not reappear at any subsequent sampling date through time $t + N$.

Since job reallocation equals creation plus destruction, these definitions imply a persistence measure for job reallocation.

Some simple examples clarify the nature of these persistence measures. Consider a plant that creates 100 jobs by increasing employment from 1,000 in March 1985 to 1,100 in March 1986. At the subsequent March samplings in 1987 and 1988, the plant's employment evolves according to one of three scenarios: (1) 1,050 in 1987 and 1,100 in 1988; (2) 1,050 in 1987 and 1,025 in 1988; (3) 1,200 in 1987 and 1,075 in 1988. According to definition 8, the one-year persistence of the 100 newly created jobs in 1986 is 50 percent in scenarios (1) and (2) and 100 percent in scenario (3). The two-year persistence rate is 50 percent in scenario (1), 25 percent in scenario (2), and 75 percent in scenario (3). Note that the persistence measures lie between 0 percent and 100 percent in each scenario, and that one-year persistence is always at least as large as two-year persistence. For both job creation and job destruction, these properties of the persistence measures hold for any pattern of plant-level employment changes.

One further remark helps to clarify the meaning of the persistence rate and its connection to the information in previous tables. The job destruction rate reported in table 2.1 equals 1 minus the one-period survival rate for the stock of existing jobs. By way of comparison, the persistence rate denotes the survival rate for new jobs. In particular, the N-period persistence rate equals the fraction of new jobs at time t that survive through period $t + N$. We use "persistence rate" to emphasize the symmetry between our treatment of newly created and newly destroyed jobs. We use "survival rate" when comparing the survival properties of new jobs with those of all existing jobs.

Table 2.3 summarizes the persistence properties of job creation and job destruction over various horizons. In the annual data, roughly seven in ten newly created jobs survive for at least one year, and roughly eight in ten newly destroyed jobs fail to reappear one year later. After two years, the persistence of annual job creation and destruction falls to 54 percent and 74 percent, respectively. The most important aspect of these results is that the annual job

Table 2.3
**Average Persistence Rates for Job Creation and Destruction
in Manufacturing**

	Annual Measures, 1973-1988	
	One Year	Two Years
Job Creation..............	70.2	54.4
Job Destruction	82.3	73.6
Job Reallocation...........	77.3	66.2

	Quarterly Measures, 1972:Q2-1988:Q4			
	One Quarter	Two Quarters	One Year	Two Years
Job Creation..............	67.8	50.4	37.7	22.6
Job Destruction	72.3	58.9	59.2	38.4
Job Reallocation...........	73.6	60.5	43.7	31.1

creation and destruction figures largely reflect persistent plant-level employment changes.[5]

The quarterly job flow figures show much smaller persistence rates than the annual figures. There are two reasons for this discrepancy. First, transitory plant-level employment movements, including seasonal movements, are much more likely to enter into the calculation of gross job flows over three-month, as opposed to twelve-month, intervals.[6] Second, over any given horizon, there are fewer sampling dates in the annual data than in the quarterly data. Thus, newly destroyed and newly created jobs must meet more stringent criteria in the quarterly data to satisfy the concept of persistence specified in definitions 8 and 9.

These remarks also reconcile the high persistence of annual job creation and destruction with some well-known facts about the importance of temporary layoffs in the U.S. manufacturing sector. For example, Lilien (1980, table III) estimates that 60–78 percent of all manufacturing layoffs ended in recall during the years 1965–76. He also reports that 92 percent of manufacturing unemployment spells ending in recall last three months or less. Most

5. A simple example suggests that the observed degree of persistence exceeds the amount associated with random walk employment behavior. Suppose, in particular, that plant-level employment follows a random walk, and assume that the increments are drawn from a continuous uniform distribution with a 0 mean. Under these assumptions, simple calculations show that the expected value of the one-year persistence rate equals 62.5 percent.
6. By "transitory" movements, we mean plant-level employment changes that are subsequently reversed, not the properties of the stochastic process describing increments to plant-level employment.

Table 2.4
Persistence Rates by Year in Manufacturing (Annual Job Flow Measures in Percent)

Year	Creation		Destruction	
	One Year	Two Years	One Year	Two Years
1975.............................	71.9	58.6	72.2	61.4
1976.............................	75.5	65.9	78.1	68.1
1977.............................	76.3		77.7	
1978.............................				
1979.............................				
1980.............................	63.6	43.5	82.3	77.0
1981.............................	57.5	41.2	87.3	82.1
1982.............................	61.0		86.4	
1983.............................				
1984.............................				
1985.............................	65.5	51.8	86.9	80.8
1986.............................	72.2	61.2	85.2	78.1
1987.............................	81.7		87.2	

of these short-duration temporary layoffs are not captured by our calculations based upon March-to-March employment changes.

Table 2.3 also reveals that job destruction is more likely than job creation to persist for one or two years. In chapter 3, we show that this pattern is pervasive across industries and across a variety of other sectoral classifications of U.S. manufacturing employment. Thus, the typical newly destroyed job represents a more persistent plant-level employment change than does the typical newly created job.

We can also compare the persistence properties of newly created and existing jobs. Table 2.1 reports a job destruction rate of about 10 percent, which is equivalent to saying that 90 percent of existing jobs survive at least one year. In comparison, table 2.3 reports that only 70.2 percent of newly created jobs survive at least one year. Hence, newly created jobs offer substantially lower one-year survival rates than do all existing jobs.

We summarize the persistence properties of existing jobs, new jobs, and lost jobs in the annual data with three statements: (1) the one-year survival rate for existing jobs is about 90 percent; (2) newly created jobs show a much smaller one-year survival rate—about 70 percent; (3) about 82 percent of newly destroyed jobs fail to reappear at the same location one year later.

Table 2.4 displays persistence measures for annual job creation and destruction by year. Figure 2.1 plots corresponding persistence measures for quarterly

Figure 2.1
Persistence of Job Creation and Destruction: Quarterly, 1972 to 1988

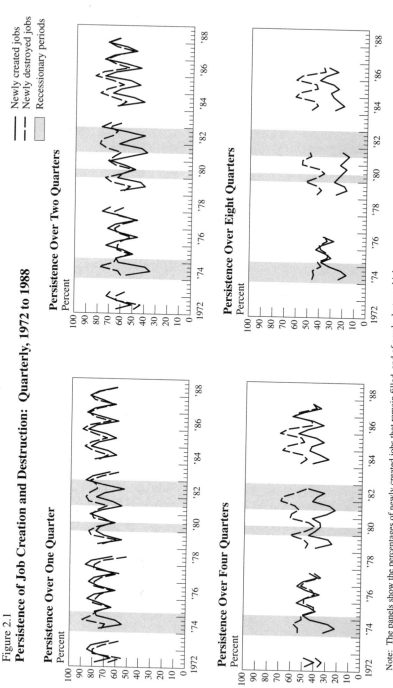

Note: The panels show the percentages of newly created jobs that remain filled, and of newly destroyed jobs that do not reappear, at subsequent quarterly sampling dates (one, two, four, or eight quarters).

job flows. The missing data points in the table and figure reflect the cross-panel linkage problems in the LRD described in chapter 1.

Two interesting patterns emerge in the data on time variation in persistence rates. First, jobs created during a recession are less likely to survive than jobs created during an expansion. Second, quarterly job creation and destruction exhibit pronounced, and virtually identical, seasonal patterns of variation. The one-quarter persistence of jobs created or destroyed in the first quarter is about 20 percentage points higher than in the third quarter.

2.3   Concentration

What role do plant births and deaths play in the creation and destruction of jobs? More generally, how are job creation and destruction distributed by plant-level employment growth rates? Do job creation and destruction primarily involve mild expansions and contractions spread among a large number of plants, or wrenching and dramatic changes at a few plants? The consequences of job creation and destruction for workers and for the communities in which they reside depend, in large part, on the answers to these questions.

In addressing these questions, we find it useful to measure plant-level growth rates in an unconventional manner. In particular, we measure a plant's growth rate in period t as the change in its employment divided by its average employment in periods $t - 1$ and t. In contrast, the conventional measure of the period-t growth rate equals the change in employment divided by employment in period $t - 1$ only.[7]

Unlike the conventional measure, our preferred growth rate measure is symmetrical about 0 and restricted to finite values. Thus, according to the conventional measure, a plant birth corresponds to a growth rate of positive infinity, and a plant death corresponds to a growth rate of -1. Under our preferred measure, plant births and deaths correspond to growth rates of $+2$ and -2,

---

7. To express these growth rate measures symbolically, let EMP_t denote a plant's employment level in period t. Then our preferred growth rate measure can be written as

$$g_t = \frac{EMP_t - EMP_{t-1}}{(1/2)\left(EMP_{t-1} + EMP_t\right)},\tag{1}$$

and the conventional growth rate measure can be written as

$$G_t = \frac{EMP_t - EMP_{t-1}}{EMP_{t-1}}.\tag{2}$$

The two growth measures are monotonically related and linked by the formula $G \equiv 2g/(2 - g)$.

respectively. Because births and deaths represent symmetrical episodes in the life cycle of a plant, we think it appropriate to assign these events symmetrical growth rate values.[8]

Figure 2.2 shows the distributions of annual job creation and destruction by absolute values of plant-level employment growth rates (g_t) for the 1973–88 period. This figure reflects the approximately 800,000 annual observations on plant-level employment changes in the LRD. The height of each rectangle in figure 2.2 equals the fraction of job creation or destruction accounted for by growth rate observations that fall into an interval spanning five percentage points. Figure 2.2 is based upon our preferred growth rate measure, as indicated by the scaling along the horizontal axis.

Figure 2.3 depicts simple pie charts that condense the information on the distribution of annual and quarterly job creation and destruction into a small number of growth rate intervals. The interval labels in the pie charts correspond to the conventional growth rate measure (G_t).

What do these figures tell us about the questions posed at the outset of this section? Figures 2.2 and 2.3 reveal that shutdowns account for 23 percent of annual job destruction, and startups account for 16 percent of annual job creation.[9] The message is plain: job creation and destruction in the manufacturing sector often involve dramatic events such as the startup of a new plant or the death of an old plant.

To elaborate upon this point, the pie charts in figure 2.3 show that two-thirds of annual job creation and destruction occur at startups, shutdowns, and continuing plants that expand or contract by at least a quarter of their initial work force. The dramatic character of much job creation and destruction in the manufacturing sector also reflects the concentration of manufacturing employment at large plants. In 1986, the average manufacturing employee worked at a facility that had nearly 1,600 workers (Davis and Haltiwanger, 1991, fig. 4.B).[10] Thus, manufacturing employment is

---

8. The symmetry and boundedness properties of the g measure are useful in formal statistical analyses of plant-level growth behavior. See Davis and Haltiwanger (1990, 1992).

9. Shutdowns and startups account for smaller fractions in the quarterly data for two reasons: (1) these events may require more than a single quarter to complete, and (2) transitory plant-level employment movements account for larger fractions of job creation and destruction in the quarterly data, as shown in the preceding sections. These transitory events are unlikely to involve complete plant shutdowns.

10. Davis (1990) provides summary statistics on the distribution of employees by establishment size for about twenty manufacturing and sixty nonmanufacturing industries that cover the nonfarm private sector of the U.S. economy. These statistics confirm that employment at large establishments is more important in manufacturing industries than in most nonmanufacturing industries.

Figure 2.2
Distributions of Job Creation and Destruction:
Annual, 1973 to 1988

Distribution of Plant-Level Job Creation

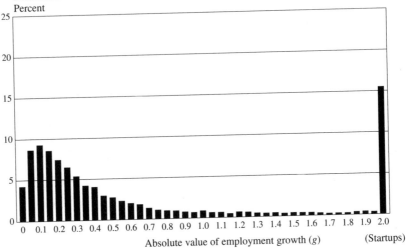

Absolute value of employment growth (g) (Startups)

Distribution of Plant-Level Job Destruction

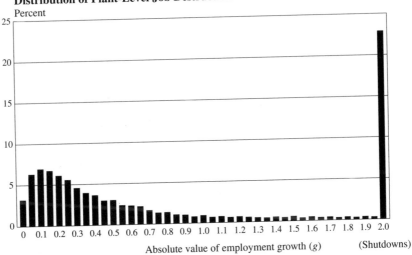

Absolute value of employment growth (g) (Shutdowns)

Note: The panels show the distributions of annual job creation and destruction by plant-level employment growth and contraction rates for the period 1973–1988.
The growth rates in this figure (g) are not the conventional measure but represent change in employment divided by the average of current and lagged employment.

Figure 2.3
Concentration of Job Creation and Destruction: 1973 to 1988

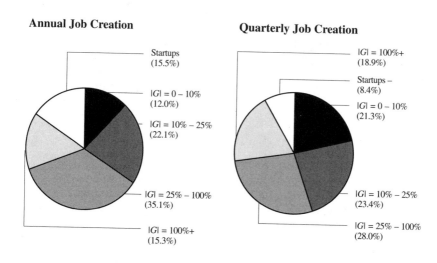

Annual Job Creation

Startups
(15.5%)

$|G| = 0 - 10\%$
(12.0%)

$|G| = 10\% - 25\%$
(22.1%)

$|G| = 25\% - 100\%$
(35.1%)

$|G| = 100\%+$
(15.3%)

Quarterly Job Creation

$|G| = 100\%+$
(18.9%)

Startups –
(8.4%)

$|G| = 0 - 10\%$
(21.3%)

$|G| = 10\% - 25\%$
(23.4%)

$|G| = 25\% - 100\%$
(28.0%)

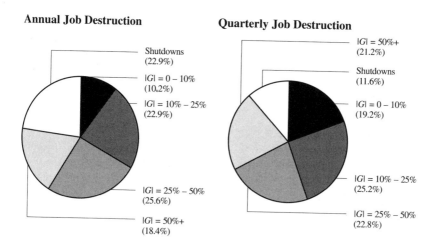

Annual Job Destruction

Shutdowns
(22.9%)

$|G| = 0 - 10\%$
(10.2%)

$|G| = 10\% - 25\%$
(22.9%)

$|G| = 25\% - 50\%$
(25.6%)

$|G| = 50\%+$
(18.4%)

Quarterly Job Destruction

$|G| = 50\%+$
(21.2%)

Shutdowns
(11.6%)

$|G| = 0 - 10\%$
(19.2%)

$|G| = 10\% - 25\%$
(25.2%)

$|G| = 25\% - 50\%$
(22.8%)

Note: The pie charts summarize the distributions of annual and quarterly job creation and destruction by plant-level employment growth and contraction rates for the period 1973–1988. The numbers in parentheses indicate shares of the total.
   The growth rates in this figure (G) are the conventional measure.

concentrated at large plants, and manufacturing job creation and destruction are concentrated at plants that experience large percentage changes in employment.

These two facts about concentration explain why job creation and destruction at manufacturing plants often have important effects on nearby communities. A dramatic employment reduction at a single large plant can flood the local labor market, which increases the economic hardship that falls upon each job loser.[11] Conversely, a sharp employment increase at a single plant can induce an in-migration of workers and their families that strains the capacity of the local community to provide such public and private goods as schooling, housing, roads, and sewers.

Another related aspect of job creation and destruction emerges most clearly in figure 2.2. A comparison of the two panels in this figure reveals that job destruction is more concentrated at plants with sharp employment changes than is job creation. The high concentration of job destruction at plant shutdowns— relative to the concentration of job creation at plant startups—is one manifestation of this general pattern. The relatively large fraction of job creation accounted for by plants that grow by at most 10 percent over the course of a year is another manifestation of the same pattern. In short, both job creation and job destruction are concentrated at plants that experience sharp employment change, but concentration is greater for job destruction.

We can tie this discussion of concentration in job creation and destruction to our previous remarks about heterogeneity in plant-level employent movements. We summarized the heterogeneity in plant-level employment movements by reporting that excess job reallocation equals 15.4 percent of employment in an average year. This figure indicates that one set of plants creates a large number of new jobs while, during the same year, another set destroys a large number of existing jobs. The concentration statistics enable us to refine this characterization. First, we note that the median growth rate among expanding (contracting) plants is about 10 percent (-10 percent) in the annual data. This means, of course, that half of the plants grow (contract) by no more than the median rate. The upper-left pie chart in figure 2.3 shows that the one-half of the expanding plants that grow by no more than 10 percent annually account for only one-eighth of annual job creation. Figure 2.3 also shows that the one-half of the contracting plants that contract by no more than 10 percent account for only one-tenth of annual job de-

---

11. See, e.g., Carrington (1993).

struction. The upshot of these observations is that job creation (destruction) is far from evenly spread among the set of growing (shrinking) plants. Instead, most job creation occurs at relatively few plants that grow much more rapidly than the typical growing plant. Likewise, most job destruction occurs at relatively few plants that contract much more sharply than the typical contracting plant.

2.4 Cyclicality

The preceding sections developed several key facts about the average behavior of gross job flows over time. This section addresses three straightforward questions about time variation in gross job flows. First, does the magnitude of gross job flows vary much over time? Second, how is time variation in gross job flows related to the business cycle? And third, do the fractions of job creation and destruction accounted for by startups and shutdowns vary over the business cycle?

Table 2.1 indicates that gross job flow rates vary considerably over time. The job reallocation rate ranges from 17 percent to 24 percent of employment per year, based on twelve-month sampling intervals, and from 8 percent to 15 percent per quarter, based on three-month sampling intervals. A noteworthy feature of the data is the relatively volatile nature of job destruction. As measured by the time-series standard deviation, job destruction varies 50 percent more than job creation in the annual data and 78 percent more in the quarterly data.

Plots of the job flow measures clearly illustrate these features of the data. Figure 2.4 depicts the evolution of annual rates of job creation, destruction, reallocation, and net employment growth from 1973 to 1988. Figure 2.5 shows how the corresponding quarterly time series evolve from 1972:Q2 to 1988:Q4. The shaded regions in figure 2.5 denote recessions, as designated by the National Bureau of Economic Research (NBER).

These figures point to distinctly different cyclical patterns for job creation and destruction. As expected, job creation tends to fall, and job destruction tends to rise, during recessions. But the cyclical behavior of these two series is not symmetrical. Job destruction rises dramatically during recessions, whereas job creation initially declines by a relatively modest amount. The quarterly plots, in particular, show some tendency toward an upturn in job creation one or two quarters after a sharp increase in job destruction. This lagging behavior of job creation probably reflects a creation of new jobs that is stimulated by a larger pool of job-seeking persons.

Figure 2.4
**Net and Gross Job Flow Rates in Manufacturing:
Annual, 1973 to 1988**

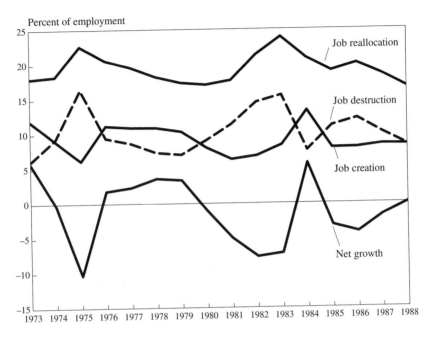

Table 2.5 presents time-series correlations involving net and gross job flow rates. The table confirms that job destruction is strongly countercyclical (i.e., negatively correlated with net employment change), and that job creation is procyclical. Especially in the quarterly data, job creation exhibits a smaller contemporaneous correlation with net employment growth than does job destruction.

Table 2.5 also documents the countercyclicality of job reallocation. In other words, large net employment contractions coincide with high rates of job reallocation. This observation restates the previous observation that the variability of job destruction exceeds that of job creation. Unlike some other aspects of time variation in the gross job flow data, the countercyclicality of job reallocation is about equally strong in both annual and quarterly data (-0.52 and -0.58).

Figure 2.6 addresses cyclical variation in the concentration of job creation and destruction by separately showing the job flows accounted for by startups, shutdowns, and continuing plants. Contrary to the impression conveyed by

Figure 2.5
**Net and Gross Job Flow Rates in Manufacturing:
Quarterly, 1972 to 1988**

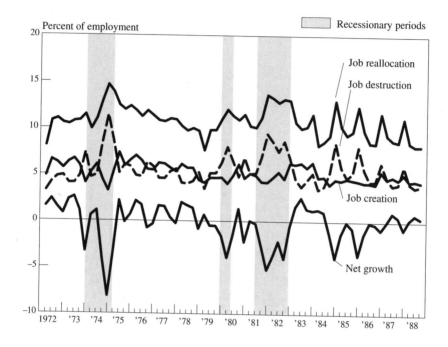

Table 2.5
Cyclical Characteristics of Job Flows in Manufacturing

Correlation Between Rates of	Annual 1973-88	Quarterly 72:Q2-88:Q4
Job Creation and Net Employment Growth..........	0.91	0.69
Job Destruction and Net Employment Growth	−0.96	−0.92
Job Reallocation and Net Employment Growth.......	−0.52	−0.58
Job Creation and Job Destruction.................	−0.75	−0.36

Figure 2.6
**Job Creation and Destruction in Manufacturing by
Recent Plant History: Quarterly, 1972 to 1988**

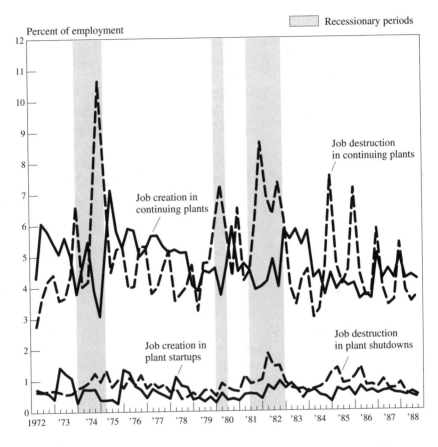

some observers, shutdowns do not account for an unusually large fraction of
job destruction during recessions, nor do startups account for an unusually
large fraction of job creation during booms.

2.5   The Connection between Job Reallocation and Worker Reallocation

We now draw together several strands of the analysis in this chapter to spell
out more fully the connection between job reallocation and worker reallocation. Our first objective is to quantify the fraction of worker reallocation
activity that is demand-driven in the sense of being induced by shifts in the dis-

tribution of job opportunities across locations. To address this issue, we compare the total number of persons who switch jobs or employment status—total worker reallocation—with the number of switches required to accommodate the reallocation of jobs.

Recall that the annual job reallocation figures are calculated from employment changes over twelve-month intervals. A meaningful comparison requires a consistent measure of worker reallocation. With this observation in mind, we calculate total worker reallocation as the sum of two pieces. The first is the number of persons who have job tenure of twelve months or less. Based on the Current Population Survey (CPS), Hall (1982, p. 717) reports that this number equals 28.2 percent of employment in 1978. The second is the number of currently jobless persons who were employed twelve months earlier. Based on our own analysis of the CPS, we estimate that this number equals 8.6 percent of employment.[12] Summing these two pieces, the total number of persons who currently have a different job or employment status than they had twelve months earlier equals 28.2 + 8.6 = 36.8 percent of employment. This figure represents our estimate of the total worker reallocation rate in an average year.

From table 2.1, the amount of worker reallocation required to accommodate job reallocation is between 11.7 percent and 19.4 percent of employment in an average year. Hence, taking the ratio of the job reallocation rates to the total worker reallocation rate, we calculate that 32 percent to 53 percent of all worker reallocation arises to accommodate shifts in the distribution of employment opportunities across locations.[13] Simply put, job reallocation accounts for between one-third and and one-half of total worker reallocation.[14]

Two observations provide further perspective on the magnitude of job reallocation's contribution to worker reallocation. First, the preceding calculation neglects secondary waves of worker reallocation initiated by job creation

---

12. This figure represents an average over the 1968–87 period. We explain our procedure for estimating this figure in Davis and Haltiwanger (1992, p. 833).

13. For a discussion of potential biases in this calculation, see Davis and Haltiwanger (1992, p. 834).

14. Studies by Lane, Isaac, and Stevens (1993) and by Anderson and Meyer (1994) also compare the magnitudes of worker reallocation and job reallocation. Both studies rely upon linked employer-worker data and are thus able to compute exact ratios rather than bounds. Using measurement procedures that are reasonably comparable with our own, Lane et al. report that job reallocation accounts for 44 percent of worker reallocation in Maryland's manufacturing sector. They also report figures for other major industry groups ranging from 28 percent in retail trade to 45 percent in transportation, communication, and utilities. Based on data for several states, Anderson and Meyer report that job reallocation accounts for only 31 percent of worker reallocation, but their measurement procedures are not closely analogous to ours. In Davis and Haltiwanger (1994a) we provide a full discussion of how the measurement procedures and calculations in these two papers relate to our own.

and destruction. For example, a person who quits an old job in favor of a newly created job potentially creates a chain of further quits as other workers reshuffle across the new set of job openings. It follows that the direct plus indirect contribution of job reallocation to worker reallocation exceeds the 32 percent to 53 percent figure derived above.

Second, a certain amount of worker reallocation inevitably arises from life cycle considerations as old workers retire and young workers enter the workforce. If the typical person works for forty-five years, then retirement and initial labor force entry directly cause transitions between employment and nonemployment equal to roughly 4.4 percent of the workforce in a typical year. It follows from our figure for total worker reallocation that simple life cycle effects account for roughly 12 percent of worker reallocation. After accounting for job reallocation and life cycle effects, the residual amount of worker reallocation equals 13.0 percent to 20.7 percent of employment, or 35 percent to 56 percent of all worker reallocation. This component of worker reallocation reflects temporary exits from the workforce and the sorting and resorting of workers across existing jobs for a variety of reasons. Thus, according to our estimates, these supply-side reasons for worker reallocation are neither more nor less important than demand-side reasons for worker reallocation.

Our facts on the concentration and persistence of gross job flows also shed light on the connection between job reallocation and worker reallocation. Since only one-third of job destruction is accounted for by establishments that shrink by less than 25 percent over the span of a year, the bulk of job destruction cannot be accommodated by normal rates of worker attrition resulting from retirements and quits. In other words, most of the job destruction we measure represents job loss from the point of view of workers. Since annual job creation and destruction primarily reflect persistent establishment-level employment changes, the bulk of annual job creation and destruction cannot be implemented by temporary layoff and recall policies. Hence, most of the job destruction we measure reflects permanent job loss that leads to a change in employer, a long-term unemployment spell, exit from the labor force, or some combination of these events.

3

Similarities and Differences by Industry and Other Sectors

This chapter describes how job creation and destruction vary among sectors within manufacturing. "Sectors" are groups of plants defined by observable characteristics such as region, industry, capital intensity, wage level, plant age, plant size, size of parent firm, degree of product differentiation, and exposure to international trade.[1] A summary of our chief findings in this chapter follows.

• *Pervasive job reallocation: Almost every sector we examine exhibits large gross job flows. Excess job reallocation rates typically exceed 10 percent of employment per year.*

• *Industry differences in job reallocation: Average annual job reallocation rates vary greatly across industries, ranging from more than 25 percent in lumber and apparel to less than 15 percent in tobacco, chemicals, and petroleum.*

• *Job stability and wages: High-wage plants exhibit smaller gross job flow rates. For example, job destruction equals 13.6 percent of employment per year in the bottom quintile of the plant-wage distribution but only 8.7 percent in the top quintile. Thus, higher-wage jobs are more durable.*

• *Job stability and international trade: Gross job flow rates show little relationship to either import-based or export-based measures of exposure to international trade.*

• *Job flows and factor intensity: Gross job flow rates decline with capital intensity. The net job growth rate increases with capital intensity but declines sharply with energy intensity.*

• *Job flows and productivity growth: Industries with high total factor productivity growth exhibit higher net employment growth and more within-industry job reallocation.*

---

1. Chapter 4 treats job creation and destruction by employer size and plant age.

3.1 Variation across Industries

The upper panel of table 3.1 displays average annual net and gross job flow rates by two-digit industry. It reveals a pattern of strikingly large gross rates of job creation and destruction in every industry. Even the leather industry, which shrank by nearly 5 percent per year on net, experienced average job creation rates of 9 percent per year. The high average rates of *excess* job reallocation in table 3.1 indicate that this pattern largely reflects simultaneous job creation and destruction within industries, not alternate years of industry expansion and contraction.

3.1.1 Implications for Worker Flows

Recall that we can use the gross job flow measures to place bounds on the number of workers who must change jobs or employment status to accommodate the reshuffling of employment opportunities across locations. This minimum amount of worker reallocation averages between 8 percent and 17 percent of employment per year for two-digit manufacturing industries. The upper bound on worker reallocation induced by job reallocation averages between 13 percent and 27 percent of employment per year. In line with our analysis in chapter 2, these figures imply that disturbances to the structure of plant-level labor demand induce large gross worker flows in every two-digit manufacturing industry.

3.1.2 Excess Job Reallocation and Plant-Level Heterogeneity

Recall, also, that excess job reallocation measures how much job creation and destruction occurs beyond the quantity required to bring about net sectoral contraction or expansion. This excess job reallocation ranges from roughly 9 to 10 percent of employment per year in the primary metals, tobacco, and paper industries to 20 percent in the apparel and lumber industries. These uniformly high rates of excess job reallocation say that every industry exhibits substantial heterogeneity among plants in the direction of employment change. In a given year, many plants expand employment while other plants in the same industry contract employment. We interpret this fact to mean that plant-level labor demand contains a large element of uncertainty that is idiosyncratic to the individual plant or firm.

One response to this interpretation is to criticize the use of two-digit industry definitions as a sectoral classification scheme. Classification schemes based on other plant characteristics, or finer industry definitions, might yield much smaller excess job reallocation rates. We consider sectoral classification

Table 3.1
Job Flows by Two-Digit Industry, 1973 to 1988

Mean Annual Rates

Industry	Job Creation	Job Destruction	Job Reallocation	Net Growth	Excess Reallocation	Minimum Worker Reallocation
Food	8.6	9.6	18.2	−1.1	16.4	10.0
Tobacco	5.7	7.9	13.6	−2.1	10.1	8.6
Textiles	7.3	9.9	17.2	−2.5	12.3	11.1
Apparel	10.8	14.4	25.2	−3.6	19.7	15.3
Lumber	12.4	14.1	26.5	−1.7	19.9	16.5
Furniture	10.1	10.8	20.9	−0.7	15.4	13.2
Paper	6.2	6.8	13.0	−0.6	10.1	8.0
Printing	8.8	8.2	17.1	0.6	15.0	9.5
Chemicals	6.6	7.5	14.1	−0.8	11.7	8.2
Petroleum	6.2	8.4	14.6	−2.2	10.9	9.1
Rubber	10.7	10.1	20.8	0.6	15.2	13.2
Leather	8.9	13.7	22.6	−4.9	16.8	14.2
Stone, Clay, Glass	9.2	11.1	20.3	−1.9	15.9	12.3
Primary Metals	6.5	9.7	16.2	−3.1	9.3	11.6
Fabricated Metals	9.5	10.9	20.5	−1.4	15.5	12.7
Nonelectric Machinery	9.9	10.8	20.7	−0.9	14.7	13.4
Electric Machinery	9.8	9.7	19.6	0.1	14.5	12.3
Transportation	9.2	9.3	18.6	−0.1	13.5	11.8
Instruments	8.7	8.9	17.6	−0.1	14.1	10.5
Miscellaneous	10.9	13.2	24.1	−2.3	19.3	14.4
Total Manufacturing	9.1	10.3	19.4	−1.1	15.4	11.7
Standard Deviation	1.5	1.9	3.1	1.3	2.6	2.1

Percentages of Manufacturing

Industry	Job Creation	Job Destruction	Employment
Food	7.6	7.6	8.1
Tobacco	0.2	0.3	0.3
Textiles	3.6	4.3	4.5
Apparel	7.8	9.3	6.6
Lumber	4.7	4.8	3.4
Furniture	2.8	2.6	2.5
Paper	2.4	2.3	3.5
Printing	6.4	5.3	6.6
Chemicals	3.5	3.5	4.8
Petroleum	0.5	0.6	0.8
Rubber	4.5	3.8	3.8
Leather	1.1	1.6	1.2
Stone, Clay, and Glass	3.1	3.3	3.1
Primary Metals	4.0	5.3	5.6
Fabricated Metals	8.7	8.9	8.3
Nonelectric Machinery	12.5	12.2	11.5
Electric Machinery	10.8	9.5	10.0
Transportation	10.0	9.0	9.9
Instruments	3.4	3.0	3.5
Miscellaneous	2.5	2.7	2.1

schemes based on other plant characteristics later. Here, we consider the consequences of finer industry definitions.

The proposition that finer industry definitions produce much smaller excess job reallocation rates within industries must, when pushed to its limit, hold true. If we define each plant as its own industry, excess job reallocation equals 0 within every industry. A more interesting exercise inquires how a standard, but highly detailed, industrial classification scheme affects the measured amount of excess job reallocation within industries. To carry out this exercise, we consider four-digit manufacturing industries, as defined in the government's Standard Industrial Classification (SIC) System. There are approximately 450 four-digit manufacturing industries under the SIC. To appreciate the level of detail captured by this sectoral classification scheme, note that the average industry has about 39,000 employees and represents only .04 percent of aggregate employment in the U.S. economy.[2]

Table 3.2 summarizes the distribution of annual excess job reallocation rates for detailed manufacturing industries. According to the upper panel, the median value for average excess job reallocation rates is 12.9 percent of employment per year. The panel also reveals that 75 percent (95 percent) of the detailed manufacturing industries exhibit average excess job reallocation rates greater than 10 percent (6 percent) of employment per year. Hence, this fine industry disaggregation of manufacturing employment fails to carry us very far toward an accounting of excess job reallocation. We infer that the typical four-digit manufacturing industry experiences simultaneously high rates of job creation and destruction in an average year.

The lower panel of table 3.2 summarizes the distribution of excess job reallocation rates over all industry-year observations from 1973 to 1988. Unlike the upper panel, it captures year-to-year variation in industry-level excess job reallocation rates. Ninety percent of all industry-year observations show excess job reallocation rates of at least 5 percent. This figure and the other entries in the lower panel point out the rarity of episodes in which plant-level employment changes in the same direction for all plants within an industry. Evidently, the typical pattern of industry performance entails considerable heterogeneity in plant-level employment changes.

3.1.3   Which Industries Create the Most Jobs?

To conclude this section, we examine the cross-industry variation in gross job flows from a different angle. Specifically, the lower panel of table 3.1 dis-

---

2. This last figure is calculated as 39,000 divided by 115 million, the number of civilian employees in 1988 (Executive Office of the President, Council of Economic Advisers, 1993, table B-31).

Table 3.2
Excess Job Reallocation Rates for Detailed Manufacturing Industries: Summary Statistics, 1973 to 1988

Average Annual Excess Reallocation Rates[a] (Percentiles of the Distribution)								
1%	5%	10%	25%	50%	75%	90%	95%	99%
4.1	6.2	7.4	9.9	12.9	15.8	19.4	21.7	25.6

Unweighted Mean: 13.2   Size-Weighted Mean: 13.2
Number of Industry Observations: 514[b]

Annual Excess Reallocation Rates[c] (Percentiles of the Distribution)								
1%	5%	10%	25%	50%	75%	90%	95%	99%
0.8	3.2	4.9	8.2	12.3	17.0	22.4	25.9	34.7

Unweighted Mean: 13.2   Size-Weighted Mean: 13.2
Number of Industry-Year Observations: 7137

Memorandum: The average number of employees per industry is 39,081 on an unweighted basis and 117,537 on a size-weighted basis.

[a]For each four-digit manufacturing industry, we computed the average annual excess job reallocation rate. Panel entries summarize the distribution of these industry-average excess reallocation rates.
[b]There are 448 distinct four-digit manufacturing industries under the 1972 SIC system and 456 under the 1987 SIC system. A total of 514 distinct industries appear under at least one of the systems.
[c]Panel entries summarize the distribution of annual excess job reallocation rates for four-digit manufacturing industries over the 1973 to 1988 period.

plays the percentage of manufacturing job creation and destruction accounted for by each two-digit industry. This table is calculated directly from information on gross job flows and employment shares in the upper panel of table 3.1. Not surprisingly, industry employment shares largely determine which industries contribute most to the creation and destruction of jobs. Four mainline manufacturing industries—fabricated metals, electric machinery, nonelectric machinery, and transportation—account for more than 40 percent of job creation and destruction in U.S. manufacturing.

3.2 Variation across Regions

Table 3.3 presents information on average net and gross job flows by census region. As the upper panel indicates, net employment growth rates vary across regions. Manufacturing employment shrank by 2.7 percent per year between 1972 and 1988 in the Middle Atlantic states while expanding by 1.0 percent per year in the Mountain states. The differences in net employment growth

Table 3.3
Net and Gross Job Flow Rates by Census Region, 1973 to 1988

Mean Annual Rates

Region	Job Creation	Job Destruction	Job Reallocation	Net Growth	Excess Reallocation	Minimum Worker Reallocation
Northeast	9.0	10.0	19.0	−1.0	14.8	11.6
Middle Atlantic	8.4	11.1	19.6	−2.7	15.7	11.7
South Atlantic	8.1	10.0	18.0	−1.9	12.8	11.6
E. South Central............	9.2	9.4	18.6	−0.2	14.5	11.3
W. South Central...........	8.8	9.1	18.0	−0.3	14.5	10.7
E. North Central............	8.9	9.5	18.4	−0.6	14.2	11.3
W. North Central...........	10.0	10.5	20.5	−0.5	16.3	12.4
Mountain	11.3	10.2	21.5	1.0	17.2	13.0
Pacific....................	11.7	11.3	23.1	0.4	18.3	13.9
Standard Deviation......	1.2	0.8	1.7	1.1	1.7	0.9

Percentages of Manufacturing

Region	Job Creation	Job Destruction	Employment
Northeast	7.2	7.2	7.3
Middle Atlantic	15.9	18.8	17.2
South Atlantic	21.0	23.3	23.8
E. South Central..............	6.8	6.2	6.8
W. South Central.............	15.0	13.9	15.5
E. North Central..............	6.8	6.6	7.0
W. North Central.............	8.4	7.9	7.7
Mountain	3.3	2.6	2.6
Pacific.......................	15.7	13.5	12.2

rates across regions are, however, dwarfed by the pace of job reallocation within each region. Excess job reallocation rates exceed 12 percent in every region. Once again, job reallocation greatly exceeds the amount required to accommodate net employment shifts between sectors.

One point of contrast between the regional and industry patterns of variation in gross job flows is captured by the cross-sectoral standard deviation of job reallocation rates. According to table 3.1, the standard deviation of job reallocation rates across industries is 3.1 percent, whereas the corresponding figure from table 3.3 for regions is only 1.7 percent. Hence, in spite of relatively large differences in net growth rates across regions, the regional variation in job reallocation rates is fairly small. This comparison indicates that the factors entering into the determination of gross job creation and destruction rates vary more among industries than among broad geographic areas.

The lower panel of table 3.3 reports the contribution of each census region to the nationwide creation and destruction of manufacturing jobs. Since job creation and destruction rates vary only mildly across regions, most regions account for shares of job creation and destruction nearly equal to their shares of employment. The Pacific region's large contribution to job creation relative to its employment share is a notable exception.

3.3   Variation by Wage Level

We now consider how job flow behavior varies with a plant's position in the plant-wage distribution. Our findings in this regard pertain to three prominent questions about the U.S. manufacturing jobs base: Has there been a disproportionate loss of high-wage manufacturing jobs during the 1970s and 1980s? Has there been a disproportionate loss of low-wage manufacturing jobs, the type of jobs likely to offer relatively attractive employment opportunities to less-skilled workers? How do wages vary with job durability? The last question involves the relationship between gross job flow rates and wages. The first two questions involve the relationship between net job growth and wages. As will become evident, our investigation here constitutes only a partial evaluation of these questions.

To carry out the investigation, we first sort plants into five groups defined by quintiles of the plant-wage distribution.[3] We carry out this sorting operation for each year in the sample. Next, we compute job flow rates for each wage group and year. Averaging across years for each wage group yields the figures reported in the top panel of table 3.4.

3.3.1   Wages and Net Job Growth

Employment contracted by 2.7 percent per year between 1973 and 1988 for plants in the top quintile and by 1.3 percent in the second highest quintile of the plant-wage distribution. Plants in the next two quintiles experienced more modest contractions or no employment change. In the bottom quintile, employment contracted by almost 1 percent per year. Thus, the U.S. manufacturing jobs base has experienced disproportionately large employment losses at the top and bottom ends of the plant-wage distribution.

---

3. We computed quintiles from the hours-weighted distribution of plants' mean hourly wages for production workers in constant 1982 dollars.

Table 3.4
Net and Gross Job Flow Rates by Level of Plant Wages, 1973 to 1988

Mean Annual Rates, Quintiles of the Plant-Wage Distribution[a]

Hourly Wage Class (1982 dollars)	Job Creation	Job Destruction	Job Reallocation	Net Growth	Excess Reallocation
Very Low (0–5.8).	12.5	13.3	25.8	–0.8	21.1
Moderately Low (5.8–7.6)	10.4	10.4	20.7	0.0	16.3
Average (7.6–9.6)	9.2	9.5	18.7	–0.4	14.6
Moderately High (9.6–12.3).	7.0	8.3	15.3	–1.3	11.8
Very High (12.3+)	6.4	9.0	15.4	–2.7	10.7
Standard Deviation.	2.2	1.7	3.9	0.9	3.7

Percentages of Manufacturing, Quintiles of the Plant-Wage Distribution[a]

	Job Creation	Job Destruction	Employment
Very Low	27.4	26.3	20.0
Moderately Low	22.9	20.5	20.0
Average	20.2	18.9	20.0
Moderately High	15.5	16.4	20.0
Very High.	14.0	17.9	20.0

Mean Annual Rates, Quintiles of the Plant-Wage Distribution within Industries[b]

	Job Creation	Job Destruction	Job Relocation	Net Growth	Excess Reallocation
Very Low.	12.4	12.6	24.9	–0.19	16.0
Moderately Low	9.8	10.0	19.8	–0.19	12.0
Average	8.7	8.9	17.7	–0.22	10.1
Moderately High.	7.4	8.7	16.1	–1.37	8.8
Very High	7.3	10.4	17.6	–3.09	9.4
Standard Deviation.	1.9	1.4	3.1	1.1	2.6

Percentages of Total, Quintiles of the Plant-Wage Distribution within Industries[b]

	Job Creation	Job Destruction	Employment
Very Low	27.0	24.7	19.9
Moderately Low	21.7	19.9	20.1
Average	19.2	17.7	20.0
Moderately High	16.2	17.3	20.0
Very High.	16.0	20.5	20.0

[a]For the two upper panels, we first coverted all wages to constant 1982 dollars using the GDP deflator for personal consumption expenditures. Second, we computed quintiles of employment-weighted distribution of plants' mean hourly production worker wages by year. (The 1973-1988 average wage class intervals are shown in parentheses.) Third, we computed job flow rates by year and wage group. Finally, to obtain the reported figures, we computed the employment-weighted means across years by wage class.
[b]For the two lower panels, we sorted plants into industry-specific wage quintiles. We first computed quintiles of the employment-weighted distribution of hourly wages by year and four-digit industry. To obtain the reported figures, we then computed for each quintile the employment-weighted mean over industry-year observations.

Although it is not shown in the table, we have also examined the relationship between the industrial wage distribution and the job growth experience of plants over the 1973–88 period.[4] These calculations reveal strong net contraction of jobs in low-wage industries but, in contrast to table 3.4, no sharp differences in net growth rates among the other wage groups.

Further evidence on the role of between- versus within-industry effects is presented in the two lower panels of table 3.4. For the lower two panels, we sort plants into quintiles of the plant-wage distribution separately for every four-digit industry. The striking result that emerges is that within four-digit industries, net employment growth at the plant level decreases sharply with plant-level wages.

Combining the unreported industry-level results with the evidence in table 3.4 yields two inferences. First, the disproportionate loss of low-wage manufacturing jobs stems from the relatively rapid employment declines in low-wage manufacturing industries. Second, the disproportionate loss of high-wage manufacturing jobs revealed by table 3.4 does *not* reflect poor employment growth in high-wage industries. Rather, high-wage plants within the typical four-digit industry suffered comparatively rapid employment losses during the 1970s and 1980s.

These findings lend credence to popular concerns about job growth performance in the U.S. manufacturing sector. The substantial net contraction of jobs in the bottom quintile of the plant-wage distribution supports the view that employment opportunities for less-skilled workers in the manufacturing sector declined significantly during the 1973–88 period. Many other studies, relying upon a variety of data and empirical strategies, also find strong evidence of declining relative demand for less-skilled workers in the U.S. manufacturing sector and in the U.S. economy as a whole. Table 3.4 adds to the weight of this evidence.[5]

---

4. We sorted each four-digit industry into one of five groups based on its 1973–88 average percentile in the employment-weighted industry wage distribution. We then computed net and gross job flow rates for plants in each industry wage category. Note that this averaging procedure differs from the one used in table 3.4. Results based on the industry wage distribution were similar across a variety of wage measures. Results were also similar when we used an averaging procedure analogous to the one that underlies table 3.4.

5. We make no attempt here to summarize this evidence or to identify the economic forces behind the declining relative demand for less-skilled workers. A large literature on these topics has emerged. See, for example, Blackburn, Bloom, and Freeman (1990), Davis and Haltiwanger (1991), Juhn, Murphy, and Topel (1991), Krueger (1991a), Bound and Johnson (1992), Davis (1992), Juhn (1992), Katz and Murphy (1992), Murphy and Welch (1992, 1993), Juhn, Murphy, and Pierce (1993), Berman, Bound, and Griliches (1993), and Lawrence and Slaughter (1993). Levy and Murnane (1992) survey the literature.

Another popular concern about job growth performance in the U.S. manufacturing sector centers on the erosion of "good," high-paying jobs. Table 3.4
reveals an erosion of high-paying manufacturing jobs in the following sense:
on average, high-wage manufacturing plants experienced employment declines of 2.7 percent per year between 1972 and 1988. Over the same time
period, total manufacturing employment shrank by 1.1 percent per year, and
civilian employment expanded by 2.1 percent per year.[6] Thus, high-wage manufacturing plants experienced sharp employment losses in both absolute and
relative terms.

This pattern of employment losses at high-wage plants should be interpreted with caution. It is not informative about changes in the number of
manufacturing jobs that offer wages above a fixed level. Two observations underlie this note of caution. First, individual plants may migrate across wage
classes in ways that relate systematically to their employment growth patterns.
For example, younger plants pay lower wages and exhibit high employment
growth rates, whereas older plants with more experienced workforces pay
higher wages and exhibit slower employment growth. Thus, the seeming erosion of the high-wage manufacturing jobs base in table 3.4 may simply reflect
the life cycle dynamics of individual plants operating in an environment with
a stationary distribution of jobs by wage level. Second, as shown in Davis and
Haltiwanger (1991), the plant-wage distribution grew increasingly dispersed
during the sample period. The hourly wage at the 80th percentile of the plant-
wage distribution rose from $11.61 in 1973 to $12.16 in 1980 and $12.85 in
1986.

3.3.2   Wages and Gross Job Flows

The upper panel of table 3.4 also shows that the magnitude of gross job flows
falls sharply with the relative level of plant wages. For example, the gross job
destruction rate in the bottom wage quintile exceeds the average rate in the top
two quintiles by more than 50 percent. Stated differently, one-year survival
rates are much higher for jobs at high-wage plants. As a second example,
excess job reallocation in the bottom wage quintile equals 21.1 percent of
employment per year, which is nearly double the corresponding rate in the top
quintile. Similar patterns hold for the other gross job flow statistics reported in
table 3.4.

---

6. Calculated from table B.31 in Executive Office of the President, Council of Economic Advisers
(1993).

Human capital theory offers a coherent explanation for these patterns in the data.[7] Workers with greater human capital—that is, a greater capacity to produce valuable goods and services—command higher wages in the market-place. In this vein, we interpret differences in mean wages across plants as largely reflecting differences in average worker levels of human capital across plants.

Human capital theory stresses that some skills and productive attributes are more valuable when applied to particular locations and firms. Furthermore, employers and workers are likely to share the returns to specific forms of human capital, an arrangement that provides each party with incentives to preserve a valuable employment relationship. By this logic, greater levels of specific human capital mean a stronger mutual attachment of employer and worker. Hence, greater levels of specific human capital imply more durable employment relationships in the face of changes and disturbances that alter the value of the employment relationship.

We can now articulate the elements of a human capital explanation for the connection between wages and gross job flows. High-wage plants operate with workers who have high average levels of human capital. Differences in average wages and human capital levels across plants partly reflect differences in plant- and firm-specific components of human capital. High levels of specific human capital at high-wage plants imply greater durability in the employment relationship and, consequently, smaller gross job flows.

3.4 Variation by Exposure to International Trade

To many critical observers, foreign competition and international trade present major threats to American jobs and job security, especially in the man-ufacturing sector. These observers stress that foreign competition exposes American firms and workers to additional sources of disturbance and a more volatile marketplace.[8] They also stress that greater openness to international trade facilitates the transfer of certain types of jobs to foreign production sites.

We address these issues here by analyzing the relationship between job flow behavior and exposure to international trade. To carry out the analysis,

---

7. Oi (1962), Becker (1975, chap. 2), Mincer and Jovanovic (1981), and Parsons (1986) are especially pertinent to the discussion at hand.

8. On theoretical grounds, the relationship between trade exposure and labor demand volatility is ambiguous. Although international trade exposes the U.S. economy to disturbances that originate in other economies, it also insulates U.S. producers from the effects of domestic product demand disturbances.

Table 3.5
Net and Gross Job Flow Rates by Measures of Foreign Trade Exposure: Mean Annual Rates, 1973 to 1986

Import Penetration Ratio of Four-Digit Industry[a]						
Import Ratio (Percentage of imports plus output)	Job Creation	Job Destruc- tion	Job Reallo- cation	Net Growth	Excess Reallo- cation	Employ- ment Share
Very Low (0–0.8)	8.9	10.1	18.9	−1.2	14.1	21.2
Moderately Low (0.8–3.3)....	9.6	10.2	19.8	−0.7	13.3	18.8
Average (3.3–6.8)	9.4	10.0	19.4	−0.6	13.0	21.4
Moderately High (6.8–13.1) ..	8.8	9.5	18.4	−0.7	11.7	21.0
Very High (over 13.1).......	9.4	12.2	21.6	−2.8	17.6	17.7
Standard Deviation......	0.3	0.9	1.1	0.8	0.8	

Export Share of Four-Digit Industry[b]						
Export Share (Percentage of output)	Job Creation	Job Destruc- tion	Job Reallo- cation	Net Growth	Excess Reallo- cation	Employ- ment Share
Very Low (0–1.3)	9.5	10.9	20.4	−1.3	15.1	22.2
Modererately Low (1.3–3.1) ..	9.3	10.9	20.1	−1.6	14.0	16.5
Average (3.1–5.8)	9.0	9.7	18.7	−0.7	12.5	17.9
Moderately High (5.8–12.5) ..	9.0	10.1	19.0	−1.1	12.3	20.1
Very High (over 12.5).......	9.2	10.2	19.3	−1.0	12.0	23.4
Standard Deviation......	0.2	0.5	0.6	0.3	1.2	

[a]Import penetration ratio is the ratio of imports to the sum of imports and domestic output for the industry. Quintiles are based on the pooled industry-year trade data. Industries are allocated to classes on an annual basis.

[b]Export share is the ratio of exports to output for the industry. Quintiles are based on the pooled industry-year trade data. Industries are allocated to classes on an annual basis.

we first sort four-digit manufacturing industries by two measures of foreign trade exposure: the import penetration ratio (imports as a fraction of imports plus domestic output) and the export share (exports as a fraction of domestic output). We then examine how net and gross job flow rates vary by these measures. Table 3.5 reports the results.[9]

Strikingly, the table shows no systematic relationship between the magnitude of gross job flows and exposure to international trade. The only aspect of table 3.5 suggesting that international trade reduces job security is the large

---

9. This analysis is conducted for the sample period 1973–86. The reason we do not use the 1987–88 gross flows data in this case is that a consistent four-digit dataset matching up the gross flows and the trade statistics is not easy to construct, given the major changes in the SIC in 1987.

rate of gross job destruction among industries with a very high import penetration ratio. However, none of the other entries in the table indicate that greater exposure to international trade reduces job security. On balance, the evidence is highly unfavorable to the view that international trade exposure systematically reduces job security.

Human capital theory provides a simple alternative explanation for higher rates of job destruction and reallocation among industries with very high import shares. In the U.S. economy, import-intensive manufacturing industries pay relatively low wages and operate with relatively unskilled workforces.[10] Thus, according to the human capital theory sketched out above, import-intensive industries in the U.S. manufacturing sector are likely to exhibit relatively high job reallocation. To test this hypothesis, we examined the relationship between four-digit industry excess reallocation rates and measures of trade exposure. After controlling for the level of wages in the industry, we found no significant relationship between excess job reallocation and measures of either export or import intensity.[11] This evidence indicates that import-intensive industries exhibit greater gross job flows because their workers have relatively low levels of specific human capital—not because foreign competition subjects these industries to unusually large and volatile disturbances.

Net job growth also exhibits no systematic relationship to measures of foreign trade exposure in table 3.5. Again, industries with a very high import share are clear outliers; they contracted by 2.8 percent per year over the 1973–86 period. The sharp employment declines in these industries accord with the view that greater openness of the U.S. economy led to the displacement of domestic employment from low-skill manufacturing activities. A full evaluation of this view lies outside the scope of this book, but we note that careful studies suggest that international trade accounts for only part—possibly a small part—of employment losses in low-skill manufacturing industries. Patterns of technological change that reduce the relative demand for less-skilled workers appear to have played a major role.[12]

---

10. See Kuhn and Wooton (1991) for evidence.

11. Using time averages of four-digit industry-level data for the 1973–86 period, we regressed the excess reallocation rate on the export share, the import penetration ratio, and various real wage measures. Also, in specifications that considered changes between the first and second halves of the decade, we found little relationship between industry-level exposure to international trade and excess job reallocation.

12. See the references in note 5 to this chapter.

3.5   Variation by Productivity Growth, Factor Intensity, and Degree of Specialization

This section summarizes how job flow rates vary by several other characteristics of plants and industries. Table 3.6 focuses on three plant-level characteristics: degree of product specialization, physical capital per worker, and energy usage per worker. Table 3.7 focuses on an industry-level characteristic: total factor productivity growth.

Job creation, destruction, and excess reallocation all increase with product specialization. The increases in job creation and destruction with specialization roughly offset, so that net employment growth shows no monotonic relationship to degree of specialization. These results support the hypothesis that relative shifts in product demand constitute an important source of job reallocation. More specialized plants are more vulnerable to relative product demand shifts, resulting in larger gross job flows. Diversified plants offer a more stable employment environment.

Turning to factor intensity categories, net employment growth increases sharply with capital intensity despite higher job creation rates among less capital-intensive plants. In other words, job destruction rates fall sharply with capital intensity. This pattern, too, emerges as a prediction of the human capital theory we sketched above, once we recognize that human capital and physical capital tend to be complementary inputs into the production process. Because more capital-intensive plants operate with more human-capital-intensive workforces, we expect them to exhibit lower job destruction and reallocation rates.

More energy-intensive plants experience lower net job growth, lower gross job creation, and higher gross job destruction rates. This pattern probably reflects the sharp energy price increases that occurred over the sample period, which led to a systematic shift of resources away from more energy-intensive plants.

The results on energy and capital intensity offer a striking contrast. Presumably, capital-intensive plants tend to be energy-intensive. Nevertheless, energy-intensive plants experienced dramatic net employment losses during the 1973–88 period, whereas capital-intensive plants were net creators of relatively stable jobs. These results identify and highlight two of the many forces that underlie the high level and variability of job flows. On the one hand, energy price increases led to a shift of employment away from energy-intensive plants. On the other hand, technological progress or other forces led to a shift of employment toward more capital-intensive plants.

Table 3.6
Job Flow Rates by Other Plant-Level Characteristics: Product Specialization, Capital Intensity and Energy Intensity: Mean Annual Rates, 1973 to 1988

Degree of Product Specialization

Specialization (Primary product as percentage of output)[a]	Job Creation	Job Destruc- tion	Net Growth	Excess Reallo- cation	Employ- ment Share
Highly Diversified (0–53)......	7.0	8.0	−1.1	11.4	14.6
Moderately Diversified (54–73) .	7.3	8.0	−0.8	11.7	16.2
Moderately Specialized (74–92).	8.1	8.2	−0.1	12.3	16.7
Highly Specialized (93–99).....	9.5	9.7	−0.3	13.8	15.4
Completely Specialized (100)...	11.1	13.1	−2.0	20.0	37.1
Standard Deviation	1.7	2.3	0.7	3.8	

Capital Intensity

Capital Intensity (Millions of dollars per worker)[b]	Job Creation	Job Destruc- tion	Net Growth	Excess Reallo- cation	Employ- ment Share
Least (0–3.0)	10.2	20.6	−10.4	20.2	10.0
Ninth (3.0–6.2)	10.7	12.2	−1.4	18.8	10.0
Eighth (6.2–9.3).............	10.1	10.6	−0.6	16.7	10.0
Seventh (9.3–12.7)...........	9.7	9.8	−0.1	15.6	10.0
Sixth (12.7–16.5)............	9.2	9.3	−0.1	14.5	10.0
Fifth (16.5–21.0)	8.9	9.0	−0.1	13.9	10.0
Fourth (21.0–26.9)...........	8.6	8.3	0.4	13.3	10.0
Third (26.9–36.8)............	8.7	8.3	0.4	13.1	10.0
Second (36.8–60.1)	8.2	7.7	0.5	12.0	10.0
Most (over 60.1)	6.9	6.2	0.7	9.9	10.0
Standard Deviation	1.1	3.8	3.2	3.0	

Energy Intensity

Energy Intensity (Energy expenditures as percentage of shipments)[c]	Job Creation	Job Destruc- tion	Net Growth	Excess Reallo- cation	Employ- ment Share
Least (0–0.4)	12.9	11.8	1.1	21.0	10.0
Ninth (0.4–0.6)	10.5	8.8	1.7	15.5	10.0
Eighth (0.6–0.8).............	9.8	8.9	0.9	15.0	10.0
Seventh (0.8–1.0)............	8.9	9.1	−0.2	14.4	10.0
Sixth (1.0–1.3).............	8.9	9.4	−0.5	14.3	10.0
Fifth (1.3–1.6)	8.7	9.6	−0.9	14.2	10.0
Fourth (1.6–2.1).............	8.5	10.1	−1.6	14.1	10.0
Third (2.1–2.9).............	8.4	11.0	−2.6	14.3	10.0
Second (2.9–5.3)	8.0	11.5	−3.4	14.8	10.0
Most (over 5.3)	6.6	11.1	−4.5	12.2	10.0
Standard Deviation	1.6	1.1	1.9	2.2	

[a]Product specialization is the extent to which a plant specializes in producing its primary five-digit SIC product. Completely specialized plants produce only one product. The other categories are based upon quartiles of the remaining non-specialized plants, using the pooled 1972-88 data.

[b]Capital intensity is the ratio of the book value of capital to the long-run average employment level of the plant. Capital intensity deciles are constructed each year for various birth cohorts. Reported figures are averages over year-cohort cells. See the Technical Appendix for more details.

[c]Energy intensity is the ratio of energy expenditures to shipments. Deciles are based upon the plant-level pooled data in 1972-88.

Table 3.7
Job Flow Rates by Total Factor Productivity Growth:
Mean Annual Rates, 1973 to 1986

Productivity Growth Quintile	Job Creation	Job Destruc- tion	Net Growth	Excess Reallo- cation	Employ- ment Share	TFP Growth
Top....................	9.8	10.6	−0.7	13.8	19.5	3.3
Second	9.7	10.5	−0.8	13.7	20.4	0.7
Third.................	9.1	10.3	−1.3	13.4	19.8	0.1
Fourth................	8.8	9.8	−1.1	12.9	19.9	−0.5
Bottom	8.7	10.5	−1.8	12.0	20.3	−1.7
Standard Deviation........	0.5	0.3	0.4	0.7		

Note: Quintiles are constructed from the employment-weighted distribution of the 1973-1986 average industry-level total factor productivity growth rates.
    Total factor productivity growth rates for four-digit SIC industries are obtained from Gray (1989).
    Within-quintile means are constructed on an employment-weighted basis.

Turning to industry-level productivity, job creation is higher in industries with high total factor productivity growth.[13] In contrast, job destruction for an industry is not systematically related to productivity growth. Together, these findings imply that net employment growth and excess reallocation increase with productivity growth. Hence, industries that experience rapid productivity growth exhibit higher net employment growth rates but also more within-industry reallocation.

3.6 Quantifying the Role of Between-Sector Employment Shifts

A striking result in tables 3.1–3.7 is that simultaneous job creation and destruction are pervasive. For every definition of sector considered thus far, the rate of excess job reallocation is high in every sector. These findings suggest that much of the job reallocation represents within-sector shifts rather than between-sector shifts.

This conjecture can be formally analyzed by decomposing excess job reallocation into two components for every sectoral definition. One component represents the contribution of reshuffling employment opportunities among sectors, and the other component represents the contribution of reshuffling employment opportunities within sectors. The component of excess job reallo-

---

13. Like table 3.5, table 3.7 is based on analysis for the period 1972–86. Table 3.7 is based on combining four-digit datasets on gross flows and productivity. A consistent four-digit dataset is difficult to construct, given the SIC change in 1987.

cation due to between-sector shifts is measured by summing across sectors the deviation of the absolute growth rate for the sector from the absolute growth rate for total manufacturing. The component of job reallocation due to within-sector shifts is measured as the sum across sectors of the excess job reallocation in each sector.[14]

Table 3.8 reports the results of decomposing excess job reallocation for sectoral classification schemes defined in terms of industry (both two-digit and four-digit) and of two-digit industry cross-classified by region, state, wage class, energy intensity class, capital intensity class, product specialization class, plant and firm size class measures, ownership type, and detailed plant age.[15]

The remarkable aspect of the results in table 3.8 is the inability of between-sector shifts to account for excess job reallocation. Employment shifts among the approximately 450 four-digit industries account for a mere 13 percent of excess job reallocation. Simultaneously cutting by two-digit industry and each of the other plant characteristics considered also yields a small contribution of between-sector shifts. In results reported elsewhere, Davis and Haltiwanger (1992) show that even when sectors are defined simultaneously by two-digit industry, region, size class, plant age class, and ownership type (which yields 14,400 sectors), between-sector shifts account for only 39 percent of excess job reallocation.[16]

These results provide little support for the view that high rates of job reallocation arise primarily because of sectoral disturbances or economywide disturbances with differential sectoral effects. Instead, the results in table 3.8 point toward the view that job reallocation is fundamentally driven by plant-level heterogeneity in labor demand.

3.7 Sectoral Variation in the Persistence of Job Creation and Destruction

Recall from chapter 2 that annual job creation and destruction largely reflect persistent plant-level employment changes. This fact means that measured gross job flows are predominantly associated with long-term joblessness and

---

14. The formulas for calculating each of these components are presented and discussed in Davis and Haltiwanger (1992).

15. The results by employer size, detailed plant age, and ownership type preview results in chapter 4. The definitions of the size and age classes can be found in chapter 4 and in the technical appendix.

16. To appreciate the level of detail captured by this sectoral classification scheme, we remark that the average nonempty "sector" contains only about five sampled plants.

Table 3.8
Fraction of Excess Job Reallocation Resulting From Employment Shifts Between Sectors: Means of Values, 1972 to 1988

Sector	Number of Groups in Sector	Fraction Resulting from Shifts Between Sectors
Four-Digit Industry	448/456[a]	0.13
Two-Digit Industry	20	0.04
Two-Digit Industry by:		
Region	180	0.05
State[a]	980	0.14
Plant Wages	100	0.07
Energy Intensity	100	0.09
Capital Intensity	100	0.12
Product Specialization	100	0.06
Current Plant Size[b]	180	0.07
Average Plant Size	180	0.07
Average Firm Size	240	0.10
Ownership Type	40	0.05
Detailed Age[c]	160	0.16

[a]See the Technical Appendix for discussion of gross flows by state.
[b]See Chapter 4 and the Technical Appendix for definitions of alternative size-class measures.
[c]See Chapter 4 and the Technical Appendix for detailed age categories. Note that gross job flows by detailed age are computed only in 1978, 1983 and 1988.

worker reallocation across plants rather than temporary layoffs and recalls. Here, we inquire how the persistence properties of gross job flows vary across different types of manufacturing plants.

Table 3.9 summarizes one-year and two-year persistence rates for newly created and newly destroyed jobs across industries, regions, plant-wage classes, product specialization categories, energy intensity classes, and capital intensity classes. The table conveys a simple and powerful message: newly created and newly destroyed jobs are highly persistent across a variety of plant types. Every two-digit industry, every census geographic region, and every plant characteristic category exhibits a one-year persistence rate for job destruction of at least 78 percent. Two-year persistence rates for job destruction equal or exceed 65 percent in every case. We infer that measured annual gross job flows reflect permanent job reallocation activity.

Another salient aspect of table 3.9 involves the relative persistence rates of job creation and destruction. According to the table, the minimum persistence

Table 3.9
Persistence Rates for Newly Created and Newly Destroyed Jobs: Summary Statistics for Mean Annual Rates, 1973 to 1988

	One-Year Persistence Rates		Two-Year Persistence Rates	
	Creation	Destruction	Creation	Destruction
Two-Digit Industries				
Mean	.69	.82	.54	.74
Standard Deviation	.03	.02	.05	.03
Minimum	.64	.79	.45	.68
Maximum	.76	.84	.63	.79
Census Regions				
Mean	.70	.82	.54	.74
Standard Deviation	.01	.02	.02	.03
Minimum	.68	.78	.51	.69
Maximum	.72	.84	.58	.77
Product Specialization Categories				
Mean	.69	.81	.54	.72
Standard Deviation	.01	.02	.02	.03
Minimum	.68	.79	.51	.69
Maximum	.70	.84	.56	.77
Plant Wage Categories				
Mean	.70	.81	.55	.73
Standard Deviation	.02	.01	.02	.02
Minimum	.67	.80	.51	.71
Maximum	.72	.82	.58	.76
Energy Intensity Categories				
Mean	.69	.82	.54	.74
Standard Deviation	.01	.02	.01	.02
Minimum	.68	.79	.53	.71
Maximum	.72	.85	.57	.78
Capital Intensity Categories				
Mean	.70	.81	.55	.72
Standard Deviation	.02	.03	.03	.05
Minimum	.65	.78	.50	.69
Maximum	.73	.89	.58	.85

Note: For each industry, region, specialization category, wage category, energy intensity category and capital intensity category, we first computed mean persistence rates for available years between 1973 and 1988. Table entries display the indicated summary statistics for these mean annual rates.

Industries, regions, and plant characterisic categories are listed in Tables 3.1, 3.3, 3.4, and 3.6.

rate for job destruction exceeds the corresponding maximum rate for job creation under all six categorizations of manufacturing plants. Thus, the two-part characterization of plant-level employment dynamics developed in chapter 2 holds across industries and regions: (1) new jobs are risky in the sense that, with relatively high probability, they fail to survive beyond one or two years; (2) lost jobs reflect relatively persistent plant-level employment movements in the sense that, with high probability, these jobs are unlikely to reopen at the same location within one or two years.

4

Differences by Size and Age of Plants and Firms

In this chapter, we describe how job creation and destruction differ by size and age of manufacturing firms and plants. We also evaluate the empirical basis for conventional claims about the job-creating prowess of small businesses. Our chief findings and conclusions fall into five categories:

• *The small business job-creation myth:* Conventional wisdom about the job-creating prowess of small businesses rests on statistical fallacies and misleading interpretations of the data.

• *The dominant role of large, mature employers:* Large, mature plants and firms account for most newly created (and newly destroyed) manufacturing jobs.

• *Job creation rates and employer size:* Smaller manufacturing firms and plants exhibit sharply higher gross job creation rates but not higher net creation rates.

• *Job reallocation intensity by employer size and age:* Job reallocation rates decline sharply with plant age, plant size, and firm size.

• *Job durability by employer size and age:* One-year survival rates for the stock of existing jobs increase sharply with employer size and age. Furthermore, the short-term survival rates of newly created jobs rise with employer size. Hence, in terms of both new jobs and the typical existing job, larger employers offer greater job durability.

4.1 Context and Motivation

Few ideas about the U.S. economy reap greater homage in public discourse than the belief that small businesses are the fountainhead of job creation. Claims about the job-creating prowess of small business appear with remarkable regularity in a wide range of public pronouncements, including speeches

by prominent politicians, newspaper columns by leading opinion makers, statements from U.S. government agencies, and assessments by well-known analysts (see Davis, Haltiwanger, and Schuh, 1993 for a sampling of these claims).[1] Claims about the role of small businesses in creating jobs are frequently presented as justification for tax incentives, regulatory policies, and other government programs that favor the small business sector.

Aside from the public discourse, three additional factors motivate our interest in the relationship of job flows to employer size and age. First, academic research has convincingly established strong connections between employer size and important economic outcomes like the level and inequality of wages, the incidence of fringe benefits, workforce quality, the pace of technological innovation, and the likelihood of unionization.[2] These findings prompt us to ask how job creation and destruction vary by employer size, a question that we address for the U.S. manufacturing sector.

Second, chapter 3 found large variation in job creation and destruction rates across industries. Because the size distributions of firms and plants differ greatly across industries, differences in job flow behavior across employers of different sizes can perhaps account for cross-industry variation in job creation and destruction rates. As a necessary condition for this explanation to hold, gross job flow behavior must vary systematically with firm and plant size. This chapter documents a systematic relationship of this sort.

Finally, chapter 3 also found high rates of excess job reallocation within industries and regions. This finding prompts us to investigate whether some other identifying characteristic of plants—such as size of plant or parent firm, or age of plant—better serves to classify plants into groups with relatively homogeneous patterns of employment change.

4.2 Measuring Employer Size and Employer Age

There are many related but distinct concepts of employer size and age. Our analysis considers one concept of employer age—plant age—and four different concepts of employer size: current plant size, average plant size, firm size, and ownership type. Plant age equals the number of years since the plant's

---

1. See also Small Business Administration (various years) and Birch (1979, 1987). The chorus of praise for the job creation performance of small businesses has been challenged by only a handful of critics. See Armington and Odle (1982a) and chapter 3 in Brown, Hamilton, and Medoff (1990). For journalistic pieces that question conventional wisdom about the small business role in creating jobs, see Wessel and Brown (1988), Marshall (1993), and Kinsley (1993).
2. Recent studies include Acs and Audretsch (1988), Brown and Medoff (1989), Brown, Hamilton, and Medoff (1990), Davis and Haltiwanger (1991, 1993), and Hansen (1992).

construction or conversion to manufacturing use. For figures computed from published data sources, current size equals the number of workers employed by the plant on a particular date during the year. For LRD-based figures, plant size equals the simple average of the plant's current employment and its employment twelve months earlier.[3] In contrast, average plant size equals the weighted mean number of employees, computed over all observations on the plant during the 1963–88 period. Firm size equals the weighted mean number of manufacturing workers employed by the plant's parent firm, computed over all the observations of the firm in the Census of Manufactures.[4] Finally, ownership type indicates whether the plant's parent firm operates one or multiple plants.

A few remarks will help to clarify the usefulness, strengths, and weaknesses of these alternative measures of employer age and size. Plant age is inherently linked to the selection process that weeds out less successful plants over time. According to various theories in the economics literature, this selection process reflects information about future profitability that the firm acquires over time as a by-product of operating the plant, as a consequence of investing in the plant, or by the simple passage of time.[5] If this selection process operates with greater intensity early in the life cycle of plants, then younger plants are likely to exhibit greater employment volatility and greater heterogeneity in employment growth paths than older plants.

Plant age also serves as a proxy for the age of the technology embodied in the plant's physical structure and equipment. To the extent that old, embodied technologies are costly to update, technological advances can contribute to the demise of older plants. The relationship between the age of a plant and the age of its technology is likely to be a crude one, however, because major renovations to existing plants often coincide with technological updating.

Plant size is a natural metric for the scale of operations at a geographically distinct production unit. Since employment often fluctuates from year to year, because of demand variation and other factors, average plant size provides a better indication of the production unit's intended scale of operations. For many purposes, we prefer average size to current size. By necessity or design, most other studies focus on a different measure of size that we describe below.

---

3. This measure of current plant size is the natural counterpart to our plant-level measures of job creation and destruction. See the technical appendix for further discussion.
4. Only in census years can we measure total employment for every manufacturing firm. The Census of Manufactures is available in the LRD for 1963, 1967, 1972, 1977, 1982, and 1987.
5. See Jovanovic (1982), Lambson (1991), Ericson and Pakes (1989), and Hopenhayn (1992).

Firm size is superior to plant size as an indicator of the overall scale of operations carried out by the plant's parent firm. Firm size corresponds closely to the notion of business size that underlies most public discourse on job creation. In addition, patterns of government regulation and business access to financial markets are more closely associated with firm size than with plant size. Smaller firms enjoy exemption from or weaker enforcement of many government regulations related to the environment, affirmative action, financial reporting, and occupational health and safety.[6] Larger firms enjoy greater access to certain forms of financial credit like equity and debt issues.[7]

Ownership type is a crude indicator of firm size. Its chief virtue lies in its widespread availability and easy use in government data on individual business establishments. Consequently, many other studies and government statistical publications report breakdowns of economic activity by ownership type. Our breakdowns by ownership type facilitate comparison with these other studies and publications.

4.3   Job Creation and Destruction Rates by Employer Size

With these remarks as background, we now turn to the empirical evidence. Table 4.1 displays average net and gross job flow rates by employer size. The table reveals strong regularities in the relationship between employer size and gross job flow rates. Consider, first, the average rates of gross job creation. By all four measures, gross job creation rates decline monotonically with employer size. The job creation rate averages 15.8 percent of employment per year for firms with fewer than 20 employees, 9.7 percent for firms with 500–999 employees, and 6.6 percent for firms with 50,000 or more employees. Similar patterns prevail for ownership type and both measures of plant size. Thus, small employers create new jobs at a much higher gross rate than large employers.

But gross job creation measures clearly reveal only part of the story. Table 4.1 also shows that gross job destruction rates decline sharply with firm and plant size. The job destruction rate averages 17.5 percent of employment per year for firms with fewer than 20 employees, 10.4 percent for firms with 500–999 employees, and 8.0 percent for firms with 50,000 or more employees. Again, similar patterns prevail for the ownership indicator and plant-size

---

6. See Brock and Evans (1986, chap. 5) and Brown, Hamilton, and Medoff (1990, pp. 82–88).
7. On the relationship between firm size and financing patterns, see Walker (1989), Gaston (1989), and Kashyap and Stein (1992).

Table 4.1
**Net and Gross Job Flow Rates by Employer Size Category:
Mean Annual Rates, 1973 to 1988**

	Job Creation	Job Destruc- tion	Job Reallo- caton	Net Growth	Excess Reallo- cation	Lower Bound	Employ- ment Share
Average Plant Size							
0 to 19 Employees.....	15.9	17.2	33.1	−1.3	27.8	19.2	4.4
20 to 49	12.6	13.8	26.4	−1.1	21.8	15.5	8.2
50 to 99	11.7	12.6	24.4	−0.9	20.2	14.2	10.1
100 to 249	10.0	11.5	21.5	−1.4	17.6	12.7	18.5
250 to 499	8.5	9.8	18.4	−1.3	14.2	11.3	16.6
500 to 999	7.5	8.5	16.1	−1.0	12.0	10.1	13.8
1,000 to 2,499	6.6	8.2	14.8	−1.6	11.1	9.3	12.5
2,500 to 4,999	6.5	8.2	14.7	−1.7	10.2	9.6	7.2
5,000 or More	5.9	6.5	12.4	−0.6	8.9	7.9	8.8
Standard Deviation...	2.5	2.6	5.1	0.3	4.8	2.7	
Current Plant Size							
0 to 19 Employees.....	18.7	23.3	42.0	−4.5	34.6	24.7	5.2
20 to 49	13.2	15.3	28.6	−2.1	23.6	16.8	8.6
50 to 99	12.2	13.5	25.6	−1.3	21.5	14.9	10.5
100 to 249	9.6	10.7	20.3	−1.1	16.1	12.3	18.5
250 to 499	7.7	8.7	16.4	−1.0	12.5	10.1	16.0
500 to 999	7.0	7.6	14.6	−0.6	10.7	9.3	13.5
1,000 to 2,499	6.3	7.3	13.5	−1.0	10.2	8.4	12.3
2,500 to 4,999	6.1	7.5	13.6	−1.3	9.7	8.8	7.0
5,000 or More	5.4	5.6	10.9	−0.2	7.7	7.1	8.4
Standard Deviation...	3.3	4.1	7.4	0.9	6.6	4.1	
Average Firm Size							
0 to 19 Employees.....	15.8	17.5	33.3	−1.6	27.5	19.6	4.2
20 to 49	11.9	13.4	25.3	−1.5	19.9	15.4	6.6
50 to 99	11.2	12.0	23.2	−0.8	18.8	13.8	6.2
100 to 249	10.7	11.1	21.9	−0.4	16.9	13.4	8.0
250 to 499	10.1	10.3	20.4	−0.2	16.5	12.1	5.9
500 to 999	9.7	10.4	20.1	−0.6	16.3	11.9	5.2
1,000 to 2,499	8.9	9.5	18.5	−0.6	14.8	11.1	7.5
2,500 to 4,999	8.4	9.5	17.9	−1.1	14.2	10.8	6.8
5,000 to 9,999	7.9	9.2	17.1	−1.3	13.3	10.5	9.2
10,000 to 24,999	7.1	8.5	15.6	−1.4	11.7	9.8	15.7
25,000 to 49,999	6.9	8.1	15.0	−1.3	11.0	9.5	11.2
50,000 or More	6.6	8.0	14.6	−1.4	9.9	9.6	13.5
Standard Deviation...	2.3	2.2	4.5	0.4	4.1	2.4	
Ownership Type							
Single-Unit...........	12.7	12.9	25.5	−0.2	20.4	15.4	22.3
Multi-Unit............	8.1	9.4	17.5	−1.3	13.7	10.7	77.7
Standard Deviation...	1.9	1.4	3.4	0.5	2.8	2.0	

measures. Thus, small employers also destroy jobs at a much higher rate than large employers.

How does net job creation vary by employer size? On this score, the empirical evidence produces no strong pattern. Net job creation rates by firm size exhibit a ∩ shape: manufacturing firms with 100–499 employees show mild net contraction rates during the 1973–88 period, whereas smaller and larger firms show sharper contraction rates. Neither plant-size measure evinces any strong relationship to net job creation rates, although the net contraction rate is substantially smaller for single-unit than multi-unit firms. In a nutshell, net job creation in the U.S. manufacturing sector exhibits no strong or simple relationship to employer size.

How can we reconcile this empirical result with the widely held belief that small businesses account for a disproportionate fraction of new jobs? One might think that the answer lies in our focus on the manufacturing sector. Perhaps in the nonmanufacturing sectors of the economy, smaller firms exhibit much higher net job creation rates than do larger firms. It is conceivable that an analysis of nonmanufacturing sectors along the lines of table 4.1 would uphold the conventional wisdom about the role of small business in job creation, but it is not this type of analysis that underlies the conventional wisdom. Rather, the conventional wisdom rests on fallacious and misleading interpretations of the data, as we explain in the next three sections.

4.4   The Size Distribution Fallacy

Many claims about the job-creating prowess of small business appear to be based upon changes over time in the size distribution of employment. We review the calculation typically performed on the size distribution data and explain why the usual interpretation of this calculation leads to fallacious inferences about job creation.

The SBA defines small businesses as firms with fewer than 500 employees, although the precise cutoff is not important to the point at hand. Given a particular cutoff, let $TOTAL_t$ and $SMALL_t$ stand for total employment and small business employment, respectively, in year t. In terms of these symbols, one can calculate the small business "contribution" to 1990 job creation as the ratio

$$\frac{SMALL_{1990} - SMALL_{1989}}{TOTAL_{1990} - TOTAL_{1989}}.$$

Box 4.1
Illustration of the size distribution fallacy

	Firm 1	Firm 2	Firm 3	Small firms	Big firms	All firms
Year 1 employment	300	550	650	300	1,200	1,500
Year 2 employment	50	340	1,210	390	1,210	1,600
Net change	−250	−210	560	90	10	100

Small-firm share of net job creation = $(390 − 300)/(1,600 − 1,500) = .9$

This illustration uses data in the three rightmost columns on the size distribution of employment to calculate job creation shares. These changes in the distribution of employment by firm size ignore the fact that firms can migrate between size categories, as shown in the three leftmost columns, resulting in a false inference about the share of job creation accounted for by small firms.

In words, the small business contribution to 1990 job creation is equated to the ratio of net employment change among small firms to total net employment change.[8]

The fallacy arises because firms can migrate between size categories from one year to the next. The example in box 4.1 illustrates this point. The example considers three firms, one of which (firm 1) satisfies the SBA definition of a small business in year 1. The largest firm (firm 3) grows dramatically in year 2, whereas the two smaller ones shrink. As it shrinks, firm 2 migrates from the large-business to the small-business category. On net, total employment increases by 100.

If one executes the typical calculation on data in the example, small business appears to contribute 90 percent of net job growth. But, as the construction of the example makes clear, this interpretation is fallacious. In the example, firm-level net job growth actually increases with firm size, an observation that can be made only by following individual employers over time, as in the calculations that underlie the net and gross job flow figures in table 4.1.

How important is such migration across firm size categories in reality? The large magnitude of gross job flows—and the concentration of job flows in plants that undergo big employment changes—indicates that migration

---

8. Zayas (1978) uses data on changes in the size distribution of employment to calculate growth rates by size of business. This calculation is also subject to the size distribution fallacy identified below.

across categories is frequent and important.[9] Especially during periods of slow employment growth, firm migration from large to small is likely to occur quite often. This pattern creates the appearance of a booming small-firm sector.

In summary, many claims about the job-creating prowess of small businesses derive from a fallacious interpretation of data on the size distribution of employment. Size distribution data cannot tell us whether small businesses systematically grew faster than large businesses.

4.5 Netting Out Reality

Sophisticated proponents of the view that small businesses create a disproportionate fraction of new jobs recognize the fallacy described above.[10] Circumventing the fallacy requires longitudinal data on individual establishments or firms—that is, data that track individual employers over time. The most widely cited studies of job creation behavior rely upon such data, but they often present results in a way that can mislead the statistically naive.[11]

To understand the potential for confusion, consider the example in box 4.2. It depicts a situation with moderate net job growth in the midst of much larger gross job flows. We know from table 4.1 that this situation typifies the experience of the U.S. manufacturing sector. It also typifies the experience in other sectors of the U.S. economy and in other industrialized nations.[12]

In the example, 100 percent of the net job increase between years 1 and 2 is accounted for by firm 1, which is classified as small on the basis of its employment in year 1. Thus, one might conclude that "small firms created virtually all new jobs" between years 1 and 2. Closer analysis reveals, however, that such a conclusion grossly mischaracterizes the distribution of newly created jobs by size of firm. In fact, in this example large firms create 80 percent of the new jobs in year 2.

Public discourse about job creation rarely distinguishes between the small business share of gross job creation (20 percent in the example) and its "share"

---

9. Table 4.1 shows that gross job creation and destruction flows are large relative to net employment changes. Chapter 2 contains additional evidence on this point and on the concentration of gross job flows at plants that undergo big employment changes.
10. Small Business Administration (1983, p. 62) clearly explains the fallacy. See also Birch and MacCracken (1983).
11. The most widely cited studies of the small-business role in creating jobs are Small Business Administration (various years) and Birch (1979, 1987).
12. See chapters 2 and 3 for a review of the evidence.

Box 4.2
Illustration of a confusion between net and gross job creation

	Firm 1	Firm 2	Firm 3	Small firms	Big firms	All firms
Year 1 employment	300	600	600	300	1,200	1,500
Year 2 employment	350	400	800	350	1,200	1,550
Net change	50	−200	200	50	0	50

Small-firm share of net job creation = 50/50 = 1
Small-firm share of gross job creation = 50/(50 + 200) = 0.2

This illustration calculates job creation shares from longitudinal data on individual firms. The calculation makes use of longitudinal data to calculate net firm-level employment changes. Those employment changes are aggregated over firms within a size class and then expressed as a fraction of the aggregate net change. Following the common practice of prominent analysts and government agencies like the U.S. Small Business Administration, continuing firms are assigned to a size category by using base-year employment. The last two lines show how the small-firm share of net job creation misrepresents the actual distribution of newly created jobs by size of firm.

of net job creation. Consequently, claims about the job creation role of small business often conjure up the image of an economy in which large firms inexorably shrink and small firms struggle valiantly to replenish the stock of jobs. This image deviates sharply from the facts set out in table 4.1 and in table 4.3, which show that both large and small employers create large numbers of new jobs.

To appreciate fully the misleading character of statements about the small business "share" of net job creation, consider a particular historical episode. Between March 1973 and March 1974, manufacturing employment as reported in the LRD increased on net by about 16,000 jobs. Over this same period, manufacturing plants with fewer than 100 employees as of March 1973 experienced a net increase of about 160,000 jobs. Thus the net increase for small plants was ten times the overall net increase. If we summarized these data in the usual phraseology of public discourse, we would say that "small employers created 1,000 percent of the new manufacturing jobs in 1974." Proponents of the small-business job creation view would likely eschew the usual phraseology in this case, because it highlights the absurdity of the underlying calculation.

Continuing with the historical episode, manufacturing plants of more than 500 employees created about 1.3 million gross new jobs between 1973 and 1974. Since net job growth was only 16,000 during this period, we could easily identify a set of large manufacturing plants that accounted for 50 percent, 100 percent, 200 percent, or 1,000 percent of net job growth. We could do so by choosing a set of large plants situated in states with robust employment growth or rapidly expanding industries. We could even identify several distinct sets of large plants, each of which accounted for, say, 100 percent of net job growth. It is unlikely that useful economic policy prescriptions would follow from these characterizations of the data. Yet it is precisely this type of data characterization and argument that underlies claims that small businesses create most jobs and—therefore—ought to receive favorable tax and regulatory treatment.

In summary, longitudinal studies that focus on the "share" of net job growth accounted for by small businesses grossly misrepresent the actual distribution of newly created jobs by size of employer. A more meaningful way to represent this distribution is to focus on the small-employer share of gross job creation.[13]

4.6 The Regression Fallacy

Most longitudinal studies of the relationship between employer size and job creation suffer from another statistical pitfall known as the regression fallacy or regression-to-the-mean bias.[14] The potential for bias arises whenever employers experience transitory fluctuations in size, or whenever measurement error introduces transitory fluctuations in observed size. Both phenomena are important features of longitudinal data on employers.

The simple example in box 4.3 illustrates the regression fallacy. It calculates growth rates for individual firms and by size of firm for years 2 and 3. Following widespread practice, firms are assigned to size classes using base-

---

13. For the record, we should note that not every statistical tabulation performed on longitudinal data by the SBA examines the small-employer share of net job creation. For example, table 13 in Small Business Administration (1988) reports gross job creation by firm size. Nonetheless, the surrounding text reverts to the misleading "net" calculation when characterizing the small-business role in job creation.

14. Friedman (1992) suggests that the regression fallacy "is the most common fallacy in the statistical analysis of economic data." Leonard (1986) explains how regression-to-the-mean bias can distort the estimated relationship between employer size and growth rates. Friedman (1992) and Quah (1992) focus on the regression fallacy in the recent literature that investigates whether per capita income levels are converging across countries.

Box 4.3
Illustration of the regression fallacy

	Firm 1	Firm 2	Firm 3	Small firms	Big firms	All firms
Year 1 employment	450	550	600	450	1,150	1,600
Year 2 employment	550	450	600	450	1,150	1,600
Year 3 employment	450	550	600	450	1,150	1,600
Year 2 growth rate	.22	−.18	0	**.22**	**−.09**	0
Year 3 growth rate	−.18	.22	0	**.22**	**−.09**	0

This illustration calculates net job creation rates for individual firms and by size class of firms. Following the common practice of prominent analysts and government agencies like the U.S. Small Business Administration, continuing firms are assigned to a size category using base-year employment. Year 1 (year 2) is the base year when calculating year 2 (year 3) growth rates. Although each firm employs the same number of workers in year 1 as in year 3, the net growth rate for small firms—as calculated—exceeds the net growth rate for big firms in years 2 and 3. This apparent puzzle reflects a bias in the estimated size-growth relationship induced by temporary changes in the level of employment at individual firms.

year employment.[15] The base year is the initial year of the time interval over which a particular growth rate is calculated.

Boldface entries in the illustration represent average employment growth rates by size class in years 2 and 3. These entries convey the impression that small firms outperform large ones in both years. Yet, closer inspection reveals that each firm is the same size in year 3 as in year 1. Evidently, the seemingly appropriate calculations underlying the boldface entries provide a misleading characterization of the size-growth rate relationship. This misleading characterization is an example of the regression fallacy.

The fallacy arises because, each year, we reclassify firms into size classes using base-year employment. The interaction between this reclassification and transitory firm-level employment movements lies at the heart of the regression fallacy. On average, firms classified as large in the base year are more likely to have experienced a recent transitory increase in employment. Since transitory movements reverse themselves, firms that are large in the base year are relatively likely to contract. Likewise, firms classified as small in the base year are

---

15. This classification practice is used, for instance, in the annual SBA reports to the president and in Birch (1979, 1987).

more likely to have experienced a recent transitory decrease in employment. Hence, firms that are small in the base year are relatively likely to expand. As in our illustration, this regression phenomenon (i.e., regression to the firm's long-run size) creates the illusion that small firms systematically outperform large ones.

The magnitude of the bias associated with the regression fallacy depends on several factors: the extent of measurement error in the data, the importance of transitory employment movements for individual employers, the size distribution of employment, and the precise size-class boundaries chosen by the analyst. As a consequence, we cannot precisely quantify the extent of regression-to-the-mean bias in previous studies without direct access to their longitudinal data. We can, however, replicate their procedure for measuring employer size in the LRD and determine the resulting relationship between size and net job growth. We can then compare this size-growth relationship with those that emerge under alternative size measures.

Table 4.2 carries out this comparison, using LRD data for the period 1973–88. Following the standard (Birch/SBA) practice described above, the first panel classifies continuing plants and plant deaths by base-year size. New plants are classified according to size in the entry year. As we have explained, the entries in this panel are subject to the regression fallacy. To avoid the regression fallacy, we measure employer size by using average plant size or current plant size. Recall that current size equals the simple average of the plant's employment in the current and previous years, and average size equals a mean computed over all sample obervations on the plant.[16] Repeating portions of table 4.1, the bottom two panels of table 4.2 display the figures for average and current plant-size measures.

The results of the comparison are striking. In the first panel, the net job creation rate declines steeply over the first five size-class intervals and then flattens out over the remaining intervals. The second panel presents a sharp contrast. It indicates that the net job creation rate shows no systematic relationship to average plant size. The third panel actually shows a positive relationship between net job creation and current plant size. The gross job creation and destruction patterns also look much more favorable for small plants under the base-year size measure (first panel) than under either

---

16. To the extent that transitory employment fluctuations require more than one year to reverse themselves, our current-size measure is subject to a milder and more subtle version of the regression fallacy. However, random errors in measuring employment levels do not produce a regression fallacy under any of our plant or firm size measures.

Table 4.2
Net and Gross Job Flow Rates by Three Measures of Plant Size:
Mean Annual Rates, 1973 to 1988

	Job Creation	Job Destruction	Net Growth	Employment Share
Birch/SBA Plant-Size Measure				
0 to 19 Employees	25.7	15.4	10.3	5.2
20 to 49	13.6	13.1	0.6	8.5
50 to 99	11.4	12.0	−0.7	10.4
100 to 249	9.5	11.1	−1.7	18.6
250 to 499	7.4	9.9	−2.5	16.0
500 to 999	6.3	9.0	−2.7	13.5
1,000 to 2,499	5.7	8.4	−2.6	12.3
2,500 to 4,999	5.4	7.9	−2.5	7.0
5,000 or more	4.7	7.1	−2.4	8.5
Average Plant-Size Measure				
0 to 19 Employees	15.9	17.2	−1.3	4.4
20 to 49	12.6	13.8	−1.1	8.2
50 to 99	11.7	12.6	−0.9	10.1
100 to 249	10.0	11.5	−1.4	18.5
250 to 499	8.5	9.8	−1.3	16.6
500 to 999	7.5	8.5	−1.0	13.8
1,000 to 2,499	6.6	8.2	−1.6	12.5
2,500 to 4,999	6.5	8.2	−1.7	7.2
5,000 or More	5.9	6.5	−0.6	8.8
Current Plant-Size Measure				
0 to 19 Employees	18.7	23.3	−4.5	5.2
20 to 49	13.2	15.3	−2.1	8.6
50 to 99	12.2	13.5	−1.3	10.5
100 to 249	9.6	10.7	−1.1	18.5
250 to 499	7.7	8.7	−1.0	16.0
500 to 999	7.0	7.6	−0.6	13.5
1,000 to 2,499	6.3	7.3	−1.0	12.3
2,500 to 4,999	6.1	7.5	−1.3	7.0
5,000 or More	5.4	5.6	−0.2	8.4

alternative measure. Evidently the regression fallacy illustrated in box 4.3 operates with powerful effect in the LRD data for the U.S. manufacturing sector.[17]

There is good reason to suspect that the regression fallacy operates with even greater effect in the longitudinal data sets used in the widely cited studies by Birch (1979, 1987) and the annual SBA reports. In particular, measurement error is almost certainly more serious in their data sets than in the LRD, a point we develop in the next section. Given their procedures for measuring firm size, the more serious measurement problems in their data suggest greater susceptibility to the regression fallacy.

In summary, the standard practice of measuring firm or plant size according to base-year employment leads to a regression fallacy, which in turn paints an overly favorable picture of the relative job growth performance of small employers. Our replication analysis with LRD data finds a substantial bias in favor of small businesses under the standard practice for measuring business size using base-year employment.

4.7 An Unsuitable Database

Still another weakness of many leading studies of the job creation process is their reliance on an unsuitable database: the Dun and Bradstreet Market Identifier (DMI) files. David Birch and associates use these data for their studies and, until recently, so did the SBA.[18] Although the Dun and Bradstreet database has many impressive attributes and represents an unparalleled source of information for many commercial purposes, it is not designed or maintained to maximize its usefulness as a tool for statistical analysis. Numerous studies

---

17. Brown et al. (1990) stress a different potential problem with the standard size measure. They argue that classifying new firms according to size in the entry year creates a bias because new firms often start small even when their intended scale of operations is large. This point clearly applies to new plants as well. However, a symmetrical point is that dying plants often contract and become small on their way toward exit. A careful reading of table 4.2 suggests that this latter effect dominates for manufacturing plants. Observe that among the smallest plants, the difference between the gross destruction rate based on current size and the gross destruction rate based on average size exceeds the corresponding difference for the gross creation rate. Observe, also, that the creation and destruction rates align more closely when comparing the current and average size measures than when comparing either of these measures with the Birch/SBA measure. This last observation indicates that the regression fallacy—not the birth problem stressed by Brown et al.— accounts for the striking contrast among panels in the table.

18. The SBA has contracted with the Bureau of the Census to longitudinally link the federal government's Standard Statistical Establishment List for the purpose of studying job creation and destruction behavior. See Census contract 61-93-41, "The Longitudinal Data Study."

have highlighted severe problems with the DMI files as a tool for measuring job creation and destruction or business births and deaths.[19]

For the purpose of investigating the job creation process, the DMI files suffer from two key problems. First, there is an enormous discrepancy between U.S. total employment as tabulated from the DMI files and the corresponding employment figures produced by the Bureau of Labor Statistics (BLS) or the Bureau of the Census. In 1986, for example, total employment tabulated from the DMI files exceeded the corresponding BLS and Census figures by 9 million persons.[20] In an economy with roughly 110 million employees, a discrepancy of this magnitude raises serious doubts about the accuracy of any statistical portrait generated from the DMI files. Furthermore, earlier research found that the most serious data problems in the DMI files involve younger and smaller businesses. This finding suggests that DMI-based claims about small business job creation should be interpreted with special caution.

Second, the DMI files do not accurately track business births and deaths or other important employment events. The U.S. General Accounting Office (GAO) has analyzed the accuracy of the DMI files in accounting for mass layoffs, with particular emphasis on layoffs due to plant closures. SBA provided GAO with a sample of mass layoffs and plant closures from the DMI files for the 1982–84 period.[21] The GAO study found that 81 percent of the mass layoff events in the DMI files were mistakenly identified. In reality, they represented some other event, such as a change in ownership structure, rather than a mass layoff or plant closure.

The DMI files also inaccurately identify plant births. A study by Birley (1984) compares three alternative sources of data for identifying new firms: the DMI file, the ES-202 data generated from administrative records maintained by state unemployment insurance agencies, and the telephone directory. She finds that the DMI files failed to identify 96 percent of the new firms found in the ES-202 data. Using a similar methodology, Aldrich et al. (1988) find that the DMI files missed 95 percent of apparently new businesses in the ES-202 data and 97 percent of those in the telephone directory.

In short, earlier research indicates that the DMI files are unsuitable for generating job creation and destruction figures. Identifying plant births and

---

19. See Armington and Odle (1982b), Birch and MacCracken (1983), Birley (1984), Howland (1988, chap. 2), Evans (1987b), Aldrich et al. (1988), and Small Business Administration (1983, 1987).

20. See Bureau of the Census (1986, p. 514).

21. The GAO defined a mass layoff as the dismissal of at least 20 percent of a plant's permanent workforce.

deaths and tracking businesses over time is most difficult in the case of small employers. Thus the DMI files are especially ill-suited for investigating the role of small business job creation.

The LRD, in contrast, is explicitly designed and maintained to avoid the types of problems that plague the DMI files. It is based on business surveys specifically designed to provide a statistical portrait of U.S. manufacturing activity. In addition, the Census Bureau draws on payroll tax records and other government data sources to verify and enhance the quality of LRD employment data.[22] Drawing on the longitudinal data in the LRD, the next two sections of the chapter report additional findings about the job creation process in the U.S. manufacturing sector.

4.8 What Fraction of New Manufacturing Jobs Did Small Employers Create?

Table 4.3 reports the percentage of manufacturing employment and job creation and destruction by employer size for the period 1973–88. As the table reveals, large employers created most new manufacturing jobs over the period. They also destroyed most of the lost manufacturing jobs. The first panel of the table reveals that plants averaging at least 100 employees accounted for roughly seven of every ten newly created and newly destroyed manufacturing jobs. The third panel shows that firms with at least 500 employees accounted for 60 percent of job creation and 61 percent of job destruction. The fourth panel shows that multiunit firms accounted for roughly seven of every ten newly created and newly destroyed manufacturing jobs.

The table also reveals why large employers play the dominant role in job creation and destruction, despite the higher creation and destruction rates among smaller employers. The reason is that large employers account for the bulk of the manufacturing jobs base. Over the 1972–88 period as a whole, firms with at least 500 employees accounted for 69 percent of manufacturing employment.

The SBA defines small businesses to include any firm with fewer than 500 employees. According to this definition, the third panel of table 4.3 re-

22. Given the need of policymakers to understand the job creation process, government statistical agencies should set a high priority on developing longitudinal establishment-level databases for other sectors of the U.S. economy. The Center for Economic Studies at the Bureau of the Census is conducting a pilot study to determine whether the federal government's Standard Statistical Establishment List can be effectively used to construct longitudinal data on firms and establishments for the entire U.S. economy.

Table 4.3

Shares of Gross Job Creation and Destruction by Employer Size Category: Annual Averages as Percentages of Employment, 1973 to 1988

	Job Creation	Job Destruction	Employment Share
Average Plant Size			
0 to 19 Employees	7.7	7.3	4.4
20 to 49	11.4	10.9	8.2
50 to 99	13.2	12.5	10.1
100 to 249	20.5	20.6	18.5
250 to 499	15.7	15.9	16.6
500 to 999	11.5	11.5	13.8
1,000 to 2,499	9.2	10.0	12.5
2,500 to 4,999	5.2	5.7	7.2
5,000 or More	5.7	5.6	8.8
Current Plant Size			
0 to 19 Employees	10.8	11.8	5.2
20 to 49	12.7	13.0	8.6
50 to 99	14.2	13.8	10.5
100 to 249	19.8	19.4	18.5
250 to 499	13.7	13.6	16.0
500 to 999	10.5	10.1	13.5
1,000 to 2,499	8.6	8.7	12.3
2,500 to 4,999	4.8	5.1	7.0
5,000 or More	5.0	4.6	8.4
Average Firm Size			
0 to 19 Employees	7.5	7.3	4.2
20 to 49	8.8	8.9	6.6
50 to 99	7.9	7.5	6.2
100 to 249	9.7	9.0	8.0
250 to 499	6.7	6.1	5.9
500 to 999	5.8	5.5	5.2
1,000 to 2,499	7.6	7.2	7.5
2,500 to 4,999	6.5	6.5	6.8
5,000 to 9,999	8.3	8.6	9.2
10,000 to 24,999	12.6	13.5	15.7
25,000 to 49,999	8.7	9.1	11.2
50,000 or More	10.1	10.9	13.5
Ownership Type			
Single-Unit	31.1	28.2	22.3
Multi-Unit	68.9	71.8	77.7

veals that small manufacturing firms account for 40 percent of job creation. This figure reflects an expansive and generous definition of the small business sector. Commentaries about the virtues of small business often bring to mind family-run businesses and struggling entrepreneurs with shoestring operations, not firms with up to 500 employees. In addition, a host of government regulations that entail exemptions for small businesses specify a cutoff level far below 500 employees. For example, Brock and Evans (1986, p. 74) note that the "Office of Federal Contract Enforcement exempts businesses with fewer than 50 employees from filing affirmative action plans." As another example, the Worker Adjustment and Retraining Notification Act of 1988 requires employers to give workers and government officials sixty days' advance notice before a plant closure or large layoff, but exempts establishments with fewer than fifty employees. The Family and Medical Leave Act of 1993 exempts employers with fewer than fifty workers. Returning to table 4.3, firms with fewer than fifty employees account for only 16 percent of gross job creation in the manufacturing sector; plants averaging fewer than fifty employees account for only 19 percent. Clearly, according to these definitions, only about one-fifth of all new manufacturing jobs are created by small employers.

Would this characterization of the small business role in job creation differ if we looked outside the manufacturing sector? Although we are currently unable to calculate gross job creation and destruction rates for nonmanufacturing industries, we know that small businesses account for a considerably larger fraction of the jobs base in most nonmanufacturing industries. This point stands out clearly in table 4.4. Drawing on several data sources, the table reports employment shares for various concepts of large and small businesses. According to SBA figures, firms with fewer than 500 workers account for 50 percent of private-sector employment but only 36 percent of manufacturing employment. According to County Business Patterns data, establishments with fewer than 100 workers account for 64 percent of nonmanufacturing employment but only 28 percent of manufacturing employment. Thus, small businesses provide a much larger share of the jobs base outside the manufacturing sector. In addition, the available evidence indicates that the gross job creation rate declines with employer size in the nonmanufacturing sector, just as it does in the manufacturing sector.[23] These facts make us confident that

---

23. Unpublished tabulations prepared by Ken Troske for the finance, insurance, and real estate sector in Wisconsin, and by Al Nucci for the U.S. nonmanufacturing sector during the 1982–87 period, indicate that gross job creation rates decline sharply with employer size. Anderson and Meyer (1994) report similar results.

Table 4.4
Share of Employment by Employer Size Category

Year	Sector	Data Source	Number of Employees			
			< 50	< 100	≤ 500	≤ 1000
Current Size of Establishment						
1988	Private	CBP	0.43	0.56	0.19	0.13
1988	Nonman.	CBP	0.51	0.64	0.14	0.09
1988	Manuf.	CBP	0.17	0.28	0.37	0.24
1988	Manuf.	LRD	0.11	0.22	0.40	0.26
Average Size of Establishment						
1988	Manuf.	LRD	0.11	0.22	0.41	0.27
Size of Firm						
1988	Private	SBA			0.50	
1988	Manuf.	SBA			0.36	
1987	Private	ES	0.28	0.36	0.51	0.29
1987	Nonman.	ES	0.36	0.45	0.59	0.21
1987	Manuf.	ES	0.12	0.18	0.32	0.48
1987	Manuf.	LRD	0.09	0.16	0.35	0.42

Year	Sector	Data Source	Single-Unit	Multi-Unit
Ownership-Type of Parent Firm				
1987....................	Private	ES	0.45	0.55
1987....................	Nonman	ES	0.54	0.46
1987....................	Manuf.	ES	0.24	0.76
1988....................	Manuf.	LRD	0.20	0.80

Note: CBP: Authors' calculations from *County Business Patterns* (1988). The CBP covers the nonfarm private sector, excluding railroad and domestic household workers.

LRD: Authors' calculations from the Longitudinal Research Database. Unlike the other data sources, the LRD excludes administrative and auxilliary establishments not directly engaged in production activity.

SBA: From Table 17 in Small Business Administration (1991).

ES: Authors' calculations from *Enterprise Statistics* (1987). The ES data exclude finance, insurance, real estate, public utilities, communications, and some service industries.

small business accounts for a larger share of job creation and destruction in most nonmanufacturing industries than in the manufacturing sector. A more precise characterization awaits the development and analysis of high-quality longitudinal data for nonmanufacturing businesses. Because the manufacturing sector accounts for a small and declining share of U.S. employment—only 19 percent in 1988—we think the development of such data merits a high priority by government statistical agencies.

4.9   Job Creation and Destruction Rates by Plant Age

Table 4.5 reports net and gross job flows by age of plant. Our age measure reflects the date of a plant's construction or conversion to manufacturing activity. Neither ownership changes nor shutdown periods influence measured plant age.

Several age-related patterns stand out in table 4.5. One clear pattern entails a net job creation rate that declines with plant age. This pattern brings to mind the replacement of old, outmoded plants by new, technologically superior plants. Although this characterization of plant life-cycle dynamics contains a germ of truth, table 4.5 indicates that other factors dominate the relationship between plant age and the creation and destruction of jobs. In particular, the table shows that gross job destruction rates decline with plant age. Contrary to an image of insecure jobs in obsolete production facilities, the typical older manufacturing plant offers jobs with unusually good prospects for continued employment.

Employment volatility also declines sharply with plant age, as indicated by the figures for total and excess job reallocation rates. For plants that are one year old in the base year, the annual job reallocation rate averages a remarkable 42 percent. It drops to 25 percent by age 3, and it declines further to 16 percent for plants that are at least fifteen years old. Unreported results reveal that this sharp relationship between plant age and the job reallocation rate is pervasive across industries, regions, plant size classes, and plant ownership types. Evidently, some systematic mechanism operates to produce a strong, positive relationship between employment stability and plant age.

One plausible explanation for this pattern stresses the selection effects associated with learning about a new plant's prospects for profitability. At the time of a plant's construction, the firm faces uncertainty regarding the plant's cost of production and the demand for goods it produces. Over time, the firm accumulates experience and information about the plant's cost and product demand. This new information leads the firm to update its assessment of the plant's longer-term profitability. A plant that accumulates favorable information about its profitability expands and survives, whereas a plant that accumulates sufficiently unfavorable information exits.[24] According to this theory,

24. Jovanovic (1982) was the first to carefully articulate this type of theory about plant-level dynamics. Ericson and Pakes (1989) developed an alternative to Jovanovic's theory that encompasses new opportunities for learning about profitability with each new investment in the plant. Several studies evaluate the empirical performance and relevance of Jovanovic's theory. See Hall (1987), Evans (1987a, 1987b), Dunne, Roberts, and Samuelson (1989a), Pakes and Ericson (1990), and Davis and Haltiwanger (1992).

Table 4.5
Net and Gross Job Flows by Plant Age, 1973 to 1988

	Mean Annual Rates						
	Job Creation	Job Destruc-tion	Job Reallo-cation	Net Growth	Excess Reallo-cation	Lower Bound	Employ-ment Share
Crude Age Categories[a]							
Young (0–1 yrs.)........	45.8	12.5	58.4	33.3	25.1	45.8	3.1
Middle-Aged (2–10).....	12.3	13.3	25.6	−1.0	21.0	15.1	18.3
Mature (10+)..........	6.9	9.4	16.3	−2.5	12.4	10.1	78.6
Standard Deviation	6.9	1.6	7.9	6.2	3.9	6.4	
Detailed Age Categories[b]							
Births................	200	0.0	200	200	0.0	200	0.6
1 Year Old............	25.6	16.3	41.9	9.3	31.9	25.9	2.4
2 Years Old...........	15.2	13.8	29.0	1.4	24.6	16.7	1.5
3 Years Old...........	13.9	10.8	24.7	3.1	21.0	14.2	1.2
4–5 Years Old.........	14.7	12.1	26.9	2.6	23.5	15.1	2.6
6–10 Years Old........	11.4	12.8	24.2	−1.5	20.7	13.9	11.3
11–14 Years Old.......	9.6	11.0	20.5	−1.4	16.6	12.2	10.7
15 Years or More	6.4	9.5	15.9	−3.2	11.8	10.0	69.7
Standard Deviation	15.2	1.7	14.9	15.7	4.8	14.8	

	Percentages of Manufacturing		
	Job Creation	Job Destruction	Employment
Crude Age Categories[a]			
Young (0–1 yrs.)	15.6	3.8	3.1
Middle-Aged (2–10 yrs.)................	24.8	24.0	18.3
Mature (10+ yrs.)......................	59.6	72.2	78.6
Detailed Age Categories[b]			
Births	12.7	0.0	0.6
1 Year Old	6.5	3.7	2.4
2 Years Old	2.5	2.1	1.5
3 Years Old	1.7	1.2	1.2
4–5 Years Old	4.2	3.1	2.6
6–10 Years Old	13.8	14.1	11.3
11–14 Years Old	11.0	11.4	10.7
15 or More Years......................	47.7	64.5	69.7

[a]Based on data for 1973 through 1988. Age ranges are approximate; the precise cutoff between middle-aged and mature plants varies by year. See the Technical Appendix for details.

[b]Based on data for the last year of complete panels: 1978, 1983, and 1988.

new plants pass through a shakeout period that reveals their longer-term profitability. Unprofitable plants exit and, hence, are selected out of the population of mature plants. Profitable plants survive to maturity and settle down to relatively stable employment levels.

4.10   The Durability of Jobs by Employer Size and Age

Laudatory claims about the role of small and new businesses in creating jobs often fail to consider how the permanence of jobs varies with employer size and age. As it turns out, this failure is a serious one, because job permanence differs greatly by employer size and age. Our earlier evidence on gross job destruction revealed that the typical existing job at younger and smaller employers has a significantly lower one-year survival probability than the typical job at older and larger employers.[25] Here, we shift the focus from the typical existing job to the typical newly created or newly destroyed job. We show how one-year and two-year persistence rates for newly created and destroyed jobs vary with employer size and age.

Table 4.6 reports the results. Based on the average plant-size measure, new jobs at larger plants are more likely to survive for at least one or two years than new jobs at smaller plants. For example, the average two-year persistence rate ranges from under 50 percent for plants with fewer than 50 employees to over 60 percent for plants with at least 2,500 employees. This evidence indicates that new jobs at larger plants offer superior short-term survival prospects.

The evidence becomes less clear-cut when we turn to the current plant size measure. Table 4.6 exhibits quite small differences by current plant size in the one-year persistence of newly created jobs. The two-year persistence rate for job creation shows only a weak positive relationship to current plant size. Based on the results by current plant size only, one might reasonably conclude that the short-term survival prospects for newly created jobs bear no strong relationship to employer size.

How can we reconcile these apparently contradictory results? To understand the reconciliation, consider some hypothetical employment histories in a simplified setting with only two size classes. Suppose a plant is small at the beginning of the sample, becomes large for one period, and then returns permanently to the small category. This plant is classified as small under the average-size measure. Under the current-size measure, it is classified as small in most periods but as large in the period that coincides with its one episode

---

25. Dunne and Roberts (1989, table 1) present evidence that five-year survival probabilities for manufacturing jobs rise sharply with plant age.

Table 4.6
Persistence Rates by Employer Size and Age: Mean Rates for Annual Job Creation and Destruction Measures, 1973 to 1988

	Creation		Destruction	
	One-Year	Two-Year	One-Year	Two-Year

Average Plant Size

0 to 19 Employees	0.62	0.44	0.84	0.78
20 to 49	0.65	0.48	0.84	0.76
50 to 99	0.69	0.51	0.82	0.75
100 to 249	0.71	0.55	0.82	0.74
250 to 499	0.71	0.56	0.80	0.72
500 to 999	0.71	0.57	0.80	0.71
1,000 to 2,499	0.71	0.57	0.82	0.74
2,500 to 4,999	0.75	0.64	0.80	0.71
5,000 or More	0.75	0.61	0.82	0.73

Current Plant Size

0 to 19 Employees	0.70	0.54	0.86	0.80
20 to 49	0.70	0.54	0.84	0.77
50 to 99	0.71	0.55	0.83	0.75
100 to 249	0.70	0.55	0.81	0.73
250 to 499	0.68	0.53	0.79	0.70
500 to 999	0.68	0.52	0.80	0.71
1,000 to 2,499	0.68	0.54	0.81	0.73
2,500 to 4,999	0.73	0.59	0.79	0.71
5,000 or More	0.71	0.57	0.83	0.72

Average Firm Size

0 to 19 Employees	0.60	0.40	0.85	0.79
20 to 49	0.64	0.46	0.82	0.75
50 to 99	0.69	0.52	0.81	0.73
100 to 249	0.70	0.56	0.80	0.71
250 to 499	0.72	0.58	0.81	0.72
500 to 999	0.71	0.58	0.80	0.73
1,000 to 2,499	0.72	0.57	0.80	0.71
2,500 to 4,999	0.70	0.57	0.82	0.73
5,000 to 9,999	0.71	0.57	0.81	0.73
10,000 to 24,999	0.72	0.58	0.80	0.72
25,000 to 49,999	0.73	0.59	0.82	0.72
50,000 or More	0.75	0.62	0.79	0.71

Ownership Type

Single-Unit Firm	0.67	0.49	0.82	0.74
Multi-Unit Firm	0.71	0.57	0.82	0.74

Plant Age

Young (0-1 yrs.)	0.79	0.67	0.88	0.84
Middle-Aged (2-10 yrs.)	0.69	0.52	0.83	0.75
Mature (10+ yrs.)	0.68	0.52	0.81	0.73

Note: Chapter 2 defines and explains the construction of the persistence measures.

Mean one-year (two-year) persistence rates are computed by averaging over the years for which we can measure one-year (two-year) persistence for all plants. Due to the five-year duration of LRD panels, we cannot compute persistence measures for all plants in certain years. For the same reason, we cannot compute long-term persistence measures for a random sample of plants. See Chapter 1 and the Technical Appendix for further details.

The precise cutoff between middle-aged and mature plants varies by year. See the Technical Appendix for details.

of job creation.[26] Consequently, this plant's employment history pulls down the persistence measure for small plants under the average-size measure, but it pulls down the persistence measure for large plants under the current-size measure.

As a second hypothetical example, consider a plant that starts out large, becomes small for one period, and then permanently returns to large status. The plant's return to large status involves an episode of persistent job creation. This episode pushes up the job-creation persistence rate for large plants under the average-size measure, but it pushes up the persistence rate for small plants under the current-size measure.

These two hypothetical employment histories illustrate a more general point: under the current-size measure, plant-level employment histories that involve occasional, temporary movements across size-class boundaries increase the job-creation persistence rates for small plants relative to large plants. Just how prevalent are these occasional boundary-crossing episodes? We know from chapter 2 that annual job creation is concentrated among plants that experience large percentage employment changes, suggesting that much job creation involves boundary crossing. We know from other research (e.g., Lilien, 1980) that temporary layoffs in the manufacturing sector are quite important, especially during cyclical downturns. These observations suggest that the second hypothetical example, in particular, captures an important aspect of plant-level employment dynamics.

These remarks reconcile the apparent discrepancy between results based on the two alternative measures of plant size, but they do not indicate which size measure is more appropriate. As we suggested earlier, the average-plant size measure is probably a more accurate proxy for the plant's intended scale of operations. More important, the average-size measure assigns each plant to a fixed category. In contrast, as our examples reveal, the current-size measure can attribute job creation to the small-plant category even though the plant is large during most periods—and vice versa.[27] This aspect of accounting for job creation by current-size class is discomfiting. Hence, we think an accounting for job creation by average size represents a more informative way to examine the data, although we recognize that the current-size measure may be more appropriate for some purposes.

---

26. Recall that our measure of current plant size equals the simple average of current-period and previous-period employment. Remarks in the text presume that the plant crosses the size-class boundary once during its job creation episode and a second time as it returns to its initial size.

27. The same problem arises if we adopt the Birch/SBA practice for measuring employer size.

Returning to table 4.6, we see that newly created jobs exhibit greater persistence at plants owned by multiunit firms. The two-year persistence rate for newly created jobs is 49 percent for single-unit firms, compared with 57 percent for multiunit firms. Based on the firm-size measure, newly created jobs are more likely to survive at larger firms. For example, the two-year persistence rate for newly created jobs ranges from under 46 percent for firms with fewer than 100 employees to greater than 57 percent at firms with more than 2,500 workers.

To summarize the discussion thus far, newly created jobs at small employers are less likely to survive for one or two years than newly created jobs at larger employers. This characterization holds for average plant size, ownership type of parent firm, and firm size. Although the relationship is weaker, table 4.6 also reveals that the persistence of newly destroyed jobs is greater for smaller employers. Finally, table 4.1 revealed that the typical existing job has poorer short-term survival prospects at smaller employers. In a nutshell, both existing and newly created jobs are less secure at small businesses than at large businesses and, once lost, small business jobs are less likely to reappear.

The last panel of table 4.6 reports persistence measures by plant age. Given the structure of LRD panels, the three-way grouping reported in the table represents the finest breakdown of persistence by plant age that we can construct for a random sample of manufacturing plants. Even though young plants tend to be small, the results indicate that newly created jobs exhibit greater one-year and two-year survival rates at younger plants. Compared with more mature plants, this result suggests that young plants create jobs only when the short-term survival prospects look quite favorable. Another interpretation is that young plants require more time to determine the long-run profitability of newly created employment positions. In any case, table 4.6 also indicates that, once lost, jobs destroyed by younger plants are less likely to return.

Although these patterns of persistence by plant age are intriguing, they are less striking than they appear. Recall from table 4.5 that "young" plants constitute only 3 percent of manufacturing employment. Moving beyond the young category, the persistence rates for job creation and destruction vary only slightly by plant age group. Thus, barring very young plants, table 4.6 provides little evidence against the hypothesis that job-creation and job-destruction persistence rates are invariant with plant age.

5   Job Flows and Business Cycles

This chapter describes several empirical regularities in the cyclical behavior of job creation and destruction. In light of these regularities, we argue that prevailing views about the nature of business cycles are unsatisfactory and incomplete, and we sketch out an alternative, richer view. Our main findings and conclusions fall into five categories:

• *Cyclical asymmetry:* *Job destruction varies much more over the business cycle than does job creation. On average, job destruction rates rise by 2.5 percentage points per quarter in recessions relative to expansions; job creation rates fall by only 0.7 percentage point.*

• *Differences in asymmetry by type of plant:* *The greater cyclical variability of job destruction is especially pronounced for larger, older, more diversified, and higher-wage plants. Smaller, younger, less specialized, and lower-wage plants exhibit much less asymmetry, and sometimes no asymmetry, between the cyclicality of creation and destruction.*

• *Differences among recessions:* *The magnitude and character of gross job flows vary considerably among business cycles. Job destruction rates showed a much more sustained rise during the recession of 1981–82 than in that of 1974–75. Job creation rates showed less sensitivity to the business cycle during the 1980s than previously.*

• *Business cycle theories:* *Prevailing interpretations of business cycles stress the role of aggregate shocks and downplay the connection between cycles and the restructuring of industries and jobs. Several aspects of gross job flow dynamics do not fit comfortably with prevailing views. Rather, the empirical evidence points to the need for a richer view of business cycles that highlights their connection with the restructuring process.*

• *A case study of the steel industry: The U.S. steel industry underwent dramatic upheaval and restructuring during the 1970s and 1980s. This experience entailed wide swings in output, a shift from integrated mills to minimills, and enormous job destruction during the 1981–82 recession. Developments related to technology, foreign competition, and energy prices underlay the restructuring process, but the timing and intensity of restructuring appear to have been strongly influenced by aggregate shocks.*

5.1 Context and Motivation

Chapter 2 shows that the ongoing, extensive process of permanent job reallocation is closely related to the business cycle. For total manufacturing, job destruction rises dramatically during recessions, whereas job creation changes relatively little. Put differently, the intensity of job reallocation is countercyclical. This chapter investigates these and related aspects of gross job flow dynamics in more detail. Part of the investigation looks at various characterizations of cyclicality in job creation and destruction for total manufacturing, and part looks at differences in cyclical patterns among industries and types of plants. The chapter also presents evidence on differences among business cycles in the magnitude and nature of gross job flows.

To structure the empirical investigation in a useful way, we first outline some important elements of prevailing views about business cycles. We then develop some evidence on gross job flow dynamics and, along the way, evaluate how closely the evidence conforms to predictions implied by prevailing interpretations of business cycles. Next, we develop several elements of a richer view of business cycles suggested by the facts. Finally, we return to the data for further investigation into the cyclical behavior of gross job flows and a case study of restructuring in the U.S. steel industry.

5.2 The Prevailing View of Business Cycles

5.2.1 The Macroeconomic Framework

According to prevailing views of business cycles, recessions are driven by shocks that adversely affect most firms at roughly the same time, thereby causing a broad reduction in production and employment. Such a shock is called an *aggregate shock.* Aggregate shocks can be positive or negative, resulting in expansions or contractions of economic activity. Examples include changes in interest rates and the availability of credit—perhaps caused

by monetary policy actions—which affect the ability of nearly all firms to invest in new buildings and equipment; changes in corporate and personal income taxes, which affect profits and spending power; and sharp changes in the prices of widely used inputs such as energy, which affect production costs.[1] Regardless of its precise source, the key feature of an aggregate shock is its widespread and broadly similar effects among most sectors and firms.

The focus on aggregate shocks leads economists to adopt a macroeconomic framework characterized by representative producers and consumers. That is, the production side of the economy is modeled as one firm whose economic behavior is thought to represent the average of all firms. Likewise, the consumption side of the economy is modeled as one household whose economic behavior represents the average of all households. This framework typically abstracts from differences in business cycle behavior among households and sectors, and among employers within sectors. By ignoring differences among households and employers, this framework reinforces prevailing views of business cycles, with their focus on aggregate shocks and their silence on the connection between reallocation and business cycles.

5.2.2 Some Empirical Underpinnings of the Prevailing View

An important empirical regularity underlying the aggregate shock view of business cycles involves comovements in employment growth among industries. Industry-level employment growth rates tend to rise and fall together over time in a highly coincident manner. Figure 5.1 illustrates this positive comovement with bar charts that depict employment growth rates for all private, nonagricultural, two-digit Standard Industrial Classification (SIC) industries during representative years of recession (1975 and 1982) and expansion (1978 and 1984). The bars plotted in figure 5.1 show the difference between an industry's actual growth rate during the indicated year and its average growth rate over time. Virtually every industry exhibits below-average growth rates in recessions and above-average rates in expansions. Moreover, the great bulk of total employment lies in contracting industries during recessions and in

---

1. An influential paper by Lucas (1977a) articulates many key elements of prevailing views about business cycles, including the notion that aggregate shocks drive cyclical fluctuations. Although most economists stress the role of aggregate shocks, they disagree widely about the relative importance of different aggregate shocks. See Cochrane (1993) for a survey of recent research on the relative importance of different shocks.

Figure 5.1
Employment Growth Rates in Two-Digit Industries in Years of Recession and Expansion

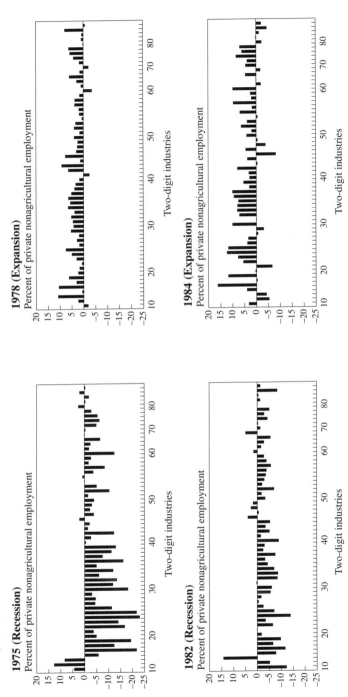

Note: The bars represent employment growth rates in individual private nonagricultural two-digit industries (Standard Industrial Classification).
The employment growth rate of an industry is the difference between the industry's actual employment growth rate and its time-series average rate, 1972–1988.

growing (relative to trend) industries during expansions.[2] Simply put, recessions and expansions are pervasive among industries.

This evidence about comovement is closely related to another empirical observation that seems supportive of prevailing views: industry-level data reveal little evidence of simultaneous job creation and destruction. To develop this point, figure 5.2 depicts the employment-weighted frequency distribution of two-digit industry growth rates for representative expansion and recession years. The height of each bar in the figure shows the percentage of employment in industries experiencing growth rates in the indicated interval.[3] Multiplying the height of each bar by its corresponding growth rate, and summing over all bars to the left (right) of 0, delivers the gross job destruction (creation) rate based on industry-level data. According to the figure, the industry-level growth rate distributions are highly concentrated about their means. These data uncover little of the simultaneous job creation and destruction so evident in the plant-level data. Consequently, the pace of restructuring in the economy looks mild and not subject to any sharp cyclical variation.

The shape of the industry-level growth rate distribution does change in a systematic way over the cycle. The variance (similarly, job reallocation rate) typically increases in recession years, and the distribution becomes somewhat more skewed to the left. However, these changes arise partly because some industries, such as durable goods, decline more than others during recessions. Furthermore, the declines are partly transitory—that is, durable goods industries increase more than others during recoveries.[4]

---

2. Industries with below-average growth rates represented 85 percent of employment in 1975 and 95 percent in 1982; industries with above-average growth rates represented 95 percent of employment in 1978 and 71 percent in 1984. Results are similar for more disaggregated data. Data for four-digit manufacturing industries show that industries with below-average growth rates represented about 90 percent of employment in 1975 and 1982; industries with above-average growth rates represented 72 percent of employment in 1978 and 82 percent in 1984.

3. The growth rates in figure 5.2 are the actual rates (g_t, defined in chapter 2), not the difference from the time-series average, as in figure 5.1.

4. Time-series data for the United States and many other countries show a positive relationship between unemployment and the variance of industry-level growth rates. Lilien (1982) argued that this relationship supports the hypothesis that sectoral labor demand shocks are important driving forces behind business cycles. Abraham and Katz (1986) countered that much of the change in the variance over the cycle reflects differences among industries in the timing and the magnitude of responses to aggregate shocks. Davis (1987), Murphy and Topel (1987), Loungani, Rush, and Tave (1990), and Brainard and Cutler (1993) also address the role of sectoral shocks as driving forces behind aggregate fluctuations. As will become clear below, plant-level data show an increase in the pace of permanent reallocation within sectors during recessions. Thus, our results are not driven by transitory distribution effects between sectors.

Figure 5.2
Two-Digit Industry-Level Growth-Rate Distributions: 1978 and 1982

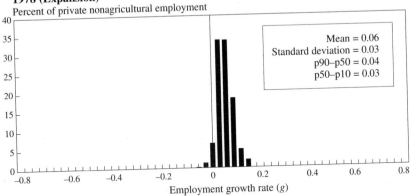

1978 (Expansion)

Percent of private nonagricultural employment

Mean = 0.06
Standard deviation = 0.03
p90–p50 = 0.04
p50–p10 = 0.03

Employment growth rate (g)

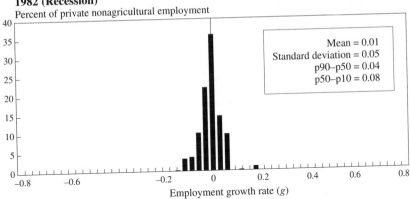

1982 (Recession)

Percent of private nonagricultural employment

Mean = 0.01
Standard deviation = 0.05
p90–p50 = 0.04
p50–p10 = 0.08

Employment growth rate (g)

Note: (p90–p50) is the 90th employment percentile minus the 50th employment percentile. (p50–p10) is the 50th employment percentile minus the 10th employment percentile.

The growth-rate distributions show the number of occurrences of each observed employment rate weighted by each industry's employment. The bars thus indicate the share of employment associated with each rate.

In this figure, the growth rate (g) is measured as the change in employment divided by the average of current and lagged employment. (See Technical Appendix.)

Let us now recapitulate some of the empirical underpinnings of the prevailing view. Fluctuations in industry-level growth rates show considerable positive comovement over the business cycle. As a related matter, the distribution of industry-level growth rates is highly concentrated and does not suggest an economy subject to continuous, large-scale job reallocation. Although the variance of industry-level growth rates rises during recessions, the increase is moderate. In addition, much of this increase appears to reflect systematic differences in industry-level responses to aggregate shocks and transitory changes in the industry distribution of employment. Although these facts can be given alternative interpretations, they fit rather comfortably with a macroeconomic framework that stresses aggregate shocks and abstracts from the connection between reallocation and business cycles.

5.2.3   Implications for Layoffs

Another feature of the prevailing view is its emphasis on the temporary nature of many layoffs that occur during recessions. To set out the story, an adverse aggregate shock induces firms to lay off workers, many of them temporarily. As the shock subsides or reverses, firms rehire many of these laid-off workers to their former jobs. This story suggests that aggregate shocks move the distribution of plant-level growth rates in much the same way that the distribution of industry-level growth rates moves. Reversal of the aggregate shocks leads the economy—and most plants—back to their original positions. The view that recessions have largely transitory effects on the distribution of employment among industries and plants fits well with the notion that expansions and recoveries are widespread. Feldstein (1975) and Lilien (1980) present evidence that seems to support this view. They find that the typical layoff is temporary, with more than two-thirds of all layoffs ending in recall.

The strong countercyclical behavior of temporary layoffs depicted in figure 5.3 provides additional support for this view. However, the figure also reveals that the increase in temporary layoffs typically accounts for less than one-third of the increase in unemployment during recessions. Thus, even this cursory examination of the role of temporary layoffs in cyclical unemployment changes raises questions about the adequacy of prevailing views about

Figure 5.3
**U.S. Temporary Layoffs and Total Unemployment:
Quarterly, 1967 to 1992**

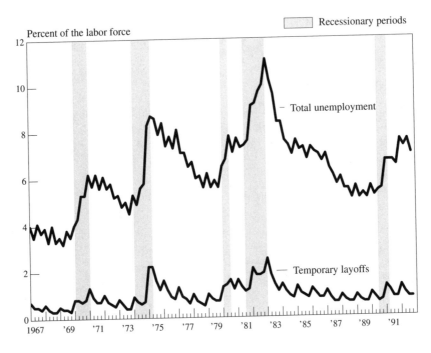

business cycles.[5] (Chapter 6 explores the connection between unemployment flows, including temporary layoffs, and gross job flows in more depth.)

5.2.4 Predictions for Job Creation and Destruction Dynamics

The prevailing view of business cycles suggests four predictions about the time-series behavior of gross job creation and destruction: (1) the correlation between creation and destruction rates is close to -1.0; (2) the changes in creation and destruction over the business cycle are of opposite sign but

---

5. The Feldstein (1975) and Lilien (1982) findings on the importance of temporary layoffs are reconciled with our evidence on the permanence of job destruction as follows. Since most temporary layoffs are of very short duration, they are unlikely to appear in our plant-level data with quarterly and annual sampling frequencies. That is, employment changes at a plant that reverse themselves within the quarter (year) are not reflected in the quarterly (annual) gross flows data.

roughly equal magnitude; (3) the variabilities of creation and destruction rates over time are similar in magnitude; and (4) the correlation between the job reallocation rate and net employment growth rate is close to 0. These predictions follow if aggregate shocks predominate and have similar growth-rate effects for all or most employers. Such shocks shift the central tendency of the plant-level growth rate distribution, but they have little effect on the shape of the distribution. The absence of any important effect on the shape of the distribution underlies the predictions.

We suggested above that aggregate shocks cause systematic, transitory differences in industry-level employment growth. Conceivably, such systematic differences among industries and other sectors in the response to aggregate shocks could account for departures from predictions (1) through (4). For example, sectoral differences in cyclical sensitivity could lead to an increased pace of job reallocation in recessions, even if this reallocation is subsequently reversed. To address this possibility, the empirical investigation below considers whether the predictions hold within detailed sectors as well as for total manufacturing.

5.3   Time-Series Evidence on Creation and Destruction

5.3.1   Total Manufacturing

As it turns out, the cyclical behavior of manufacturing job flows does not conform well to the predictions of the prevailing view. Chapter 2 described the countercyclicality of job reallocation, one fact that does not fit comfortably with the prevailing view. Other aspects of job flow behavior also run counter to the predictions of that view. Table 5.1 contrasts theory and evidence by juxtaposing predictions of the prevailing view against the empirical evidence. The first piece of evidence is the correlation between job creation and destruction. The prevailing view predicts a correlation close to -1.0, but the actual correlation is -0.36. Evidence that creation and destruction do not always move in opposite directions over the cycle appears in figure 5.4, which replicates figure 2.5. A particularly interesting period is the recession of 1981:Q2 to 1982:Q4. Rather remarkably, the gross job creation rate fell little at the onset of this severe recession, and then rose moderately over the remaining course of the recession.

The second piece of evidence is the ratio of cyclical changes in job destruction and creation. Cyclical change equals the difference between the average

Table 5.1
Gross Job Flow Dynamics: Predictions of the Prevailing View vs. the Data, 1972 to 1988

Property	Prediction (Approximation)	Actual[a]
Correlation between Job Creation and Job Destruction..	−1	−0.36
Ratio of Cyclical Change in Job Destruction to Cyclical Change in Job Creation...........................	−1	−3.68
Ratio of Variance of Job Destruction to Variance of Job Creation...................................	1	3.35
Correlation between Job Reallocation and Net Employment Growth............................	0	−0.57

[a]Based on quarterly data, 1972:Q2 to 1988:Q4.

rate during recessions and the average rate during expansions.[6] The prevailing view predicts a cyclical change ratio (destruction to creation) close to −1.0, but the actual ratio is −3.7: during recessions, job destruction rises by nearly four times as much as job creation declines. During the 1981–82 recession, the quarterly rate of job destruction rose from about 5 percent to nearly 10 percent, while job creation remained essentially unchanged at about 5 percent. During the recession of 1973–75, job destruction rose (4.1 to 11.4 percent) by much more than job creation fell (6.7 to 3.2 percent).

The third piece of evidence is the ratio of variances of job destruction and creation. The prevailing view predicts a variance ratio (destruction to creation) close to 1.0, but the actual ratio is 3.4: destruction is more variable than creation in terms of recession-versus-expansion comparisons, as indicated by the relative cyclical change, and on average over all quarters. If job creation were more variable than destruction during expansions, then this variance would offset the large recessionary increase in destruction, and the ratio would still be close to 1.0. However, figure 5.4 clearly shows that during expansions the variances of creation and destruction are much more similar (the ratio is 1.4). Consequently, the cyclical imbalance between changes in creation and destruction during recessions dominates the variance ratio.

The fourth and final piece of evidence is the correlation between job reallocation and net employment growth. The prevailing view predicts a correlation

---

6. As in chapter 2, we use the recessions and expansions defined by the National Bureau of Economic Research (NBER) in this analysis. We examine this measure in more detail below, in the section dealing with business cycles.

Figure 5.4
**Net and Gross Job Flow Rates in Manufacturing:
Quarterly, 1972 to 1988**

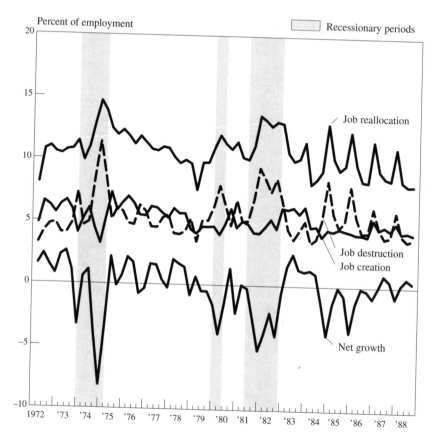

close to 0, but the actual correlation is −0.57. Large increases in job reallo-cation characterize each recessionary period between 1972 and 1988, as well as other periods with manufacturing employment declines that are not offi-cially classified as recessions. Furthermore, job reallocation tends to decline over long expansionary periods (1975–80 and 1983–88).

In summary, the prevailing view of business cycles, which is based upon the notion that most or all firms respond similarly to the cycle, is not supported by the evidence on job flows in the manufacturing sector. We turn next to a similar analysis at the sectoral level.

5.3.2   Variation among Sectors and Plant Types

By examining the cyclical behavior of job creation and destruction at the sectoral level, we can determine whether the results above simply reflect differences among sectors in the timing and magnitude of cyclical responses to aggregate shocks. Perhaps more important, the analysis in this section develops a set of facts about how the cyclical behavior of gross job flows varies with observable characteristics of individual employers.

Tables 5.2 through 5.4 report evidence on the cyclical behavior of job flows by sector and plant type.[7] For each statistic, the weight of evidence follows the pattern observed in data for total manufacturing. In this respect, the detailed sectoral results reinforce the previous results. Thus, sectoral differences in cyclical responses do not account for the evidence against the prevailing view of business cycles.[8] We now take a closer look at the sectoral differences in the cyclical behavior of job creation and destruction.

5.3.2.1   *Correlation between Job Creation and Destruction*

The correlation between job creation and destruction (column 1 of tables 5.2 through 5.4) is substantially different from the predicted value of -1.0 for all sectors and plant types. Only one correlation, in the tobacco industry, is much below -0.5, and even that (-0.68) is still far from -1.0. The majority of correlations lie in the range of -0.2 to -0.5. Many industries, regions, and plant types show correlations near -0.5: the food, primary metals, and transportation industries; the East South Central and Pacific regions; and some plants (certain medium-size, highly diversified, and average-wage plants). Although these correlations depart from the prediction of the prevailing view, they still suggest that shocks common to all plants in the sector play a major role.

Some sectors and plant types, however, exhibit correlations between creation and destruction that are 0 or even positive—behavior that differs radically from the prediction of the prevailing view. The apparel and printing industries, very small plants, and single-unit plants exhibit significantly positive correlations. The chemicals and instruments industries, West North Cen-

---

7. The tables present results only for the average plant-size measure, but similar results hold for current plant size and firm size.

8. In related work (Davis and Haltiwanger, 1990, 1992), we more thoroughly investigate whether departures from the predictions of the prevailing view can be explained by sectoral differences in cyclical responses. We find that they cannot.

Table 5.2
Cyclical Properties of Gross Flow Rates by Two-Digit Industry: Quarterly, 1972 to 1988

Industry	Correlation of Creation, Destruction[a]	Cyclical Change Ratio[b]	Variance Ratio of Destruction to Creation[c]	Correlation of Net, Reallocation[d]
Food	−0.46	2.36	0.72	0.18
Tobacco	−0.68	−2.55	0.61	0.32
Textiles	−0.19	−5.20	3.66	−0.58
Apparel	0.16	−4.11	2.62	−0.45
Lumber	−0.35	−20.03	1.54	−0.23
Furniture	−0.32	−2.85	2.83	−0.50
Paper	−0.38	−3.28	3.45	−0.58
Printing	0.48	−3.03	3.03	−0.55
Chemicals	−0.11	−8,45	1.89	−0.31
Petroleum	−0.34	4.25	1.21	−0.10
Rubber	−0.33	−3.36	3.18	−0.54
Leather	−0.38	−2.26	2.53	−0.46
Stone, Clay, and Glass	−0.44	−4.29	1.61	−0.26
Primary Metals	−0.51	−2.61	4.14	−0.67
Fabricated Metal	−0.33	−3.10	2.76	−0.49
Nonelectric Machinery	−0.36	−2.19	3.30	−0.56
Electric Machinery	−0.44	−2.95	4.03	−0.64
Transportation	−0.47	−8.27	1.71	−0.29
Instruments	−0.03	−2.84	1.85	−0.30
Miscellaneous	−0.40	−1.97	3.13	−0.55
Total Manufacturing	−0.36	−3.74	3.44	−0.58

[a] Correlation between job creation and job destruction.
[b] Ratio of cyclical change in job destruction to cyclical change in job creation.
[c] Ratio of variance of job destruction to variance of job creation.
[d] Correlation between job reallocation and net employment growth.

tral and Middle Atlantic regions, young, low-wage, and completely specialized plants exhibit essentially 0 correlations. Shocks that induce bursts of simultaneous job creation and destruction are apparently quite important for these sectors and plant types.

The sharpest differences in the correlation between creation and destruction occur among plant types. Small, young, single-unit, specialized, and low-wage plants exhibit a 0 or even positive correlation. In contrast, large, old, multiunit, diversified, and high-wage plants typically exhibit a large negative correlation. These results suggest that there are systematic differences in the driving forces underlying time variation in job creation and job destruction among plant types. We return to this theme below.

Table 5.3
Cyclical Properties of Gross Flow Rates by Region: Quarterly, 1972 to 1988

Region	Correlation of Creation, Destruction[a]	Cyclical Change Ratio[b]	Variance Ratio of Destruction to Creation[c]	Correlation of Net, Reallocation[d]
Northeast	−0.21	−3.99	3.53	−0.57
Middle Atlantic	−0.12	−3.34	4.17	−0.62
South Atlantic	−0.44	−4.11	3.53	−0.60
East South Central.............	−0.47	−3.94	2.43	−0.46
West South Central	−0.18	−3.46	3.01	−0.51
East North Central.............	−0.36	−2.84	2.69	−0.48
West North Central	−0.11	−3.62	2.62	−0.45
Mountain	−0.19	−2.96	1.61	−0.24
Pacific.......................	−0.46	−4.55	1.42	−0.19

[a] Correlation between job creation and job destruction.
[b] Ratio of cyclical change in job destruction to cyclical change in job creation.
[c] Ratio of variance of job destruction to variance of job creation.
[d] Correlation between job reallocation and net employment growth.

5.3.2.2   Ratio of Cyclical Changes in Job Creation and Destruction
The ratio of cyclical changes (column 2 of tables 5.2 through 5.4) differs sharply from the predicted value of −1.0 for all sectors and plant types. The ratio closest to −1.0 is twice as large in magnitude: −2.0 in the miscellaneous industry sector (SIC 39). Most ratios are close to −3.0 or even lower. Some ratios are −7.0 or lower: in the lumber, chemicals, and transportation industries; in the second largest plant size; in moderately specialized plants; and in the highest-wage plants. For two industries (food and petroleum) the ratio is actually positive, so that job creation rises during recessions but not by as much as job destruction. In short, the cyclical asymmetry between creation and destruction is widespread among sectors and plant types.

Although the cyclical asymmetry is pervasive among plant types, it is somewhat more pronounced for large, old, and multiunit plants. The ratio of cyclical change for these large plants is about −4.0 or lower, which means they experience greater cyclical asymmetry than the average for total manufacturing. In contrast, the ratio for small, young, and single-unit plants is much closer to −2.5, that is, there is less cyclical asymmetry for these plants. This difference between large and small plants captures the tendency for large plants to experience much larger than average increases in job destruction during recessions.

Table 5.4
Cyclical Properties of Gross Flow Rates by Plant Characteristics: Quarterly, 1972 to 1988

Plant Characteristics	Correlation of Creation, Destruction[a]	Cyclical Change Ratio[b]	Variance Ratio of Destruction to Creation[c]	Correlation of Net, Reallocation[d]
Plant Type				
Single-Unit Firm	0.34	−2.74	1.98	−0.35
Multi-Unit Firm...............	−0.46	−4.01	3.43	−0.59
Plant Age[e]				
Young (0–10 yrs.)	0.04	−2.63	1.32	−0.14
Mature (10+ yrs.)..............	−0.41	−3.83	4.18	−0.65
Average Size				
0 to 19 employees	0.45	−4.87	1.13	−0.07
20 to 49	0.11	−3.44	1.77	−0.28
50 to 99	−0.15	−5.48	2.41	−0.42
100 to 249	−0.47	−4.13	2.78	−0.52
250 to 499	−0.47	−3.06	3.06	−0.56
500 to 999	−0.44	−2.80	3.04	−0.55
1,000 to 2,499	−0.40	−3.34	3.66	−0.60
2,500 to 4,999	−0.43	−7.07	1.65	−0.27
5,000 or More	−0.46	−5.17	1.74	−0.30
Product Specialization				
Highly Diversified	−0.48	−4.01	3.21	−0.57
Moderately Diversified	−0.40	−3.24	2.34	−0.43
Moderately Specialized	−0.28	−7.10	3.73	−0.59
Highly Specialized.............	−0.31	−4.00	3.01	−0.52
Completely Specialized	−0.01	−6.17	1.92	−0.32
Level of Plant Wages				
Very Low....................	−0.00	−2.93	2.19	−0.37
Moderately Low...............	−0.31	−3.11	2.60	−0.46
Average	−0.49	−2.71	2.88	−0.54
Moderately High	−0.41	−4.04	3.44	−0.59
Very High....................	−0.39	−8.28	2.74	−0.50

[a] Correlation between job creation and job destruction.
[b] Ratio of cyclical change in job destruction to cyclical change in job creation.
[c] Ratio of variance of job destruction to variance of job creation.
[d] Correlation between job reallocation and net employment growth.
[e]The young and middle-aged categories have been combined.

5.3.2.3 Ratio of Variances of Job Creation and Destruction

The variance ratios (column 3 of tables 5.2 through 5.4) differ substantially from the predicted value of 1.0 for most—but not all—sectors and plant types. Several sectors and plant types exhibit ratios close to the predicted value. Ratios of 1.4 or less hold for the food, tobacco, and petroleum industries; the Pacific region; young plants; and the smallest plant size. Several others are less than 2.0. However, for most industries and sectors, the job destruction variance is at least twice as large as the creation variance.

Although the variance ratios uniformly exceed 1.0, they are systematically greater for larger and older employers. This difference is especially pronounced for single-unit versus multi-unit plants and for old versus young plants. Among plant sizes, the variance ratio peaks for large, but not the largest, plants. This result contrasts with the ratio of cyclical changes. Apparently the largest plants experience the biggest changes in destruction during recessions, but they also experience rather large changes in creation during expansions.

5.3.2.4 Countercyclicality of Job Reallocation

A pervasive pattern among industries and sectors is the negative correlation between rates of net employment growth and job reallocation (column 4 of tables 5.2 through 5.4). Every correlation is lower than -0.1 except for three industries (food, tobacco, and petroleum) and the very smallest size class (0–19 employees). Food and tobacco actually exhibit positive correlations—that is, job reallocation declines during recessions. But most correlations tend to be significantly negative, and there is less variation among sectors and plant types than for the other statistics.

Interestingly, the correlations between net employment growth and job reallocation for sectors and plant types are rarely much lower than the correlation for total manufacturing (-0.57). Only four correlations (primary metals and electric machinery industries, Middle Atlantic region, and old plants) lie below -0.60. In contrast, many correlations are much larger (closer to 0). Thus, unlike the other statistics, deviations from the total manufacturing statistic tend to be one-sided.

Once again, differences appear most clearly among plant types. In particular, large, old, multiunit, diversified, and high-wage plants tend to exhibit strong negative correlations, whereas small, young, single-unit, specialized, and low-wage plants tend to exhibit milder negative correlations. But these differences do not alter the conclusion that job reallocation rates increase during downturns for virtually every sector and every plant type.

5.3.3   A Summary of the LRD Evidence

One way to summarize how the data differ from the prevailing view is to look at the dynamics of the plant-level growth rate distribution. Figure 5.5 illustrates how the annual empirical distribution changes between an expansion (1978) and a recession (1982).[9] This figure is similar to figure 5.2, except that the growth rates are for plants rather than two-digit industries. The most striking aspect of the figure is the enormous variance of plant-level growth rates. (Figure 5.5 has the same scale as figure 5.2.) Many plants grow sharply in recessions and many contract sharply in expansions.

The prevailing view of business cycles emphasizes the role of aggregate shocks with similar effects among plants, but figure 5.5 shows that the shape of the growth rate distribution changes between recessions and expansions. In the expansion year, the distribution looks nearly symmetrical and not unlike the industry distribution (except that it is more dispersed). However, two main features of the recession distribution distinguish it from the expansion distribution. First, the distribution becomes skewed to the left, so that job destruction rises more sharply than would be implied by a shift in the mean alone. Second, the distribution becomes more spread out, so that job reallocation rises. The systematic cyclical variation in the shape of the plant-level growth rate distribution is difficult to square with the prevailing view. Instead, it points toward a richer view of business cycles that emphasizes their connection to the pace of job reallocation and economic restructuring.

5.3.4   Evidence Based on Other Data Sources

We have seen that job reallocation in manufacturing was closely linked to business cycles during the 1970s and 1980s. An obvious question is whether the results extend to other time periods, other sectors, and other countries. Recent studies, partly stimulated by our previous work, shed some light on this question.

Let us first consider some evidence for a longer time period. Annual and quarterly data are not available in the LRD prior to 1972, but data on worker accessions and separations in the monthly BLS Manufacturing Turnover Survey can be used to generate time series for job creation and destruction. These data are available from 1951 through 1981.

---

9. As in the industry distributions, these years are fairly representative and were chosen only to illustrate the general principle. Figure 5.5 is a size-weighted growth rate distribution.

Figure 5.5
Plant-Level Employment Growth-Rate Distributions: 1978 and 1982

1978 (Expansion)

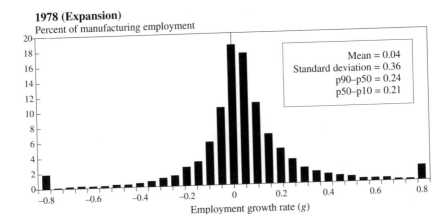

Percent of manufacturing employment

Mean = 0.04
Standard deviation = 0.36
p90–p50 = 0.24
p50–p10 = 0.21

Employment growth rate (g)

1982 (Recession)

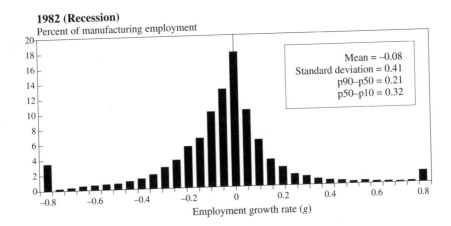

Percent of manufacturing employment

Mean = –0.08
Standard deviation = 0.41
p90–p50 = 0.21
p50–p10 = 0.32

Employment growth rate (g)

Note: (p90–p50) is the 90th employment percentile minus the 50th employment percentile. (p50–p10) is the 50th employment percentile minus the 10th employment percentile.

The growth-rate distributions show the number of occurrences of each observed employment rate weighted by each plant's employment. The bars thus indicate the share of employment associated with each rate.

In this figure, the growth rate (g) is measured as the change in employment divided by the average of current and lagged employment. (See Technical Appendix.)

Following Blanchard and Diamond (1990), we adjust the BLS data on accessions and separations to account for time variation in quits and vacancies and to remove seasonality.[10] Because the BLS data directly measure worker flows, the procedure for generating job flow series is subject to potentially important measurement errors. One can gauge the accuracy of the BLS-based time series on gross job flows by comparing them with the LRD-based series for the overlapping time period.

Figure 5.6 plots the BLS-based creation and destruction rates for the period 1951:Q1 to 1981:Q4. These quarterly rates are cumulated from monthly rates. Thus, plant-level employment changes that reverse themselves within a quarter are captured by the BLS-based job flow series, but they are not captured by the LRD-based series reported throughout this book.

Several features of the figure merit attention. First, as in the LRD-based data, job destruction is more variable than job creation; the two series have a variance ratio of 1.7. However, the volatility of job creation in the 1950s is much higher than in later periods and about as volatile as job destruction. Thus, figure 5.6 suggests the possibility that the greater volatility of job destruction represents a relatively recent development in the U.S. economy.

Second, every recession exhibits a spike in job destruction, confirming a prominent feature of business cycles in the LRD-based data. Unlike the period since 1970, however, job creation rates also increase sharply shortly after the onset of the three recessions in the 1950s and early 1960s. Sharp declines in job creation rates preceded the onset of each recession by a few quarters. Thus, the decoupling of job destruction and creation intensity, a striking feature of business cycles in the manufacturing sector during the 1970s and 1980s, does not characterize the experience of the manufacturing sector in the two preceding decades.[11] An open question is whether the nearly simultaneous increases in creation and destruction during these earlier recessions primarily reflect permanent job reallocation or a pattern of temporary layoffs and recalls.

Third, the secular decline in manufacturing employment has been brought about primarily by a decrease in the job creation rate rather than by an increase in the destruction rate. Although we do not explore the issue here, the

10. See Blanchard and Diamond (1990) for a full discussion of the adjustment procedure.
11. The analysis in Caballero and Hammour (1994b) suggests that the recent evolution toward decoupling of destruction and creation may reflect a deterioration in the economic efficiency of the reallocation process.

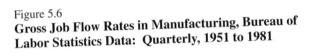

Figure 5.6
**Gross Job Flow Rates in Manufacturing, Bureau of
Labor Statistics Data: Quarterly, 1951 to 1981**

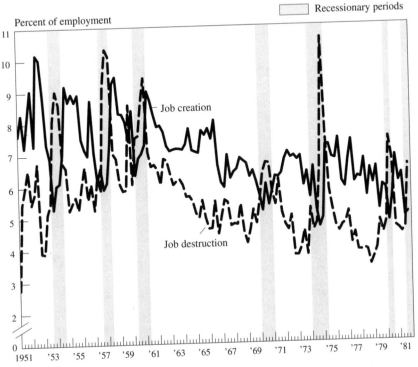

Note: The job creation and destruction measures depicted here are constructed from data on worker
separations and accessions using the Bureau of Labor Statistics manufacturing turnover survey.

creation and destruction rates for detailed industries and regions that we have
constructed from the LRD could be used to explore whether this pattern is typical of the way in which secular employment changes occur.

Evidence on the time-series properties of gross job flows for other sectors
in the United States and other countries is sparse. Studies of gross job flows
for nonmanufacturing sectors in the United States are usually limited to annual or lower frequency data, short sample periods, and often a single state or
region.[12] Because of data limitations, these studies also raise concerns about

---

12. See, e.g., Leonard (1987), Lane, Isaac, and Stevens (1993), and Anderson and Meyer (1994).

spurious time-series patterns in the gross job flow measures.[13] Similar limitations hamper most studies of time variation in gross job flows for other countries as well.[14]

An exception is the study by Baldwin, Dunne, and Haltiwanger (1994), which compares annual gross job flows between the United States and Canada for the 1972–86 period. It uses annual gross job flow series for Canada that are based upon longitudinal establishment data of quality comparable with that of the LRD. The authors find that job reallocation in the manufacturing sector in Canada is countercyclical, but to a somewhat lesser degree than in the United States.

One U.S. study that has a reasonably long time series is the preliminary work by Bronars (1990), which is based on BLS 790 data for the 1972–89 period. Based on continuing establishments only, Bronars found that job reallocation rates exhibit even greater countercylicality in U.S. nonmanufacturing sectors than in the manufacturing sector. Although this finding conforms to our evidence for the manufacturing sector over the same time period, the preliminary nature of the work and the questions about data quality argue for interpreting the results with caution.

The bottom line is that we do not know very much about the cyclical properties of job creation and destruction for other sectors, time periods, and countries. The striking cyclical dynamics of job creation and destruction in the U.S. manufacturing sector during the 1970s and 1980s, and their failure to conform to the predictions of prevailing business cycle interpretations, suggest a clear need for the development of appropriate databases for other sectors and countries.

5.4   Some Theoretical Elements of a Richer View of Recessions

The inconsistencies between the time-series evidence and the prevailing view of business cycles raise several questions: What forces cause gross job flow

---

13. As stressed in the introduction and technical appendix, most other studies of gross job flow behavior rely upon datasets with a questionable ability to track establishments accurately through time in the face of mergers, ownership transfers, changes in taxpayer identification number or location of payroll offices, and changes in how multiunit firms choose to report employment. These problems inflate measured gross job flow rates and, to the extent that the incidence of these problems varies over time, cause spurious time variation.

14. See, e.g., Contini and Revelli (1992), Boeri and Cramer (1992), Regev (1990), and Blanchflower and Burgess (1993).

behavior to differ from the predictions of the prevailing view? How should the prevailing view be modified? What alternative view of recessions does the evidence favor? This section attempts to supply preliminary answers to these questions and, in doing so, to develop some building blocks of a richer view of recessions. We discuss several ideas that seem to us likely to be important elements in successful theories of gross job flows and their connection to business cycles. Because we think it important to communicate these ideas to a wide audience, we carry out the discussion at an informal and nontechnical level, although we recognize that this expositional choice involves some sacrifice of precision and clarity. For readers who crave more rigorous analyses, we provide references to the relevant literature.

5.4.1   The Role of Heterogeneity and Reallocation Frictions

In recent years, some economists have begun developing theories to explain the magnitude and cyclical behavior of job and worker flows and their connection to aggregate fluctuations.[15] These theories start from the premise that the economy is subject to a continuous stream of *allocative shocks*—shocks that cause idiosyncratic variation in profitability among job sites and worker–job matches. The continuous stream of allocative shocks generates the large-scale job and worker reallocation activity observed in the data. To model the job and worker reallocation process explicitly, these theories incorporate heterogeneity among workers and firms along one or more dimensions. The theories also emphasize search costs, moving costs, sunk investments, or other frictions that impede the free reallocation of factor inputs.[16] The combination of frictions and heterogeneity gives rise to potentially important roles for allocative shocks and the reallocation process in aggregate economic fluctuations.

---

15. See Aghion and Blanchard (1994), Andolfatto (1993), Blanchard and Diamond (1989, 1990), Burda and Wyplosz (1994), Caballero (1992), Caballero and Hammour (1994a, 1994b), Campbell (1994), Davis and Haltiwanger (1990), Gautier and Broersma (1993), Greenwood, MacDonald, and Zhang (1994), Hall (1991), Hosios (1994), Mortensen (1992), Mortensen and Pissarides (1992, 1994), and Yashiv (1994).

16. A sunk investment expenditure is one that cannot be (fully) recovered if the action associated with the original expenditure is subsequently reversed or altered. For example, once a firm constructs a manufacturing plant at one location, it cannot costlessly move the plant to another location revealed to be superior by later information. As another example, a worker who relocates his or her family to pursue job opportunities in a new place incurs expenses that cannot be recovered if the new location proves undesirable. As these examples suggest, a sunk investment creates an "asset" that has additional value when applied to a specific activity, firm, location, industry, or sector.

The idea that some shocks create incentives to reallocate jobs and workers across products, locations, and activities lies at the heart of many theoretical models of unemployment and other labor market phenomena. In these models, unemployment arises becase it takes time, effort, and expense for job seekers to find appropriate new jobs. Reallocation of capital inputs also requires time and sunk investments. Early theoretical studies that analyze the connections among allocative shocks, the resulting search and reallocation process, and the determination of unemployment include Lucas and Prescott (1974), Hall (1979), Diamond (1981), and Mortensen (1982).

The basic ideas articulated in these early studies have strongly influenced many subseqent analyses and intepretations of unemployment and job vacancies, the reallocation of workers and jobs, job shopping and career mobility patterns, and individual wage growth.[17] However, despite the wide diffusion of ideas related to theories of search and reallocation in the economics literature, most analyses of business cycles and aggregate fluctuations ignore or downplay the role of allocative shocks and reallocation frictions. In our view, greater attention to the reallocation process will lead to a firmer understanding of the driving forces behind aggregate fluctuations, the mechanisms through which aggregate shocks affect the economy, and the social and economic costs of business cycles.

Among recent theories of cyclical fluctuations in job and worker flows, two broad types have received the most attention. One type treats fluctuations over time in the intensity of allocative shocks as an important driving force behind aggregate fluctuations. The second type maintains that although allocative shocks and reallocation frictions are important, aggregate shocks drive business cycles and fluctuations in the pace of worker and job reallocation. Although different in emphasis, the two types of theories offer complementary views of labor market dynamics and business cycles, and both types point toward a rich set of interactions between aggregate fluctuations and the reallocation process. A third type of theory emphasizes the endogenous accumulation and revelation of information related to allocative shocks. This type of theory has yet to see a formal development directed toward the analysis of business cycles, but it offers interesting insights and the prospect of more fully understanding the connection between reallocation and aggregate fluctuations. We turn now to a fuller discussion of some key elements in these theories.

---

17. Pissarides (1990) offers an excellent development and synthesis of several important theoretical ideas in this literature. Devine and Kiefer (1991) nicely survey empirical research in labor economics that adopts a search approach.

5.4.2 Allocative Shocks as Driving Forces behind Aggregate Fluctuations

One can think of allocative shocks as events that alter the closeness of the match between the desired and actual characteristics of labor and capital inputs (Black, 1982). Here, "closeness" refers to physical distance and other aspects of geography, the complement and distribution of skills embodied in workers, the productive attributes of plant and equipment, and the way in which labor and capital inputs are organized to produce goods and services. "Events" refer to any shock or new piece of information that bears on the current or future closeness of the match between the desired and actual characteristics of factor inputs.

For example, the OPEC oil price shock of 1973 increased the demand for small, fuel-efficient cars and simultaneously reduced the demand for larger cars. American automobile companies were poorly situated to respond to this shock, because their capital stock and workforce were primarily directed toward the production of large cars. Consequently, capacity utilization and output fell in the wake of the oil price shock, even though a handful of plants equipped to produce small cars operated at peak capacity (Bresnahan and Ramey, 1993).

The oil price shock adversely affected the closeness between the desired and actual characteristics of factor inputs in the auto industry along several dimensions. First, much of the physical capital in the auto industry was dedicated to the production of larger rather than smaller cars. Second, U.S. auto workers had accumulated skills that were specialized in the production of particular models, and these tended to be larger vehicles. Third, many autoworkers laid off from large-car plants could not take up employment at small-car plants without a costly relocation. Fourth, the dealership network and sales force of the U.S. auto industry had evolved under an era of thriving large-car sales, and they were probably better suited to market, distribute, and service larger cars. Fifth, the knowledge base and the research and design personnel at U.S. auto companies had specialized in engineering larger cars. The development of smaller, more fuel-efficient cars required a costly and time-consuming reorientation of the knowledge base, and the development of new skills by research and design personnel.

These remarks suggest how reallocation frictions led to reduced output and employment in the auto industry in the wake of the first OPEC oil price shock. Similar remarks could be fashioned for many other industries. Coupled with the magnitude and widespread impact of oil price shocks during the 1970s and 1980s, these remarks about reallocation frictions also suggest how oil price shocks could cause large aggregate fluctuations by upsetting established

patterns of production. Several studies investigate the hypothesis that oil price shocks drove large aggregate fluctuations by upsetting established patterns of production.[18]

As another example, the immediate impact of recent U.S. defense spending cutbacks is extremely uneven among regions, firms, and workers. In the short run, their uneven character contributes to a slowdown in aggregate economic activity, because it renders obsolete much of the specialized plant and equipment in the defense industry, and because it heightens the mismatch between the location and skills of defense workers and the location and skill requirements of available jobs. Other examples of allocative disturbances with potentially important aggregate consequences include major weather events, technological progress that upsets established patterns of production, and government policy changes that alter the desired allocation of capital and labor inputs.

To this point, our discussion emphasizes the impact of allocative shocks on the closeness between the desired and actual characteristics of tangible factor inputs such as capital and labor. Yet some of the most important aggregate consequences of allocative shocks probably arise because these shocks destroy or devalue intangible inputs to the production process. These intangible inputs include the information capital embodied in an efficient sorting and matching of heterogeneous workers and jobs, knowledge about how to work productively with coworkers, knowledge about suitable locations for particular business activities and about idiosyncratic attributes of those locations, the information capital embodied in long-term customer–supplier and debtor–creditor relationships, and the organization capital embodied in sales, product distribution, and job-finding networks. The terms "information capital" and "organization capital" reflect the time and expense required to discover and develop efficient configurations of factor inputs when workers, capital inputs, technologies, and firms exhibit heterogeneity along many dimensions.

When allocative shocks upset established patterns of production, they devalue information and organization capital specific to that pattern of production (Caplin and Leahy, 1993b). Re-creating information and organization capital suited to the new pattern of production requires experimentation, time,

---

18. See, e.g., Davis (1985), Loungani (1986), and Mork (1989). In related work, Davis, Loungani, and Mahidhara (1994) find that oil price shocks were major driving forces behind regional unemployment cycles in the postwar U.S. economy. Hamilton (1988) analyzes a model with reallocation frictions that is motivated by the apparent impact of oil price shocks on aggregate economic activity. Many of the other theoretical and empirical studies referenced in this chapter also bear on the issue of whether oil price shocks drive aggregate fluctuations by upsetting established patterns of production.

and expense. Meanwhile, the productive potential of the economy is reduced by the obsolescence of old information and organization capital. Atkeson and Kehoe (1992) pursue this theme in their analysis of the transition from statist to capitalist economies in Eastern and Central Europe.[19]

Our account of how allocative shocks influence aggregate economic activity stresses the role of reallocation frictions, but other mechanisms may also be at play. Upstream and downstream linkages in the input–output structure of the economy can transmit a sector-specific shock throughout the economy, with potentially important aggregate consequences.[20] In this type of theory, the heterogeneity of intermediate factor inputs plays a central role in aggregate fluctuations, but the reallocation of jobs and workers does not. Hence, although this type of theory seems promising as a vehicle for understanding the aggregate output consequences of allocative shocks, its current formulations offer little insight into the relationship among worker flows, job flows, and business cycles.

The magnitude of job reallocation documented in this book and other studies shows that allocative shocks strike the economy continuously and with considerable intensity. Our remarks in this section make clear why the economic adjustments to these shocks are often costly and time-consuming. It follows that sharp time variation in the intensity of allocative shocks can cause large fluctuations in gross job flows and in conventional measures of aggregate economic activity, such as the output growth rate and the unemployment rate. Whether time variation in the intensity of allocative shocks has actually been a major driving force behind aggregate economic fluctuations is an important empirical issue.[21]

---

19. Information and organization capital appear as important concepts in many different guises and in a wide range of economic applications. The seminal analysis of the informational capital embodied in worker-job matches appears in Jovanovic (1979). Another influential paper by Jovanovic (1982) considers the information capital that arises as an industry evolves toward a set of relatively efficient production sites. Jovanovic and Moffitt (1990) develop a theoretical model of and a procedure for estimating the value of (worker-employer) match-specific information in the economy. Montgomery (1991) and Mortensen and Vishwanath (1994) model the role of job-finding networks in labor market search and wage growth. Firm-specific human capital that accumulates with learning by doing or from learning how to work more productively with coworkers is another important form of information and organization capital. See, e.g., Rosen (1972) and Prescott and Boyd (1986) for analysis.

20. See Bak et al. (1992), Cooper and Haltiwanger (1993), and Horvath (1994).

21. A provocative paper by Lilien (1982) stimulated considerable interest in this issue. Lilien focused on the role of shocks to the industry structure of labor demand. More recent research focuses on allocative shocks that drive large gross flows of workers and jobs across locations within and between industries. See Blanchard and Diamond (1989, 1990), Davis and Haltiwanger (1990, 1994b), and Caballero, Engel, and Haltiwanger (1994b).

5.4.3   Aggregate Shocks and Reallocation Timing Effects

The second type of theory maintains that aggregate shocks drive business cycles, including cyclical movements in gross job flows. Unlike the prevailing
view of business cycles, this type of theory stresses how aggregate shocks
interact with allocative shocks and reallocation frictions to influence the timing of worker and job reallocation.[22] In turn, worker and job reallocation responses to an adverse aggregate shock strongly influence the character, depth,
and duration of the resulting recession. This type of theory also highlights the
role of reallocation frictions in generating persistent output and unemployment
responses to aggregate shocks.

There are at least four reasons why adverse aggregate shocks lead to
a concentration of certain reallocation activities during recessions. First, a
large adverse aggregate shock can push many declining and dying plants
over an adjustment threshold. During boom times, a firm may choose to
continue operating a plant that fails to recover its long-run average cost
because short-run revenues exceed short-run costs, or because of a sufficiently large option value to retaining the plant and its workforce.[23] An
adverse aggregate shock may sufficiently reduce current revenues or the option value of continued operation so as to push the plant across the shutdown
threshold.

Second, the reallocation of specialized labor and capital inputs involves
forgone production due to lost work time (e.g., unemployment or additional
schooling), worker retraining, the retooling of plant and equipment, the adoption of new technology, and the organization of new patterns of production and
distribution. On average across firms and workers, the value of forgone production tends to fluctuate procyclically, rising during expansions and falling
during recessions. Observable indicators of procyclical movements in the
value of forgone production include the procyclicality of real wages and real
interest rates, procyclical movements in other indicators of credit availability, procyclical inventory fluctuations, and countercyclical movements in sales
and marketing costs. The cyclicality of these variables points to the incentives
that both workers and firms have to concentrate costly reallocation activity

---

22. See Caballero and Hammour (1993), Cooper and Haltiwanger (1993), Davis (1987), Davis
and Haltiwanger (1990), Gautier and Broersma (1993), and Hall (1991).

23. When the firm is uncertain about future demand for the plant's output, a deferral of the
shutdown decision preserves the valuable option to produce and sell the plant's output in favorable
future circumstances without incurring the costs of reopening the plant, training a new work force,
etc. See Dixit and Pindyck (1994) for a systematic analysis of how sunk costs and uncertainty
influence the timing of investment decisions.

during recessions, when the opportunity cost of the resulting forgone production is relatively low. Some aspects of government policy reinforce incentives to concentrate reallocation activity during downturns. An example is greater generosity or duration of unemployment insurance benefits during economic downturns.

Third, the curtailment of credit availability that often accompanies a recession causes investment cutbacks, employment declines, and business failures among firms with imperfect access to credit markets, especially if those firms simultaneously experience declines in cash flow. To some extent, the cutbacks and failures induced by a credit crunch will be concentrated among firms with weaker prospects for future profitability, but they will also be concentrated among firms that—for whatever reason—face greater difficulties in overcoming informational problems that impede the flow of credit. Thus, a credit crunch induces a reallocation of capital and employment away from credit-sensitive sectors and firms and toward sectors and firms that are less dependent upon outside sources of credit to fund current operations and investments.

Fourth, adverse aggregate shocks may trigger the revelation of accumulated pieces of information that bear upon the desired allocation of jobs, workers, and capital inputs. In other words, an adverse aggregate shock can lead to an increase in the intensity of allocative shocks. The next subsection explains how such a connection between aggregate shocks and the intensity of allocative shocks might arise.

5.4.4   Information Spillovers, Allocative Shocks, and Aggregate Fluctuations

As suggested by our remarks on information capital, information acquisition often plays a central role in the search and reallocation process. Job-seeking workers need to acquire information about the location of suitable job opportunities; how the prospects for promotion, job security, and wage growth differ among available jobs; the fit between their own skills and the skill demands of particular jobs; whether to leave the labor force to acquire new skills, and, if so, what type of skills to acquire. A firm seeking to locate a new plant needs to acquire information about the suitability of the local workforce, the degree of access to prospective customers, the tax and regulatory policies of local authorities, and the local availability and cost of intermediate inputs. A firm considering the adoption of a new technology needs to acquire infor-

mation about its compatibility with the firm's existing capital stock and work force.

Firms and workers gather information through costly search and experimentation, and by relying upon information that others have acquired through their own costly efforts or by happenstance.[24] Information spillovers—in our context, the possibility of learning from search, experimentation, and reallocation by others—affect individual incentives and generate potentially important dynamics in the accumulation and public revelation of information about the desired allocation of factor inputs.

Caplin and Leahy (1993a) analyze the role of information spillovers in the search and reallocation of a group of displaced workers. They stress that information spillovers are likely to be important when two conditions hold: (1) when workers lack perfect channels of information concerning the best available jobs, so that they value the information they can obtain from others; (2) when there is a group of workers with sufficiently similar characteristics that they can learn from each other's search and job experience. As Caplin and Leahy point out, the evidence in chapter 2 on the concentration of job destruction at plants that undergo sharp employment declines implies that many displaced workers have a "natural peer group of fellow unemployed workers with similar skills and characteristics."

In their analysis, Caplin and Leahy show how information spillovers can lead to inefficiently high unemployment and slow reallocation as each displaced worker attempts to free ride on the information generated by the search activity and experience of others. Information spillovers also encourage a bunching of reallocation, because a single worker's discovery of an attractive job opportunity leads other displaced workers in the group to pursue the same type of job.[25] Instead of displaced workers considering search and mobility decisions, one can easily imagine similar effects operating for a group of firms faced with informationally related investment decisions.

These remarks indicate how reallocation activity can reveal information that begets more reallocation activity. An event or shock that directly induces

---

24. Holzer (1988) and Staiger (1990) contain evidence on the role of personal connections in job search and wage growth patterns, and provide references to related literature.
25. The extreme bunching of reallocation in Caplin and Leahy's model reflects particular assumptions about worker homogeneity and information transmission among displaced workers, but the tendency for informational spillovers to generate bunching in reallocation activity, broadly defined, is more general. See, for example, the analyses in Banerjee (1992), Bikhchandani, Hirshleifer, and Welch (1992), Caplin and Leahy (1993c), and Chamley and Gale (1994).

a burst of reallocation activity reveals information that triggers a secondary wave of reallocation activity, which leads to a tertiary wave of reallocation activity, and so on. Consequently, if information spillovers are an important aspect of reallocation processes, the intertemporal bunching of job flows, worker flows, and other forms of reallocation is a natural outcome.

We have already suggested how an initial burst of reallocation activity might be triggered by an oil price shock, a change in the spatial distribution of military expenditures, the introduction of a new technology, or other events. Our discussion of information spillovers suggests how the initial allocative effects of such events might be magnified and further propagated through time.

We have also pointed out several channels through which aggregate shocks influence the timing of reallocation. In particular, we have stressed how adverse aggregate shocks lead to a bunching of reallocation during recessions even in the absence of information spillovers related to the reallocation process. Because adverse aggregate shocks intensify reallocation activity, and informational spillovers imply that reallocation reveals information about desired factor allocations, it follows that aggregate shocks and the intensity of allocative shocks are intimately connected at a deep level.

5.5 A Case Study: Restructuring in the Steel Industry

We turn now to a dramatic restructuring episode in one major manufacturing industry—the U.S. steel industry.[26] The economic upheaval in this industry during the 1970s and 1980s has attracted considerable attention from researchers, journalists, and policymakers, and it points toward the potential importance of some theoretical elements of the richer view of business cycles.

During the period under study, the U.S. steel industry experienced a major decline in demand for its products, sharp increases in energy prices, tough competition from foreign producers, the introduction of a new production technology, and marked uncertainty about the profitability of new capital investment. These developments sparked a major reallocation of jobs and capital within the industry—reallocation that was related to the business cycle and ultimately led to sharp increases in productivity.

---

26. Our description of events in the steel industry draws heavily on Barnett and Crandall (1986).

Demand for U.S. raw steel production suffered two precipitous declines during the recessions of 1973–75 and 1981–82. In the earlier recession, during which energy prices soared, annual production declined from 151 million tons to 117 million tons. Although production rose somewhat during the expansion of 1975–79, it never returned to its earlier levels. In the later recession, during which the dollar began to appreciate and foreign steel producers became increasingly competitive, production declined from 120 million tons to 75 million tons. Production stayed below 93 million tons throughout the mid-1980s. Thus, steel industry output shrank by more than one-third in the span of a decade.

Concurrent with this massive two-step contraction of steel output, the industry underwent a major structural change highlighted by the emergence of a new breed of steel plant. The new plants, called minimills, use a streamlined production process driven by an electric furnace to produce smaller, lower-grade steel products.[27] The old plants, called integrated mills, use a more complicated production process driven by a blast furnace to produce all types of steel products. Throughout the 1970s and 1980s, output grew in minimills as they seized control of the low-grade market, while output at integrated firms declined.

Minimills successfully challenged the integrated firms with technological superiority and greater specialization. The minimills' electric furnace technology is more energy-efficient and labor-productive than the blast furnace technology. Perhaps more important, minimills have a much lower minimum efficient scale of operations.[28] When steel demand dropped precipitously, it became difficult for integrated mills to meet their minimum efficiency levels of production, and they suffered large losses and plant closures. The losses hampered their ability to undertake the large expenditures required to upgrade their plant and equipment and to adopt newer, more efficient technologies. Minimills, on the other hand, are less expensive to modernize and are designed for shorter economic life spans.

Minimills have other advantages. They use scrap metal and electricity, which are relatively inexpensive, as primary inputs. They developed a largely nonunionized workforce driven by productivity incentives, which gave them

27. "Low grade" means that the metallurgy process is less sophisticated, or that the metal contains relatively more impurities, not necessarily that the final product is inferior.
28. Whereas integrated plants typically need to produce about 3 million tons per year to be efficient, some minimills have minimum efficient scales of less than 200,000 tons per year.

a lower unit labor cost. And minimills concentrated on the lower end of the steel market (wire rods and bars), where they could—and did—compete very effectively with integrated firms.

Minimills nearly drove integrated firms from the low-grade end of the domestic market. Most closures of integrated firms' production facilities were of plants producing rods, bars, and other low-end products. Whereas the integrated firms lost market share in high-end products to foreign competitors during the 1980s, minimills' production costs remained favorable relative to those of foreign competitors even at peak 1985 exchange rates.

Restructuring in the steel industry, primarily in the form of job destruction at integrated plants and job creation at minimills, is reflected in the gross job flows data (see figure 5.7).[29] Four facts are worth stressing. First, although the shift to minimills was continuous, a major portion of the reallocation occurred in the early 1980s, when job destruction reached an astonishing rate of 34 percent. Second, destruction remained high between 1982 and 1988, averaging 75 percent more than before 1982. Third, the coworker mean (i.e., the number of workers at the average worker's plant) shrank by more than one-third, from 7,000 workers in 1981 to fewer than 4,500 in 1985. Fourth, the time-series properties for the steel industry are broadly similar to those for total manufacturing (see table 5.5).

At first glance, remarkably high job destruction and the virtual absence of job creation during the early 1980s appeared to augur the complete demise of the U.S. steel industry. Although employment continued to contract during the mid-1980s, the steel industry showed impressive gains in labor productivity beginning in 1983.[30] (See figure 5.8.) Through 1982, labor productivity growth averaged 2.3 percent per year (excluding the trough years 1975 and 1982), but afterward it rose to 13.7 percent per year. The relationship between the job reallocation rate and labor productivity growth in the steel industry reflects the shift away from integrated firms to minimills.

A question arises about the relationship between job reallocation and labor productivity growth: Why was reallocation (especially destruction) so highly concentrated in 1982–83? Domestic steel output declined 22 percent in the 1973–75 recession and 37 percent in the 1981–82 recession. Yet the job de-

---

29. Figures 5.7 and 5.8 contain annual data because some of the time series are available only at that frequency.

30. Labor productivity is an index of the quantity of steel output per worker calculated from the Wayne Gray ASM data base.

Figure 5.7
**Job Flow Rates and Downsizing in the Steel Industry:
Annual, 1973 to 1988**

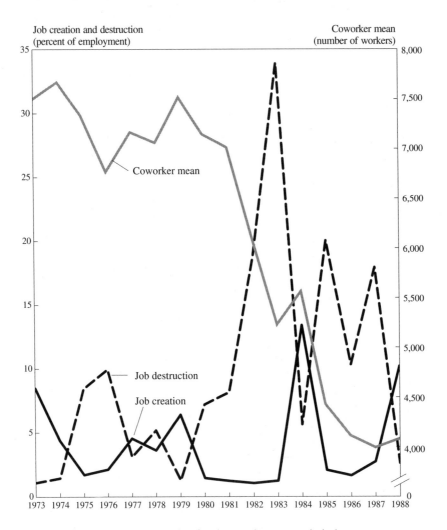

Note: The coworker mean is the number of employees at the average worker's plant.

Table 5.5
Statistics on Gross Flow Rates in the Steel Industry: Quarterly, 1972 to 1988

Statistic	1972-1988	1972-1981	1982-1988
Average Job Creation	2.67	2.55	2.98
Average Job Destruction	3.99	3.30	5.80
Average Net Employment Growth	−1.32	−0.75	−2.83
Average Job Reallocation	6.66	5.86	8.78
Correlation of Creation, Destruction[a]	−0.42	−0.51	−0.43
Cyclical Change Ratio[b]	−2.51	−1.95	−4.48
Variance Ratio of Destruction to Creation[c] . . .	3.49	3.00	3.52
Correlation of Net, Reallocation[d]	−0.59	−0.56	−0.60

[a] Correlation between job creation and job destruction.
[b] Ratio of cyclical change in job destruction to cyclical change in job creation.
[c] Ratio of variance of job destruction to variance of job creation.
[d] Correlation between job reallocation and net employment growth.

struction rate was only 10 percent in the earlier recession and 34 percent in the later one. Severity of the recession (in terms of the decline in industry output) cannot fully account for differences in job destruction rates. The shift to minimills seems an unlikely explanation because their rise was steady, not concentrated in recessions. In fact, many integrated firms suffered large losses during the second half of the 1970s and began reducing capacity as early as 1977.

The richer view of recessions suggests two related explanations for this puzzle. The first is that integrated firms were unsure whether the demand decline in 1973–75 was permanent, and were waiting for (perhaps even expecting) demand to return to the high levels that had made their plants efficient and competitive. Had they closed plants or shifted to alternative production technologies, the consequences might have been extremely costly if demand had recovered. The second recession eliminated any expectation of a return to high demand levels in the near-term future, whereupon integrated firms suddenly closed or scaled back many inefficient plants that would have been closed earlier had they been more certain about future demand. Thus, according to this interpretation, the timing of plant closure and job destruction by the integrated firms was sharply influenced by aggregate business cycle developments.

The second explanation is related to the first. An important reason why integrated firms were able to postpone reallocation is that aggregate de-

Figure 5.8
**Job Reallocation and Productivity Growth in the Steel
Industry: Annual, 1973 to 1988**

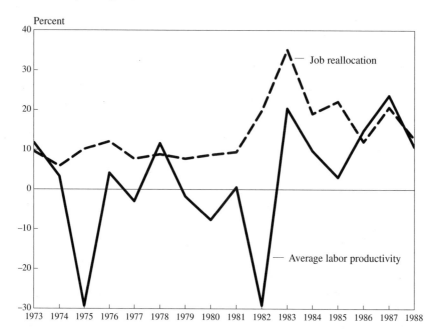

Note: Job reallocation is measured as a percentage of employment.

mand was high during the expansion of 1975–79. During this time, the
Federal Reserve pursued a stimulative monetary policy, and real gross domestic product (GDP) grew by 3.5 percent annually. Given the ac-
celerating inflation rates that also characterized this period, an indefinite
continuation of stimulative monetary policies was probably perceived as unlikely. According to this scenario, the late 1970s was not a propitious time
to curtail or reallocate steel industry output, because the opportunity cost
of forgone production during this period was higher than it was likely to
be in the near future. Put another way, temporarily strong aggregate demand encouraged integrated firms to postpone the restructuring process that
would eventually occur in response to the longer-term developments described
above.

We regard this interpretation of the restructuring and reallocation process in the U.S. steel industry, and its connection to aggregate business cycle developments, as tentative and incomplete. More thorough studies of the steel industry and other industries that underwent major restructuring episodes are needed in order to develop a richer empirical foundation for understanding the connections among restructuring, gross job flows, and business cycles.

5.6 Differences among Recessions

We close this chapter with a brief description of differences in gross job flow patterns among recessions. Economists often investigate differences among recessions in an attempt to better understand business cycles.[31] These investigations take many forms. The simplest method is to classify recessions by their depth and duration. Another method examines whether a particular component of national income—such as consumption, investment, or net exports—accounts for the recession. A third method examines whether a particular government policy intervention—such as a tax change—was responsible. Still another method looks for unexpected, exogenous events such as oil price shocks, wars, political changes, or weather disturbances. This section illustrates a new way to identify potentially important differences among business cycle episodes.

Figure 5.9 shows the post–World War II history of GDP and employment. Despite some differences in depth, duration, and symmetry, most recessions appear as fairly small, regular deviations from long-run growth. In contrast, the decomposition of net employment into gross job creation and destruction produces fairly pronounced differences among recessions, as seen in figures 5.4 and 5.6. The recessions and expansions of the 1970s and 1980s exhibit striking differences in the behavior of gross job flows. The BLS-based data that we examined earlier also pointed to sharp differences in gross job flow behavior among recessions.

One clear difference in job flows among recessions is that the cyclical sensitivity of creation has declined over time. The decline in the 1980s relative to the 1970s is seen in tables 5.6 through 5.8, which contain the cyclical changes (average in recession minus average in expansion) in creation and destruction for various sectors and plant types. The tables show that cyclical changes in

---

31. For example, Blanchard (1993), Hall (1993), Hansen and Prescott (1993), and Perry and Schultze (1993) highlight peculiarities of the 1990–91 recession.

Figure 5.9
**U.S. Output and Employment Since World War II:
Macroeconomic Measures**

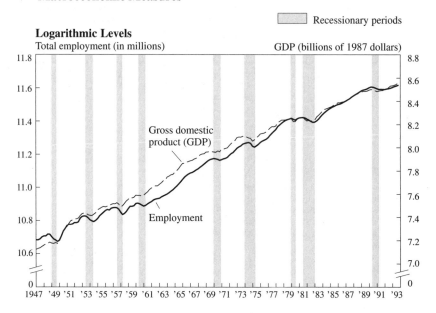

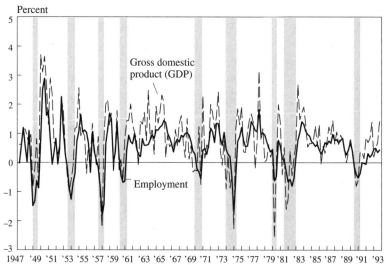

Table 5.6
Recession-Minus-Expansion Differences in Gross Flows by Two-Digit Industry: Quarterly, 1972 to 1988

Industry	Job Creation[a]			Job Destruction[b]		
	Total	1970s	1980s	Total	1970s	1980s
Food	0.33	−1.81	2.10	0.77	0.26	1.28
Tobacco	−0.48	−1.85	0.78	1.22	2.40	0.60
Textiles..................	−0.41	−0.47	−0.31	2.13	3.12	1.43
Apparel..................	−0.34	−0.73	0.05	1.39	2.60	0.49
Lumber..................	−0.20	−0.87	0.45	3.98	4.26	3.82
Furniture.................	−1.09	−1.59	−0.64	3.11	4.36	2.24
Paper....................	−0.53	−0.96	−0.15	1.73	2.48	1.22
Printing..................	−0.31	−0.59	−0.03	0.94	1.21	0.75
Chemicals................	−0.17	−0.09	−0.13	1.47	1.92	1.15
Petroleum	0.41	−0.27	0.91	1.74	0.83	2.20
Rubber	−1.03	−1.58	−0.55	3.47	4.16	3.00
Leather	−0.38	−0.42	−0.30	0.86	1.97	−0.04
Stone, Clay, and Glass.......	−0.66	−0.56	−0.63	2.83	3.01	2.64
Primary Metals............	−1.48	−1.40	−1.55	3.86	2.49	4.64
Fabricated Metals...........	−1.01	−1.32	−0.67	3.12	3.18	3.03
Nonelectric Machinery.......	−1.20	−1.25	−1.07	2.62	2.03	2.87
Electric Machinery..........	−1.05	−1.62	−0.55	3.10	4.68	1.93
Transportation	−0.54	−0.44	−0.50	4.43	3.61	5.03
Instruments...............	−0.56	−1.05	−0.06	1.59	2.43	0.91
Miscellaneous..............	−1.28	−1.59	−0.91	2.52	3.28	1.98
Total Manufacturing	−0.68	−1.08	−0.29	2.54	2.76	2.35

[a] Average job creation rate in recession minus average job creation rate in expansion.
[b] Average job destruction rate in recession minus average job destruction rate in expansion.

creation declined in absolute value in the 1980s; hence creation was less sensitive to the business cycle. For total manufacturing, job creation was nearly four times more cyclically sensitive in the 1970s than in the 1980s. In fact, job creation experienced almost no change (−0.3 percentage point) between recessions and expansions in the 1980s.

Job creation also became less cyclically sensitive among a broad range of sectors and plant types. For eighteen of twenty two-digit industries, all regions, and all plant types except the largest size class, the recession-minus-expansion differences rose.[32] Furthermore, whereas the cyclical change in job creation

---

32. The primary metals industry is an exception. Both job creation and job destruction in this industry were more cyclically sensitive in the 1980s than in the 1970s.

Table 5.7
Recession-Minus-Expansion Differences in Gross Flows by Region: Quarterly, 1972 to 1988

Region	Job Creation[a]			Job Destruction[b]		
	Total	1970s	1980s	Total	1970s	1980s
Northeast	−0.49	−1.21	0.16	1.94	2.67	1.37
Middle Atlantic	−0.64	−1.11	−0.21	2.14	2.58	1.79
South Atlantic	−0.91	−1.00	−0.76	3.72	3.44	3.87
East South Central	−0.68	−0.72	−0.52	2.68	2.53	2.79
West South Central	−0.60	−0.93	−0.26	2.07	2.72	1.62
East North Central	−0.87	−1.04	−0.70	2.46	2.74	2.25
West North Central	−0.52	−0.70	−0.25	1.90	2.22	1.59
Mountain	−0.78	−1.15	−0.25	2.31	2.44	2.23
Pacific....................	−0.47	−1.61	0.59	2.15	1.97	2.29

[a] Average job creation rate in recession minus average job creation rate in expansion.
[b] Average job destruction rate in recession minus average job destruction rate in expansion.

was always negative in the 1970s, it was occasionally positive in the 1980s. That is, during the 1980s job creation was actually higher during recessions than during expansions for five industries, two regions, and certain smaller, more specialized plant types. Nowhere is this difference more evident than for large versus small plants: the decline in the cyclical sensitivity of job creation between the two decades was far more dramatic for small plants than for large ones. When combined with the evidence for earlier decades in figure 5.6, the data suggest that rising or relatively high gross job creation rates during recessions are not unusual.

The cyclical sensitivity of job destruction, on the other hand, changed little between the two decades. For total manufacturing, job destruction was only 16 percent more cyclically sensitive in the 1970s. Cyclical sensitivity of destruction did decrease for small plants and increased for large plants in the 1980s. Most notably, plants with 2,500–4,999 workers and those in the highest wage interval experienced dramatically higher job destruction rates during recessions than during expansions in the 1980s.

Another distinct difference in job flows among recessions is found in the behavior of reallocation (see figure 5.4). In the recession of 1973–75, job reallocation rose sharply and then declined almost immediately (though not quite as quickly as it had risen). In the recessions spanning 1980–82, job

Table 5.8
Recession-Minus-Expansion Differences in Gross Flows by Plant Characteristics

Plant Characteristics	Job Creation[a]			Job Destruction[b]		
	Total	1970s	1980s	Total	1970s	1980s
Plant Type						
Single-Unit Firms..........	−0.73	−1.32	−0.10	2.00	2.40	1.73
Multi-Unit Firms	−0.67	−1.01	−0.37	2.70	2.85	2.56
Plant Age						
Young Plants (0–10 yrs.).....	−0.98	−1.81	−0.19	2.57	3.09	2.20
Mature Plants (10+ yrs.)	−0.65	−0.99	−0.35	2.48	2.53	2.39
Average Size						
0 to 19 employees	−0.37	−0.79	0.40	1.81	2.20	1.73
20 to 49	−0.65	−1.68	0.34	2.22	2.60	2.00
50 to 99	−0.46	−1.38	0.36	2.50	2.52	2.49
100 to 249	−0.63	−1.31	−0.03	2.60	3.00	2.32
250 to 499	−0.79	−1.18	−0.43	2.40	2.93	1.99
500 to 999	−0.85	−1.10	−0.63	2.39	2.77	2.05
1,000 to 2,499	−0.74	−0.78	−0.67	2.46	2.55	2.32
2,500 to 4,999	−0.54	−0.61	−0.49	3.85	3.05	4.33
5,000 or More	−0.60	−0.40	−0.70	3.10	3.00	3.10
Product Specialization						
Highly Diversified	−0.56	−0.88	−0.27	2.24	2.17	2.23
Moderately Diversified	−0.70	−1.16	−0.30	2.27	2.13	2.33
Moderately Specialized	−0.41	−0.90	0.06	2.89	2.95	2.85
Highly Specialized..........	−0.79	−1.36	−0.25	3.17	2.96	3.34
Completely Specialized	−0.45	−0.96	0.13	2.75	3.47	2.30
Level of Plant Wages						
Very Low.................	−0.68	−1.31	−0.07	1.99	2.93	1.32
Moderately Low............	−0.80	−1.40	−0.25	2.50	3.36	1.91
Average	−0.93	−1.44	−0.46	2.51	2.87	2.24
Moderately High	−0.56	−0.98	−0.20	2.27	2.23	2.25
Very High................	−0.44	−0.45	−0.36	3.63	2.89	4.09

[a] Average job creation rate in recession minus average job creation rate in expansion.
[b] Average job destruction rate in recession minus average job destruction rate in expansion.

reallocation also rose sharply but remained high for a much longer period of time. Thus the spike-shaped versus hump-shaped patterns of reallocation suggest that the total volume of reallocation varies among recessions. In this sense, the recessions of the 1980s involved more restructuring than did the recession of the 1970s.

Besides varying in volume, reallocation also varies in type across cyclical episodes. For example, chapter 2 showed that plant-level destruction was more persistent in the recession of the early 1980s than in the 1974–75 recession.[33] Creation, however, was much less persistent in the later recessions.

---

33. This finding matches up well with the fact that permanent layoffs became more important in the 1980s, as documented in chapter 6.

6

Job Flows, Worker Flows, and Unemployment over the Business Cycle

This chapter examines the cyclical behavior of job and worker flows, and their connection to unemployment rate movements. The main results fall into five categories.

• *Unemployment inflows and outflows: Flows into and out of unemployment rise during recessions. This increased passage of workers through the unemployment pool suggests that cyclical downturns are times of unusually intense restructuring in the economy.*

• *Job destruction and unemployment inflows: Sharp increases in job destruction during recessions coincide with sharply higher flows into the unemployment pool. The wide swings in unemployment inflows, in turn, drive the cyclical variation in the number of unemployed persons.*

• *Composition of the unemployment pool: During good times, unemployment is dominated by new entrants and reentrants into the labor market. During recessions, the rise in unemployment is dominated by increases in the number of laid-off persons and an accompanying increase in the share of unemployment accounted for by workers aged twenty-five to fifty-four.*

• *Rising role of permanent layoffs: Temporary layoffs accounted for most of the unemployment increase during the recession of the mid-1970s. In contrast, permanent layoffs accounted for most of the unemployment increase during the recessions of the early 1980s and early 1990s.*

• *The link to long-term joblessness: Increases in the persistence of plant-level job destruction and rising unemployment inflows of permanently laid-off persons underlie much of the secular and cyclical increases in long-term joblessness since 1980.*

6.1   Context and Motivation

Job reallocation accounts for a large fraction of observed worker reallocation, as shown in chapter 2. This fraction of worker reallocation takes many forms. Some job-losing workers immediately find another job. Others experience unemployment during the transition from job to job. Some exit the labor force, and others enter the labor force to fill newly created jobs at expanding establishments. Of course, a large fraction of worker reallocation is not a direct response to job reallocation. Persons enter the labor market when young, exit when old, and often temporarily exit to attend school or raise children. Workers also switch jobs for reasons unrelated to job reallocation, such as career advancement, higher pay or more attractive benefits, a more agreeable work environment, a change in family circumstances, or the relocation of a spouse.

Ideally, a study of the connections between worker flows and job flows would draw upon data that link workers to employers and follow both over time. At present, comprehensive data of this sort are not available for the U.S. economy.[1] Lacking ideal data, we combine information on worker flows from the Current Population Survey (CPS) with the job flows we have constructed from the Longitudinal Research Database (LRD). We focus on the connection between job flows and the flow of workers into and out of the unemployment pool, but we also provide some analysis of worker flows into and out of employment.

Given our focus on unemployment flows, we begin with a description of the relationship between job flows and the rate of unemployment. This provides a useful transition to the connection between unemployment flows and job flows.

6.2   The Relationship between Job Flows and the Unemployment Rate

Figure 6.1 depicts job creation and destruction rates for manufacturing, the aggregate unemployment rate, and the manufacturing unemployment rate on a quarterly basis from 1972 to 1988. The manufacturing unemployment rate captures persons who flowed into the unemployment pool from jobs in the manufacturing sector.[2] The figure shows a strong positive relationship

---

1. Chapter 8 describes prospects for developing such data.
2. The manufacturing unemployment rate equals the number of unemployed persons who previously worked in the manufacturing sector divided by the sum of this number and manufacturing employment. Thus, this rate is not intended to measure the number of persons who seek or ultimately find manufacturing jobs.

Figure 6.1
Unemployment Rates and Job Flow Rates: Quarterly, 1972 to 1988

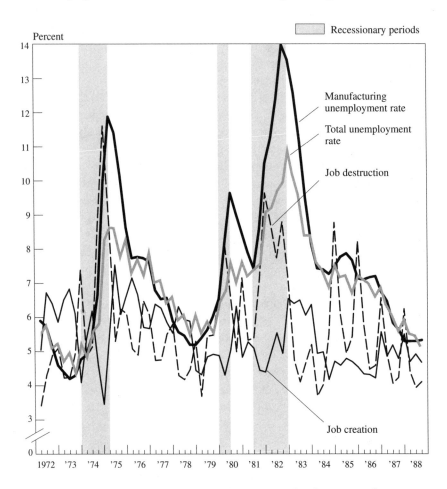

Note: Job creation and destruction are measured as percentages of employment; unemployment
rates are measured as percentages of the labor force.

between job destruction and unemployment: job destruction has a contemporaneous correlation of 0.44 with the aggregate unemployment rate and 0.50 with the manufacturing unemployment rate. The correlation between the aggregate unemployment rate and the manufacturing unemployment rate is 0.92.[3]

In addition to this contemporaneous correlation, there is a strong lead-lag relationship between job destruction and unemployment. In the two major cyclical downturns over this period, the peak in job destruction clearly leads the peak in unemployment. Job destruction rises rapidly in downturns and falls sharply in recoveries. Unemployment peaks a couple of quarters after the peak in job destruction and falls slowly during the recovery.

Interestingly, there is a weak positive correlation between job creation and unemployment. The contemporaneous correlation is 0.12. This weak correlation reflects the relatively acyclical behavior of job creation. It also reflects the fact that job creation recovers more quickly in recessions than does unemployment. As noted in chapter 5, job creation actually rose in the recession of the early 1980s. One natural interpretation of this finding is that a larger unemployment pool facilitates hiring by employers. Empirical studies of the matching process in the labor market typically find a positive relationship between hiring rates and the level of unemployment and vacancies (e.g., Blanchard and Diamond, 1989).

These observations summarize the comovements between job flow rates and the unemployment rate. Movements in the unemployment rate reflect time variation in the underlying flows into and out of the unemployment pool. The rest of the chapter examines the nature of these inflows and outflows, other worker flows, and their connection to job creation and destruction.

6.3   Gross Worker Flows—Concepts and Magnitudes

Many events induce transitions, or flows, of workers among employment, unemployment, and not in the labor market. Layoffs and quits induce transitions from employment to unemployment or not in the labor force. Transitions out of unemployment occur when workers find jobs or decide to leave the labor force. Transitions from not in the labor force occur when new workers enter

---

3. Much of the analysis in this chapter combines information on unemployment and employment flows for the aggregate economy with the job creation and destruction measures we have developed for the manufacturing sector. The close relationship between aggregate unemployment and manufacturing unemployment mitigates concerns that arise from using worker and job flow statistics that differ in coverage.

the labor force, or when workers reenter after an absence (e.g., for school or child rearing) to take a job or search for one.

It is important to stress that employment inflows and outflows are not the same as job creation and destruction. For example, suppose a worker quits and becomes unemployed, and the firm hires another worker from the pool of the unemployed. These events generate simultaneous employment inflow and outflow, as well as unemployment inflow and outflow, but no job creation or destruction. Alternatively, job creation and destruction can occur without any corresponding employment or unemployment flows. If one employer destroys a job, and the job-losing worker immediately takes another job with an expanding employer, then these events involve simultaneous creation and destruction of jobs but no flows into or out of employment or unemployment.

Worker flows among labor market states can be measured from the CPS by matching the records of individuals over adjacent months and tracking changes in labor market status.[4] Based on these records, the unemployment inflow at time t equals the number of persons who are unemployed at time t but were not unemployed at time $t - 1$. The unemployment outflow at time t equals the number of persons who were unemployed at time $t - 1$ but are not unemployed at time t. Analogous definitions hold for flows involving employment and not in the labor force.

Figure 6.2 presents evidence on the magnitude of these worker flows drawn from an in-depth study by Blanchard and Diamond (1990).[5] The quarterly flows reported in figure 6.2 are cumulations of monthly flows. The figure reveals large quarterly gross worker flows across labor market states. Paralleling previous comparisons of net and gross job flows, gross worker flows among labor market states dwarf the corresponding net flows. In much of what follows, we shall characterize these worker flows as rates of change. We express unemployment flows as rates by dividing through by the labor force, and we express employment flows as rates by dividing through by employment.

An alternative method exists for measuring unemployment flows. Instead of measuring gross worker flows by matching individual records across time, one can use CPS data on unemployment duration. In this method, the monthly

---

4. A number of problems with these measures are documented at length in Abowd and Zellner (1985) and Poterba and Summers (1986). Misclassification of labor market status is a key problem, especially misclassification between unemployed and not in the labor force. Adjustments to correct for misclassification and other problems have been developed by Abowd and Zellner (1985) and Poterba and Summers (1986). We use the adjusted series developed by Abowd and Zellner, which are available from 1968 to 1986.

5. We are grateful to Olivier Blanchard and Peter Diamond for providing us with data used in their study.

Figure 6.2
Labor Market States and Flows of Workers Among Them:
Quarterly, 1968 to 1986
(In millions of workers)

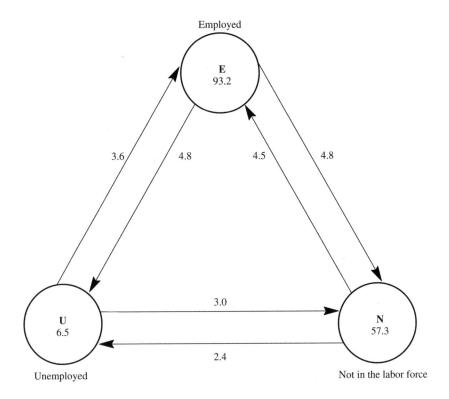

Note: The numbers in the circles represent average numbers of employed workers (E), unemployed workers
(U), and workers not in the labor force (N). The arrows represent flows of workers between states of being
employed, unemployed, and not in the labor force.
Source: Blanchard and Diamond (1990), Figure 1, based on the Abowd–Zellner adjusted gross flow series.
The quarterly flows are cumulative monthly flows.

unemployment inflow is measured as the number of currently unemployed persons who report an unemployment duration of five or fewer weeks. The monthly unemployment outflow equals the number of unemployed persons in the previous month minus the number of currently unemployed persons who report an unemployment duration of greater than five weeks. This method generates unemployment flows that correspond to movements in the official unemployment rate because it uses the entire CPS sample, whereas the other method uses only persons who can be matched across months.[6]

In what follows, we calculate worker flows by using both methods for two reasons. First, because they are subject to error, it is useful to employ each method as a check on the other. Second, each method has distinct advantages and disadvantages. The gross worker flows method allows us to measure employment flows as well as unemployment flows. However, the Abowd-Zellner adjusted series are readily available only for 1968 to 1986, and the unadjusted series are very noisy and viewed as unreliable. In contrast, unemployment flows based on duration data are available from 1948 to 1992. Further, unemployment flows calculated via this method can be decomposed by reason for unemployment (i.e., temporary layoffs, permanent layoffs, quits, and entrants).

Figure 6.3 presents quarterly unemployment inflow and outflow rates using both methods. Because the quarterly rates are just the cumulative sum of the monthly rates, there is some "double-counting" of flows for workers who have multiple spells of unemployment within a quarter. Further, these quarterly flows incorporate short spells of unemployment that are absent from our job creation and destruction series. For example, if a worker is temporarily laid off and then recalled within a quarter—which is not atypical; the average duration of a temporary layoff is approximately two months—these transitions show up in the unemployment flows but not in the job flows. For both reasons, the measured quarterly unemployment flows should be interpreted as upper bounds for quarterly unemployment flows that correspond precisely to our gross job flows. To maintain consistency with our gross job flow measures, the unemployment flow rates in figure 6.3 treat December, March, June, and September as the first month of the respective quarters.

Unemployment flows computed from gross worker transitions show a slightly lower mean and a slightly higher variance than the duration-based unemployment flows. The correlation between the respective inflow rates is 0.92, as is that between the respective outflow rates. A striking feature of the

---

6. See Darby, Haltiwanger, and Plant (1985, 1986) and Davis (1987) for discussions of the issues that arise in measuring unemployment flows from data on unemployment duration.

Figure 6.3
Unemployment Inflows and Outflows: Quarterly, 1948 to 1992

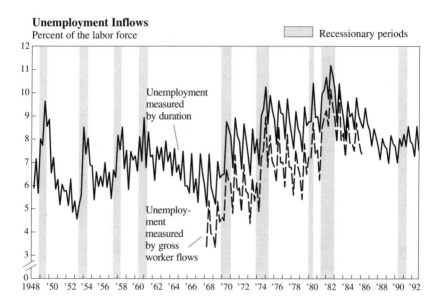

Unemployment Inflows
Percent of the labor force

Unemployment
measured
by duration

Unemploy-
ment
measured
by gross
worker flows

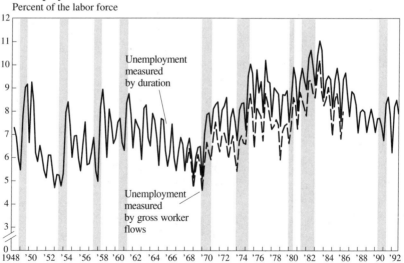

Unemployment Outflows
Percent of the labor force

Unemployment
measured
by duration

Unemployment
measured
by gross worker
flows

Table 6.1
Average Quarterly Employment Flows, Unemployment Flows, and Job Flows

	Inflows Rate	Outflows Rate
Unemployment Flows (Duration-based)[a]	8.8	8.8
Unemployment Flows (Abowd-Zellner)[b]	7.3	7.7
Employment Flows (Abowd-Zellner)	9.7	9.2
	Creation	Destruction
Job Flows	5.2	5.5

[a]Duration-based flows are measured in percentages of the labor force, as discussed in the text. These data are for 1972:Q1-1988:Q4.

[b]Abowd-Zellner flows are measured by tracking changes in the labor-market status of individuals, adjusted for problems of misclassification. These data are for 1972:Q1-1986:Q4.

series under both methods is their pronounced seasonality. As shown in the appendix to this chapter, the seasonality largely reflects strong seasonal inflows and outflows of new entrants and reentrants in the summer months. Given our focus on cyclical and lower-frequency secular movements, we carry out the analysis in the remainder of the chapter using seasonally adjusted worker and job flow rates.[7]

Table 6.1 presents time averages of the unemployment flows, employment flows, and job flows. In an average quarter, about 8 percent of the labor force flows into unemployment and 8 percent flows out. The average employment inflow rate (measured as a percent of employment) is almost 10 percent per quarter, and the employment outflow rate exceeds 9 percent. Direct comparisons of the magnitudes of these flows to job creation and destruction rates are hampered by sectoral differences in coverage and the cumulative nature of the worker flows. Nevertheless, a rough comparison suggests that gross job creation and destruction account for a substantial component of the flows into and out of employment and unemployment. The gross job flow rates are more than half the magnitude of the gross employment and unemployment flows.

With these observations about the magnitude of gross worker and job flows in mind, we now examine their comovement over time and their connection to unemployment.

---

7. Our analysis of the seasonally adjusted gross worker and job flows follows Blanchard and Diamond (1990). In addition to a desire to abstract from seasonality, their motivation for using seasonally adjusted series involved concerns that the Abowd-Zellner adjustment methodology failed to treat systematic, seasonally related measurement error.

6.4   The Time-Series Relationship between Worker and Job Flows

6.4.1   Total Unemployment Flows

The upper panel of figure 6.4 depicts the quarterly unemployment rate from 1948 to 1992, and the lower panel, the corresponding unemployment inflow and outflow rates.[8] The most striking pattern is that both inflow and outflow rates increase in recessions. The contemporaneous correlation between unemployment inflow and outflow rates is 0.79. The countercyclical behavior of both inflows and outflows is consistent with the view that recessions are periods of intense restructuring activity in the economy.[9]

The unemployment rate and the inflow and outflow rates are higher in the 1970s and 1980s than in earlier periods. For example, at the cyclical peak in late 1969, the unemployment rate was 3.93 percent, the quarterly inflow rate was 6.40 percent, and the quarterly outflow rate was 6.43 percent. In contrast, at the cyclical peak in early 1980, the unemployment rate was 6.08 percent, the quarterly inflow rate was 8.65 percent, and the quarterly outflow rate was 8.84 percent. This comparison provides some support for the view that the labor market became more turbulent between 1969 and 1980. However, inflow and outflow rates began to fall during the sustained growth of the middle and late 1980s. At the cyclical peak in 1990, the quarterly inflow and outflow rates were 7.75 percent and 7.31 percent, respectively. These rates are high compared with those of the 1960s but low relative to the late 1970s and early 1980s.[10]

Figure 6.5 and table 6.2 provide information about the cyclical variation in unemployment flows, employment flows, and gross job flows. They show that the connection between job destruction and worker flows is stronger than that between job creation and worker flows. Job destruction and unemployment inflows rise sharply during recessions, and they exhibit a high contemporaneous correlation (0.71). Employment outflows show less cyclical variation, but they also show a positive correlation with the job destruction rate (0.47). Looking at the other side of the flows, unemployment outflows and employment inflows

8. The duration-based method of measuring unemployment flows is used here to exploit as long a time series as possible.
9. Blanchard and Diamond (1990), Darby, Haltiwanger, and Plant (1985, 1986), and Davis (1987) consider the implications of countercyclicality in unemployment flows for unemployment rate dynamics and the interpretation of business cycles.
10. As will become clear below, these patterns are partly accounted for by the changing demographic composition of the labor force.

Figure 6.4
**Unemployment Rate and Flows in the U.S. Economy:
Quarterly, 1948 to 1992**
(Seasonally adjusted)

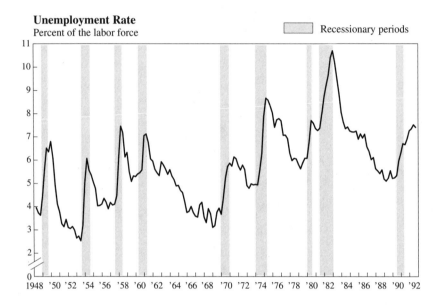

Unemployment Rate
Percent of the labor force

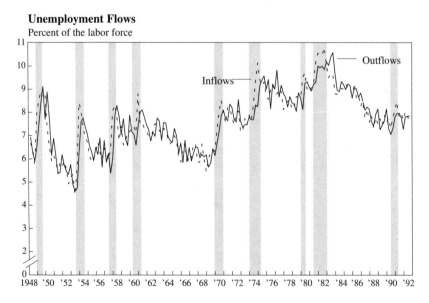

Unemployment Flows
Percent of the labor force

Figure 6.5
**Unemployment Flows, Employment Flows, and Gross Job Flows:
Quarterly, 1972 to 1988**
(Seasonally adjusted)

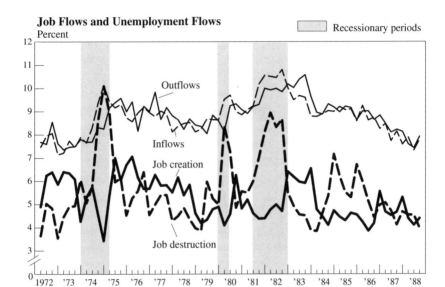

Job Flows and Unemployment Flows

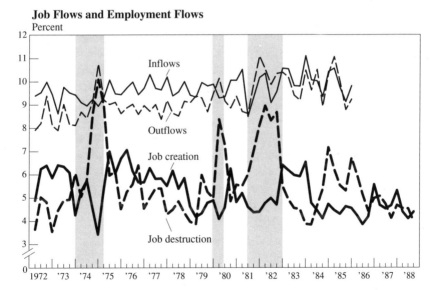

Job Flows and Employment Flows

Note: Job creation, job destruction, and employment flows are measured as percentages of employment; unemployment flows are measured as percentages of the labor force.

Table 6.2

Cyclical Variation and Comovements in Job Flows, Unemployment Flows, and Employment Flows

Correlation Between Job Flows and Worker Flows

	Job Creation	Job Destruction
Unemployment Inflows......................	−0.15	0.71
Unemployment Outflows.....................	0.16	0.27
Employment Inflows.........................	0.22	−0.17
Employment Outflows........................	−0.38	0.47

Cyclical Variation in Worker and Job Flows (Cyclical Average)

	Periods of Expansion	Periods of Recession
Unemployment Inflows......................	8.58	9.37
Unemployment Outflows.....................	8.77	8.79
Employment Inflows.........................	9.83	9.38
Employment Outflows........................	9.14	9.48
Job Creation.................................	5.34	4.75
Job Destruction	4.96	7.34

Note: In the upper panel, correlations for unemployment flows are for the period 1972:Q2-1988:Q4. Those for employment flows are for the period 1972:Q2-1986:Q4.
   In the lower panel, statistics for unemployment flows are for the period 1972:Q2-1988:Q4. Those for employment flows are for the period 1972:Q1-1986:Q4.

show only weak positive correlations with job creation (0.16 and 0.22). As shown in the bottom panel of table 6.2, these latter three series vary less, on average, over the business cycle than the former three. Indeed, unemployment outflow rates are virtually unchanged from recessions to expansions, although they rise considerably from the final phase of a recession through the initial phase of a recovery.

These time-series patterns show that unemployment inflows and employment outflows account for most of the cyclical variation in employment and unemployment. During recessions, unemployment inflows and employment outflows rise dramatically. Unemployment outflows and employment inflows also rise during recessions, but by less than their counterparts and not until later in a recession. In fact, it is easy to see from the lead-lag relationship between unemployment inflows and outflows why the unemployment rate rises sharply in recessions but declines more slowly for a longer period afterward.

These worker flow patterns also bear out the mirror image quality of worker flow and job flow dynamics. Chapters 2 and 5 show that job destruction rises

sharply in recessions, whereas job creation remains relatively constant over the business cycle. In a similar manner, the components of worker flows most closely related to job destruction—unemployment inflows and employment outflows—rise sharply in recessions. But the components most closely related to job creation—unemployment outflows and employment inflows—are relatively unchanged over the business cycle.

6.4.2   Unemployment Flows by Reason

Unemployment rates can be decomposed by reason of unemployment beginning in 1967.[11] This decomposition of unemployment is based upon responses to questions about why persons are unemployed. We use the following four-way classification: temporary layoffs (laid off with expectation of recall), permanent layoffs (laid off without expectation of recall), quits (voluntarily left previous job and seeking another), and entrants (new entrants plus reentrants). The decomposition of layoffs reflects recall expectations at the survey date rather than at the layoff date or the actual event of recall.[12]

The decomposition of cyclical unemployment changes by reason appears in table 6.3. Temporary and permanent layoffs account for most of the cyclical changes in unemployment, except for the brief recession in the first half of 1980. Permanent layoffs play a larger role in the recessions of 1981:7 to 1982:11 and 1990:7 to 1991:3 than in the recession of 1973:11 to 1975:3. This finding fits well with the evidence in chapters 2 and 5 that job destruction persistence rates were especially high in the recession of the early 1980s. The evidence in table 6.3 on the dominant role of permanent layoffs in the recession of the early 1990s suggests that job destruction persistence rates were high during this most recent recession. Echoing the view expressed in chapter 5, this evidence suggests that the two most recent recessions involved a different type or intensity of restructuring than the recession of the mid-1970s.[13]

---

11. Unfortunately, unemployment by duration and reason simultaneously does not become available until 1976.

12. Katz and Meyer (1990) explore the relationship between ex ante temporary layoffs (workers who expect recall) and ex post temporary layoffs (workers who are recalled). They find that ex ante temporary layoffs are much larger than ex post temporary layoffs. Workers who initially expect recall probably revise their expectations over the course of a long unemployment spell, so that part of the movements in the CPS-based temporary and permanent layoff series may reflect changes in expectations by continuously unemployed persons. The findings of Katz and Meyer suggest that revisions of expectations are potentially important for understanding the observed dynamics of unemployment by reason.

13. Retooling and restructuring within plants may involve temporary layoffs. Cooper and Haltiwanger (1993) provide evidence that this type of restructuring is important in the auto industry.

Table 6.3
Cyclical Changes in Unemployment by Reason (All Workers)

Fraction of Change in Unemployment Due to:	Trough to Peak	Peak to Trough
	Average, 1970:11–1992:12	
Temporary Layoffs	0.58	0.32
Permanent Layoffs	0.33	0.46
Quits	−0.06	0.02
Entrants	0.14	0.21
Average Change in Unemployment	−2.7	2.8
	1970:11–1975:3	
	(70:11–73:11)	**(73:11–75:3)**
Temporary Layoffs	0.50	0.44
Permanent Layoffs	0.29	0.40
Quits	−0.18	0.00
Entrants	0.38	0.16
Change in Unemployment	−1.0	4.6
	1975:3–1980:7	
	(75:3–80:1)	**(80:1–80:7)**
Temporary Layoffs	0.44	0.19
Permanent Layoffs	0.42	0.26
Quits	0.03	0.05
Entrants	0.11	0.50
Change in Unemployment	−2.3	1.0
	1980:7–1982:11	
	(80:7–81:7)	**(81:7–82:11)**
Temporary Layoffs	1.11	0.32
Permanent Layoffs	0.08	0.65
Quits	−0.05	−0.05
Entrants	0.14	0.09
Change in Unemployment	−0.5	3.0
	1982:11–1991:3	
	(82:11–90:7)	**(90:7–91:3)**
Temporary Layoffs	0.28	0.46
Permanent Layoffs	0.54	0.67
Quits	−0.03	−0.02
Entrants	0.21	−0.11
Change in Unemployment	−4.9	1.6

Figure 6.6 and table 6.4 present information about the connection between job flows and unemployment flows by reason. Sharp increases in job destruction during recessions coincide with increased inflows into unemployment of temporarily and permanently laid-off persons. The prolonged increase in job destruction in the early 1980s was accompanied by a prolonged increase in the inflow to unemployment, especially via permanent layoffs. Unemployment in-

Figure 6.6
**Unemployment Flows and Job Flows by Reason:
Quarterly, 1976 to 1992**
(Seasonally adjusted)

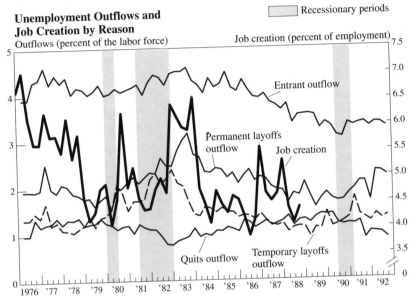

**Unemployment Outflows and
Job Creation by Reason**
Outflows (percent of the labor force)

Job creation (percent of employment)

Recessionary periods

Entrant outflow

Permanent layoffs
outflow

Job creation

Quits outflow

Temporary layoffs
outflow

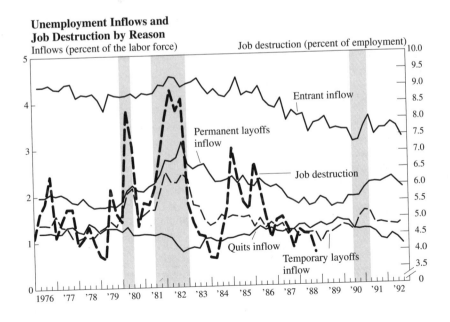

**Unemployment Inflows and
Job Destruction by Reason**
Inflows (percent of the labor force)

Job destruction (percent of employment)

Entrant inflow

Permanent layoffs
inflow

Job destruction

Quits inflow

Temporary layoffs
inflow

Table 6.4
Relationship Between Unemployment Flows by Reason and Job Flows

Correlation Between Unemployment Flows and Job Flows

	Job Creation	Job Destruction
Inflows (All workers)	−0.15	0.71
Inflows (Temporary layoffs)	−0.08	0.77
Inflows (Permanent layoffs)	0.08	0.58
Inflows (Quits)	−0.17	−0.25
Inflows (Entrants)	0.38	0.48
Outflows (All workers)	0.16	0.27
Outflows (Temporary layoffs)	0.16	0.60
Outflows (Permanent layoffs)	0.31	0.07
Outflows (Quits)	−0.10	−0.26
Outflows (Entrants)	0.44	0.23

Cyclical Variation in Unemployment and Job Flows (Cyclical average)

	Periods of Expansion	Periods of Recession
Inflows (All)	8.58	9.37
Inflows (Temporary layoffs)	1.36	2.09
Inflows (Permanent layoffs)	2.08	2.46
Inflows (Quits)	1.16	1.10
Inflows (Entrants)	4.10	4.30
Outflows (All)	8.77	8.79
Outflows (Temporary layoffs)	1.41	1.91
Outflows (Permanent layoffs)	2.16	2.16
Outflows (Quits)	1.16	1.09
Outflows (Entrants)	4.14	4.19
Job Creation	5.34	4.75
Job Destruction	4.96	7.34

Note: In the upper panel, the correlations for all workers are for the period 1972:Q2-1988:Q4. Correlations by reason are for the period 1976:Q3-1988:Q4. In the lower panel, the unemployment statistics and job flows for all workers are for the period 1972:Q2-1988:Q4. Statistics for unemployment by reason are for the period 1976:Q4-1988:Q4.

flows and outflows due to quits decline moderately during recessions, which indicates that quits play little role in the sharply higher job destruction during cyclical downturns.

Job creation covaries positively with unemployment outflows by permanently and temporarily laid-off persons and, especially, with outflows by new entrants. However, neither job creation nor any of these unemployment outflows by reason (except quits) varies as much over the cycle as do their counterparts on the job destruction and unemployment inflow side (see the bottom panel of table 6.4).

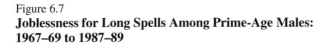

Figure 6.7
**Joblessness for Long Spells Among Prime-Age Males:
1967–69 to 1987–89**

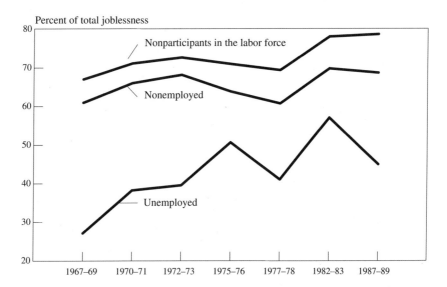

Note: The figure represents joblessness for at least six months among males aged 25–54. Nonemployed workers include those unemployed and those not in the labor force.

The phenomena of prolonged, persistent job destruction and the larger role of permanent layoffs since the early 1980s are linked to the rise in long-term joblessness documented by other researchers. Drawing on work by Juhn, Murphy, and Topel (1991), figure 6.7 illustrates the rising shares of unemployment, nonparticipation in the labor force, and nonemployment accounted for by long spells among prime-age males.[14] Based on any of these three measures, the share of joblessness accounted for by men who were jobless for at least half of the year rose dramatically after the late 1960s. Most of the secular increase in long-term unemployment occurred between the expansionary periods of 1967–69 and 1977–79. However, the role of long-term joblessness in terms of nonemployment and nonparticipation rose sharply in the early 1980s. Although the secular increase in long-term unemployment between 1977–79 and 1987–89 is relatively modest, the recession years of the early 1980s show an especially large fraction of unemployment accounted for by long spells.

---

14. Nonemployment includes unemployment and nonparticipation in the labor force.

Figure 6.8 provides further perspective on the role of permanent layoffs in the rising importance of long-term joblessness. The upper panel shows that the escape rate from unemployment is much lower for permanently laid-off persons than for unemployed persons.[15] The lower panel shows a secular increase in the fraction of unemployed persons accounted for by permanent layoffs. The share of unemployment accounted for by permanent layoffs rose to new heights in the early 1990s. Taken together, these two panels indicate that the growing importance of permanent layoffs accounts for part of the secular and cyclical increases in long-term joblessness.[16]

To recapitulate, sharp increases in job destruction during recessions are accompanied by increased flows through the unemployment pool. These increased flows primarily involve job-losing workers. Since the deep recession of 1981–82, permanent layoffs have played the dominant role in accounting for cyclical unemployment swings. The rising importance of permanent layoffs, coupled with the low unemployment escape rate of permanently laid-off persons, contributed to secular and cyclical increases in long-term joblessness.

6.4.3 Unemployment Flows by Age and Sex

Another useful decomposition breaks down unemployment flows by sex and age groups. Figure 6.9 displays shares of unemployment by sex and age group over the period 1948–92.[17] Women and young workers (16–24 years of age) account for a sharply rising share of unemployment over much of the 1960s and 1970s. The first effect reflects the sharp increases in labor force participation rates of women, and the second effect reflects the labor force entry of the baby boom cohorts. As the entry of the baby boom cohorts subsided in the 1980s, the share of unemployment accounted for by young men and young women fell steadily.

These changes in unemployment shares by sex and age help us to understand changes over time in the level of unemployment inflows and outflows. In particular, the entry into the labor market of the baby boom cohorts and

---

15. In figure 6.8, the escape rate equals the fraction of unemployed workers who exit unemployment within a month. The reported values are quarterly averages of monthly rates. The typical worker has an escape rate of just under 0.50 each month, which implies that the typical duration of an unemployment spell is about two months.

16. See Darby, Haltiwanger, and Plant (1985, 1986) for a more extended analysis of cyclical changes in the composition of the unemployment pool.

17. The inflow and outflow rates by age and sex are the flows divided by the total labor force. Accordingly, summing the inflow (outflow) rates across all age and sex categories yields the aggregate inflow (outflow) rate.

Figure 6.8
**Escape Rates From Unemployment and Shares of Unemployment
by Reason: Quarterly, 1967 to 1992**
(Seasonally adjusted)

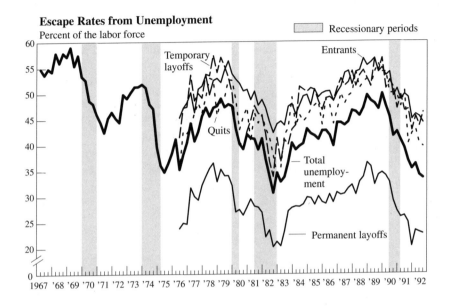

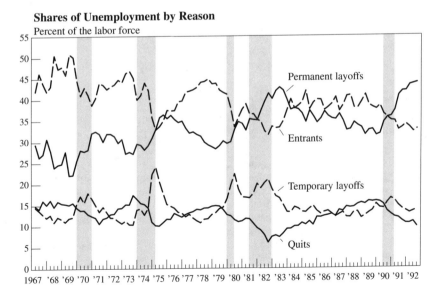

Figure 6.9
Shares of Unemployment by Sex and Age Group:
Quarterly, 1948 to 1992
(Seasonally adjusted)

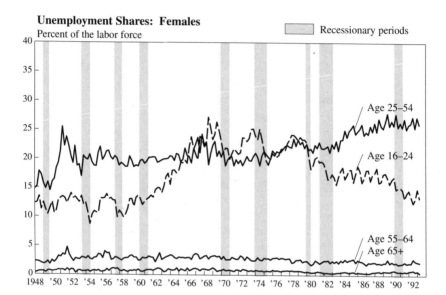

Unemployment Shares: Females

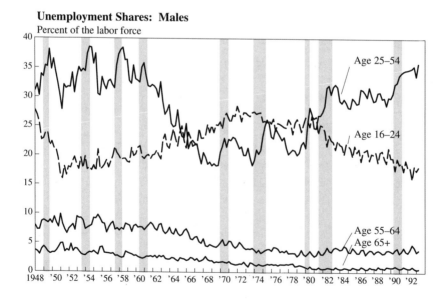

Unemployment Shares: Males

the increased participation by women underlie the high unemployment inflow and outflow rates experienced during the 1970s. New and recent entrants and reentrants to the labor market typically engage in job-shopping behavior that is associated with frequent short employment and unemployment spells. Darby, Haltiwanger, and Plant (1985) develop this theme at greater length and provide references to related literature.

Beyond these factors underlying the secular changes in unemployment flows, there is an important connection between cyclical movements in the composition of unemployment and the behavior of gross job flows. Figure 6.9 shows that immediately before and during recessions, the share of unemployment accounted for by prime-age (25–54) men rises sharply. Figure 6.10 and table 6.5 show further that the unemployment inflows and outflows for prime-age men also rise sharply in recessions. Unemployment flows for prime-age women increase somewhat during recessions, but their unemployment shares do not. The sharp increases in unemployment rates and inflows for prime-age males during recessions coincide with sharp increases in job destruction.

6.4.4 Putting the Pieces Together

When we consider the evidence on unemployment by reason and by demographic characteristics, we see an important connection between job flow dynamics and cyclical variation in the composition of the unemployment pool. During good times, unemployment is dominated by entrants, quitters, and young people. These workers transit across states of the labor market to accommodate life cycle entry and exit, and normal search for an appropriate job match. During recessions, increases in unemployment are dominated by permanent and temporary layoffs as firms restructure their employment positions. These layoffs are accompanied by an increase in the share of unemployment of prime-age workers (especially men), most of whom have considerable work experience and strong attachment to the labor force.[18]

This interpretation of unemployment rate dynamics offers an interesting parallel to the observed job flow dynamics. Job flow dynamics in good times are dominated by the creation and destruction of jobs among relatively young and small plants. These younger and smaller plants are, like young workers, trying to determine whether and where they fit into the marketplace. During recessions, older and larger plants experience sharply higher job destruction

---

18. Young workers also face increased layoffs in recessions. Table 6.5 and figure 6.10 show that the inflow rate into unemployment for young workers rises in recessions. However, unemployment and unemployment inflows of prime-age workers rise disproportionately.

Figure 6.10
Job Flows and Unemployment Flows by Age and Sex: Quarterly, 1976 to 1992
(Seasonally adjusted)

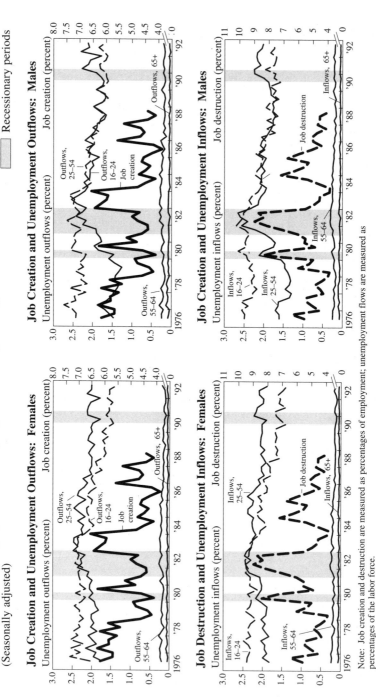

Note: Job creation and destruction are measured as percentages of employment; unemployment flows are measured as percentages of the labor force.

Table 6.5
Relationship Between Unemployment Flows by Age and Sex, and Job Flows

Correlation Between Unemployment Flows and Job Flows

	Job Creation	Job Destruction
Inflows (All workers)	−0.15	0.71
Inflows (Females, 16–24)	0.40	0.44
Inflows (Females, 25–54)	−0.24	0.52
Inflows (Females, 55–64)	0.28	0.38
Inflows (Females, 65+)	0.00	−0.09
Inflows (Males, 16–24)	0.31	0.54
Inflows (Males, 25–54)	−0.21	0.61
Inflows (Males, 55–64)	0.10	0.64
Inflows (Males, 65+)	0.37	0.04
Outflows (All workers)	0.16	0.27
Outflows (Females, 16–24)	0.45	0.30
Outflows (Females, 25–54)	−0.10	0.14
Outflows (Females, 55–64)	0.33	0.13
Outflows (Females, 65+)	−0.01	−0.07
Outflows (Males, 16–24)	0.54	0.28
Outflows (Males, 25–54)	0.03	0.22
Outflows (Males, 55–64)	0.35	0.30
Outflows (Males, 65+)	0.49	−0.05

Cyclical Variation in Unemployment, by Age and Sex, and in Job Flows (Cyclical average)

	Periods of Expansion	Periods of Recession
Inflows (All)	8.58	9.37
Inflows (Females, 16–24)	2.13	2.37
Inflows (Females, 25–54)	2.09	2.26
Inflows (Females, 55–64)	0.19	0.20
Inflows (Females, 65+)	0.05	0.05
Inflows (Males, 16–24)	2.18	2.52
Inflows (Males, 25–54)	1.79	2.23
Inflows (Males, 55–64)	0.21	0.27
Inflows (Males, 65+)	0.06	0.07
Outflows (All)	8.77	8.79
Outflows (Females, 16–24)	2.16	2.32
Outflows (Females, 25–54)	2.12	2.14
Outflows (Females, 55–64)	0.19	0.19
Outflows (Females, 65+)	0.05	0.05
Outflows (Males, 16–24)	2.23	2.40
Outflows (Males, 25–54)	1.85	1.98
Outflows (Males, 55–64)	0.22	0.24
Outflows (Males, 65+)	0.07	0.06
Job Creation	5.34	4.75
Job Destruction	4.96	7.34

Note: In the upper panel, the correlation for all workers is for the period 1972:Q2-1988:Q4. Correlations by age and sex are for the period 1976:Q3-1988:Q4. In the lower panel, the unemployment statistics and job flows for all workers are for the period 1972:Q2-1988:Q4. The statistics for unemployment by age and sex are for the period 1976:Q4-1988:Q4.

rates, so that their contribution to the job and worker reallocation process rises. This time of intense job destruction by older and larger plants coincides with the rise in layoff unemployment, especially among prime-age workers.[19]

6.4.5 Some Missing Pieces

This story has some missing pieces. An important component of worker reallocation that is missing from the flows we examine is quits by workers who move directly from one job to another. As emphasized by Akerlof, Rose, and Yellen (1988), large numbers of workers move between jobs without experiencing any unemployment. Many of these transitions relate to job satisfaction or other factors that do not involve job creation and destruction. These job-to-job transitions have interesting dynamics of their own. An initial job-to-job transition can set off a chain of vacancies and a reshuffling of workers among existing jobs.

How important is this component for understanding the cyclical variation in worker reallocation? The work of Akerlof, Rose, and Yellen shows that total worker reallocation (including employment-to-employment transitions) is acyclical or perhaps mildly procyclical. Given that the part of worker reallocation driven by job reallocation is strongly countercyclical, the remaining component must be strongly procyclical. The evidence from unemployment flows suggests that the component of worker reallocation attributable to life cycle entry and exit from the labor force is essentially acyclical.[20] These observations imply that employment-to-employment quits are an important and highly procyclical component of worker reallocation. Direct evidence on quit rates for the manufacturing sector confirms this inference.

To put this conclusion in perspective, recall the evidence in chapter 2 on the role of job reallocation in worker reallocation. Chapter 2 presented evidence that job reallocation accounts, on average, for approximately 32 percent to 53 percent of worker reallocation. The remainder of worker reallocation reflects life cycle entry and exit (which we estimated to account for roughly 12 percent of worker reallocation) and the sorting and resorting of workers across a given set of jobs for a variety of reasons. Since total worker reallocation is acyclical or mildly procyclical, whereas job reallocation is highly countercyclical, the percentage of worker reallocation induced by job reallocation is probably

---

19. We believe that older plants disproportionately employ older workers, but we know of no direct evidence on this issue.

20. The evidence in Blanchard and Diamond (1990) also suggests that the flows into and out of the labor force are not an important factor in accounting for cyclical variation in total worker reallocation.

much higher than 32 percent to 53 percent during recessions, and considerably lower during expansions. The evidence compiled and reviewed in this chapter suggests that the primary driving force behind worker reallocation activity during recessions is the reshuffling of job opportunities across locations.

To sum up, job reallocation is countercyclical—the economy restructures the organization of employment positions in recessions. This restructuring involves large flows of workers through the unemployment pool as the result of layoffs. Total worker reallocation, however, is not countercyclical, because direct employment-to-employment transitions associated with quits are strongly procyclical. In other words, the intensity with which workers sort across a given set of employment positions increases in booms, a point stressed by Akerlof, Rose, and Yellen. These two important but distinct components of worker reallocation thus have strikingly different cyclical properties.

6.5 Appendix: Seasonal Variation in the Flows

The strong seasonal patterns in worker and job flow rates are shown in table 6.6. These seasonal patterns were obtained by regressing the quarterly flow rates on quarterly seasonal dummies. The seasonally adjusted data examined in the chapter are the residuals from these regressions added to the sample mean for each series.

The first quarter (measured as December–February) is a time of high unemployment inflow, low unemployment outflow, high job destruction, low job creation, high employment outflow, and low employment inflow. The breakdown by reason of unemployment shows that these characteristics are associated with high unemployment inflow and low outflow from layoffs (both temporary and permanent).

The second quarter (March–May) is a time of low inflow and high outflow from unemployment, moderate job creation and low job destruction, moderate employment inflow and low employment outflow. Again, this is associated with similar seasonal variation in the inflow and outflow rates from layoffs.

The third quarter (June–August) is a time of very high unemployment inflow and outflow rates, very high employment inflow and outflow rates, high job creation and low job destruction. This pattern is driven by high inflow and outflow rates from entrants. This third-quarter seasonal variation in the inflow and outflow rates for entrants dominates the seasonal pattern of the total inflow and outflow rates.

The fourth quarter (September–November) is a time of moderate unemployment inflow and outflow, moderate employment inflow, high employment outflow, and moderate job creation and destruction.

Table 6.6
Seasonal Variation in Unemployment Flows, Employment Flows, and Job Flows

	First Quarter	Second Quarter	Third Quarter	Fourth Quarter
Unemployment Flows				
Abowd-Zellner Inflows..............	6.75	5.89	7.82	6.81
Abowd-Zellner Outflows	6.39	7.56	7.89	7.35
Inflows (Duration-Based)............	7.72	6.84	8.31	7.54
Inflows (Temporary layoffs)..........	1.83	1.24	1.33	1.32
Inflows (Permanent layoffs)..........	2.21	1.91	2.08	2.19
Inflows (Quits)	1.04	0.99	1.25	1.27
Inflows (Entrants).................	3.49	3.62	4.65	3.91
Outflows (Duration-Based)...........	6.52	7.94	8.21	7.62
Outflows (Temporary layoffs)	1.36	1.74	1.32	1.30
Outflows (Permanent layoffs).........	1.82	2.29	2.14	2.10
Outflows (Quits)...................	1.04	1.08	1.11	1.34
Outflows (Entrants)................	3.41	3.62	4.60	4.06
Employment Flows				
Abowd-Zellner Inflows..............	7.31	9.44	11.65	9.99
Abowd-Zellner Outflows	8.92	6.86	9.67	11.02
Job Creation and Destruction				
Creation.........................	5.03	5.16	5.53	5.08
Destruction	6.86	5.16	4.72	5.47

Note: Duration-based unemployment flows (all workers) and job-flow statistics are for the period 1972:Q1-1988:Q4. Statistics for unemployment by reason are for the period 1976:Q3-1988:Q4. Abowd-Zellner flows are measured by tracking changes in the labor-market status of individuals, adjusted for problems of misclassification. These data are for 1972:Q1-1986:Q4.

As noted, the peaks in the unemployment and employment flows occur in the third quarter, driven by inflows and outflows of entrants. Since entrants are not closely connected to job creation and destruction, the third quarter has especially high unemployment and employment flows but not especially high job reallocation. In the chapter, we abstract from this seasonality, because it is not the focus of the chapter and because it is not closely connected with the job flow patterns.

In addition to the third-quarter seasonal effect, it is apparent from table 6.6 that the seasonality in the worker flows generally is greater than that in the job flows in all quarters. Job creation, in particular, exhibits relatively little change among quarters. Thus the seasonal adjustment procedure also smooths the worker flows more than the job flows throughout the year.

7   Economic and Policy Implications

Chapters 2 through 6 constructed a detailed statistical portrait of gross job flow behavior in the U.S. manufacturing sector and of the connection between job and worker flows. We now draw upon this statistical portrait to develop several implications for economic policy and, more generally, to illustrate how the measurement and analysis of job and worker flows inform our thinking about the economy. Our chief points fall into the following categories:

• ***Dominance of idiosyncratic factors:*** *Idiosyncratic factors dominate the determination of gross job creation and destruction. Easily observable systematic factors related to industry, region, wages, employer size and age, capital and energy intensity, and foreign competition account for little of the heterogeneity in plant-level job growth outcomes.*

• ***Ignorance about idiosyncratic factors:*** *Economists can point to several reasons for the importance of idiosyncratic factors in business performance, but the current state of economic science provides little knowledge about the relative importance of these various factors or the precise reasons why they generate such heterogeneity in outcomes.*

• ***Economics of targeted industrial and commercial policies:*** *The dominant role of idiosyncratic factors in business performance hampers the evaluation of targeted industrial and commercial policies by making it more difficult and costly to discern policy effects. The design of targeted policies is hampered by differences in policy responses among businesses, because these differences necessitate more complex policy design and greater monitoring efforts.*

• ***Political economy of targeted policies:*** *The central role of job destruction and business failure in the process of economic growth and change amplifies the severity of two problems that arise with targeted policies. First, they engender the formation of special interest groups that tend to undermine the*

application of economic efficiency criteria. Second, targeted policy programs tend to persist beyond the point of economic desirability, because government officials are reluctant to acknowledge policy failures. Both problems inhibit efficient political responses to economic "losers" underwritten by targeted policies.

• **Preferential treatment based on job growth performance:** *Factual claims about job growth performance by particular classes of employers (e.g., small businesses) do not provide a sound basis for preferential policy treatment. Such claims neither identify the market failure that preferential policies are intended to address nor quantify how the number and quality of jobs would respond to a policy intervention.*

• **Workforce flexibility:** *High job destruction rates in almost all sectors of the economy underscore the economic importance of a flexible workforce able to adapt to changes in the location and skill requirements of available jobs.*

• **International trade and job security:** *Cross-industry differences in gross job flow behavior do not support the view that greater international openness undermines job security by exposing American firms and workers to additional sources of disturbances.*

• **Aggregate stabilization policies:** *This book's evidence on the connection between restructuring activity and business cycles raises several questions about traditional perspectives on the consequences and wisdom of aggregate stabilization policies.*

7.1   The Limitations of Our Statistical Portrait

Before developing economic and policy lessons from our statistical portrait, it is important to recognize its limitations, especially as a tool for policy evaluation. We spell out the chief limitations in this section.

One important limitation is the sharp focus of our statistical portrait on job creation and destruction activity. Although job growth receives enormous attention in economic policy discussions, this attention is sometimes misplaced. Indeed, the mere creation of jobs is not, by itself, an appropriate economic policy objective. Instead, policy is appropriately directed toward wealth creation and the expansion of consumption opportunities. Here, we mean "consumption opportunities" in a broad sense that encompasses not just material goods but also the many factors that influence the quality of life.

The focus on job growth as a policy objective probably stems from a perceived link between high (or rising) employment and high (or rising) real

income. Real income, in turn, is seen as closely linked to consumption opportunities and, hence, economic well-being. Although these links hold in
many historical circumstances, other episodes point to their tenuous nature.
For example, rapid U.S. employment expansion during much of the 1980s
coincided with stagnant or declining real hourly wages and annual earnings
for large segments of the workforce (Cutler and Katz, 1991; Levy and Murnane, 1992). Furthermore, in the face of rapid employment expansion, real
consumption fell during the 1980s for households headed by less-educated
workers (Attanasio and Davis, 1994). Thus, the experience of the 1980s be-
lies the belief in a tight chain of causation running from employment to real
income to consumption and economic well-being. In short, high employment
and rapid job growth are very imperfect indicators of economic welfare, so
they should not be treated as ultimate policy objectives or the primary yard-
sticks of policy evaluation.

An important corollary to this conclusion involves the quality of jobs. Policy discussions frequently focus on prospects for job creation and destruction
while giving little attention to such important aspects of job quality as productivity, compensation, stability, opportunities for skill acquisition, and working
conditions. The frequent neglect of job quality undermines the formulation
and implementation of welfare-enhancing economic policies.

Unfortunately, the need to consider job quality complicates the task of policy evaluation in two ways. First, many aspects of job quality are difficult
to measure. Our statistical portrait reflects this difficulty: average production
worker wages and job survival rates are the only dimensions of job quality
considered in this book. Second, measurable indicators of job quality reflect
outcomes that depend on both worker and job characteristics. Because productivity, compensation, skill acquisition, and working conditions all depend
on the distributions of worker and employer attributes, *and* on a variety of labor market institutions, it can be quite difficult to determine the distinct effects
of a particular policy on the types of work environments and jobs provided
by employers. However severe these impediments to the evaluation of policy
effects on job quality may be, they do not lend greater credibility to policy
evaluations that ignore job quality.

One other limitation of our statistical portrait merits emphasis. With respect
to employment, policy evaluation requires an analysis of how job numbers
and quality respond to actual or proposed policy interventions. The mere fact
that, historically, some particular class of employers created jobs at a relatively
rapid or slow pace does not ensure a strong or weak response by that class to a
policy intervention or other change in the economic environment. A concrete

example illustrates this point. Chapter 4 reports that smaller employers exhibit sharply higher job destruction rates than larger employers. Yet chapter 5 finds that larger employers exhibit more cyclically sensitive job destruction rates. Evidently, the job destruction rates of large employers show *greater sensitivity to the changes* in the economic environment associated with business cycles, even though they exhibit much *smaller average* job destruction rates. More generally, statistics on average creation and destruction behavior do not, by themselves, generate reliable predictions about the response to policy interventions or other changes in the economic environment.

Having laid out some important limitations of our statistical portrait, we do not want to leave the impression that jobs and job growth are unimportant. For most people, jobs are the primary means of providing for consumption and accumulating wealth. Jobs and job creation also contribute to economic and social well-being in ways not captured by statistics on income and production. Besides a paycheck, the benefits to job holding often include better health, greater self-esteem, a favorable social status, opportunities for friendship, membership in a community, opportunities for professional and personal growth, and the sense of participating in a larger society.[1] Although difficult to measure, these nonpecuniary personal rewards of jobs are real and important. In addition to the personal rewards of jobholding, job creation often brings positive social consequences, and job loss or a lack of job opportunities can cause or exacerbate social problems. Wilson (1987), for example, argues that a large-scale loss of urban manufacturing jobs underlies much of the economic and social strife that afflicts inner city life in the United States.

A complete evaluation of how job creation and destruction affect economic and social welfare, and how job flows are affected by government policies, would require careful, explicit models of the economy and society. This book does not engage in formal model building, but many discussions in this chapter and elsewhere in the book draw upon lessons that emanate from formal and informal economic models. In the remainder of this chapter, we deliberately focus on issues that can be illuminated by combining the facts developed in this book with an informal treatment of economic ideas and models. We steer clear of topics or lines of analysis that call for formal model building. Formal model building and the integration of theoretical models with the

---

1. There is a large medical sociology literature on the physical and mental health consequences of unemployment and job loss. See, e.g., Platt (1984), Forcier (1988), Ezzy (1993), and Ettner (1994).

facts developed in this book are important activities that we leave for other occasions.

In summary, job numbers and quality affect economic and social well-being, but job creation is not the ultimate objective of economic policy. Simple statistics about job creation and destruction behavior inform our thinking about the economy, and they serve as useful inputs into the design and evaluation of economic policies, but policy design and evaluation also require economic models. With these remarks and caveats in mind, we now proceed to a discussion of how the evidence on job creation and destruction relates to our understanding of the economy and to several economic policy issues.

7.2   Heterogeneity in Job Growth Outcomes

7.2.1   The Magnitude and Pervasiveness of Job Reallocation

We begin by recalling a key empirical regularity developed in chapters 2, 3, and 4: high job reallocation rates characterize virtually every type of plant and firm that we identified in the data. This large-scale, pervasive, and continuous reshuffling of job opportunities bespeaks a constant reallocation of production activity in the U.S. economy and—according to the available evidence summarized in chapter 2—other advanced market economies.

Especially as regards the more detailed U.S. evidence, the magnitude and pervasiveness of job reallocation fit imperfectly with common conceptions of the extent and nature of structural adjustment in the economy. To be sure, it is widely understood that market economies reallocate employment and other factor inputs in response to the emergence of new products and new production techniques, changes in the scope and composition of international trade, changes in economic policies and patterns of government expenditure, and many other events. Sectors facing favorable changes in cost and demand conditions expand, whereas sectors facing unfavorable changes contract. In recent years, much has been made of employment shifts away from basic manufacturing industries (e.g., steel and autos) and toward advanced technology (e.g., computers) and service industries.

Although these between-sector employment shifts are often important, our statistical portrait shows rather strikingly that they are dwarfed by the magnitude of within-sector shifts in employment across plants. Chapters 3 and 4 document large within-sector employment reallocation regardless of whether sectors are defined in terms of industry, region, plant age, plant or firm size,

wage level, degree of product specialization, energy intensity, capital intensity, or degree of exposure to foreign competition. In short, employment growth outcomes exhibit enormous heterogeneity among plants and firms that operate in the same classifiable sectors.

The heterogeneity of job growth outcomes within narrowly defined sectors parallels recent findings on plant-level productivity growth patterns. Drawing on the LRD, Baily, Bartelsman, and Haltiwanger (1994) document large within-sector differences in productivity growth for a variety of widely used sectoral classifications. Hence, most of the variation in job *and* productivity growth rates across plants reflects within- rather than between-sector differences. This empirical evidence about the heterogeneity of outcomes within observable sectoral classifications is a key point of departure for several of our remarks below.

7.2.2   Reasons for Heterogeneity

The magnitude of within-sector heterogeneity implies that idiosyncratic factors dominate the determination of which plants create and destroy jobs, and which plants achieve rapid productivity growth or suffer productivity declines. One likely reason for heterogeneity in plant-level outcomes is the considerable uncertainty that surrounds the development, adoption, distribution, marketing, and regulation of new products and production techniques. Uncertainty about the demand for new products or the cost-effectiveness of alternative technologies encourages firms to experiment with different technologies, goods, and production facilities (Roberts and Weitzman, 1981). Experimentation, in turn, generates differences in outcomes (Jovanovic, 1982; Ericson and Pakes, 1989). Even when motives for experimentation are absent, uncertainty about future cost or demand conditions encourages firms to differentiate their choice of current products and technology so as to position themselves optimally for possible future circumstances (Lambson, 1991).

Another likely reason is that differences in entrepreneurial and managerial ability lead to differences in job and productivity growth rates among firms and plants. These differences include the ability to identify and develop new products, the ability to organize production activity, the ability to motivate workers, and the ability to adapt to changing circumstances. There seems to be little doubt that these and other ability differences among managers generate much of the observed heterogeneity in plant-level outcomes. Business magazines and newspapers regularly portray the decisions and actions of particular management teams or individuals as crucial determinants of success or fail-

ure. High levels of compensation, often heavily skewed toward various forms of incentive pay, also suggest that senior managers play key roles in business performance, including productivity and job growth outcomes.[2]

Other factors that drive heterogeneity in plant-level productivity and job growth outcomes involve plant- and firm-specific circumstances and disturbances. For example, energy costs and labor costs vary over space and time. Cost differences induce different employment and investment decisions among otherwise similar plants and firms. These decisions, in addition, influence the size and type of labor force and capital stock that a business carries into the future. Thus, current differences in cost and demand conditions induce contemporaneous heterogeneity in plant-level job and productivity growth. They also cause businesses to differentiate themselves in ways that lead to heterogeneous responses to common shocks in the future.[3]

Slow diffusion of information about technology, distribution channels, marketing strategies, and consumer tastes is another important source of plant-level heterogeneity in productivity and job growth. Nasbeth and Ray (1974) and Rogers (1983) document multi-year lags in the diffusion of knowledge about new technologies among firms producing related products. Mansfield et al. (1981) and Pakes and Schankerman (1984) provide evidence of long imitation and product development lags. Rhee et al. (1984) report that foreign buyers and sellers were important transmitters of technical information in the Korean industrialization process. The remarkable proliferation of differentiated computerware suggests important roles both for information diffusion in the production and use of computer products and for vintage capital effects in computer usage and product development patterns.[4]

7.2.3   Heterogeneity, Ignorance, and Economic Policy

Coupled with the empirical evidence of pervasive within-sector job reallocation activity, and parallel findings for plant-level productivity behavior, these remarks about sources of heterogeneity among seemingly similar businesses

---

2. Many economic analyses attribute a key role to managerial ability in the organization of firms and production units. Lucas (1977b), for example, provides an early and influential formal treatment.

3. Chari and Hopenhayn (1991) model the role of vintage capital effects as a source of firm-level heterogeneity in factor input usage.

4. Knowledge diffusion plays a key role in many theories of firm-level dynamics, industrial evolution, economic growth, and international trade. See, e.g., Grossman and Helpman (1991), Jovanovic and Rob (1989), and Jovanovic and MacDonald (1994).

underscore the remarkable complexity of economic growth and change. They underscore the continuous, large-scale job creation and destruction activity required to allocate resources toward their highest value uses. And they underscore the extremely limited degree to which the precise patterns of job creation and destruction can be explained in terms of business characteristics that are easily observable to economists and policymakers. Indeed, the current state of economic science provides little knowledge about the relative importance of various idiosyncratic factors or the precise reasons why they generate such tremendous heterogeneity in outcomes.[5]

The predominant role of idiosyncratic factors in job creation and destruction, and our highly incomplete understanding of these factors, incline us toward a prudent stance regarding economic policy interventions intended to create more or better jobs. Absent an understanding of which factors drive employer decisions about job creation and destruction, policy interventions may impede the allocation of workers and other inputs to their highest value uses.

One can certainly argue that understanding the idiosyncratic factors that underlie most job creation and destruction activity is inessential for the design of welfare-enhancing policy interventions. In principle, policy interventions can have predictable consequences for aggregate or industry-level net job creation, even when they have unknown consequences for gross job creation and destruction.

We doubt whether this principle provides a sound basis for the design and evaluation of many economic policy interventions, in part on the basis of evidence in this book. Indeed, the intimate connection between aggregate job growth and the dispersion of job growth rates among employers documented in chapter 5 suggests that the real world economy exhibits no clean separation between aggregate outcomes and the dispersion of outcomes among employers. In other contexts, such as fluctuations in aggregate business investment and expenditures on consumer durables, work by Bertola and Caballero (1990), Eberly (1994), and others makes clear that modeling and understanding the cross-sectional distribution of outcomes among individual agents is

---

5. Davis and Haltiwanger (1992) attempt to systematically explain the heterogeneity in job creation and destruction rates among plants, with only limited success. Of course, business analysts and policymakers typically have access to much information that is not easily quantified or systematically incorporated into datasets. Thus, the empirical evidence in our earlier work and in this book may exaggerate the importance of unexplained heterogeneity. Although we are sympathetic to this line of argument, one should bear in mind that business analysts and policymakers lack real-time access to a comprehensive, probability-based sample of plants and firms like the one we use.

important for understanding aggregate developments. This research indicates that the aggregate response to a policy intervention depends on the nature of cross-sectional heterogeneity among economic agents. For example, the impact of a temporary investment tax credit depends on the vintage distribution of the existing capital stock.

7.3   Targeted Industrial and Commercial Policies

Many government policies target specific sectors or types of firms for preferential treatment. The stated objectives of such policies typically include job creation, the prevention of job loss, or improvements in the "competitiveness" and productivity of "crucial" sectors. These policies involve preferential taxes or subsidies, protection from foreign competition, special regulatory treatment, and preferential treatment in bidding for government contracts. Actual and proposed targets of preferential treatment include advanced technology products, heavy manufacturing industries, alternative energy sources, agricultural products, major transportation industries, economically depressed communities, and particular types of firms, such as small or minority-owned businesses. Box 7.1 cites many specific examples that illustrate the great range and ubiquity of targeted commercial policies.

7.3.1   Arguments for Targeted Policies

Arguments for targeted commercial policies often appeal to the potential for improvements in economic efficiency—that is, a reallocation of labor, capital, and other inputs toward uses with higher economic returns.[6] One common economic argument for targeting rests on the claim that inefficiently low production arises in certain sectors because of imperfections in product or labor markets. For example, excessively high wages in some sectors of the economy lead to inefficient distributions of employment and output. Excessively high wages can arise from the institutional environment governing the wage-setting process, employer responses to problems of motivating workers, and employer efforts to attract and retain high-quality workers.[7]

---

6. See, e.g., the discussions in Krugman (1986, 1987a, 1987b), Cohen and Noll (1991, chap. 2), and Tyson (1992).

7. Katz and Summers (1989) consider several reasons why wages might be excessively high in certain sectors of the economy, and they review the related theoretical and empirical literatures. Weiss (1990a) and many others argue that employer efforts to motivate workers and to attract and retain high-quality workers lead to socially inefficient wage structures that, in turn, induce an inefficient sectoral distribution of employment and output.

Box 7.1
Examples of targeted commercial policies

Subsidies to Commercialize Advanced Technology Products

• The supersonic transport (SST) program, headed by the Federal Aviation Administration, received nearly $1 billion in funding over the course of its ten-year life (Cohen and Noll, 1991, p. 97).

• An important aspect of U.S. semiconductor policy was the 1987 formation of Sematech, a consortium of computer chip manufacturers jointly funded by participants and the federal government. In addition to government subsidies of approximately $100 million per year, Sematech participants benefit from reduced exposure to antitrust violations under the National Cooperative Research Act of 1984. See Office of Technology Assessment (1990), Tyson (1992), Flamm (1993), and Richards (1991).

• The National Flat Panel Display Initiative proposes to spend $587 million over five years to encourage the development and production of high-definition, flat-panel video devices (Business Wire, 1994). Unlike Sematech, this initiative proposes to underwrite marketing and plant construction costs as well as research and development. See Bradsher (1994) and *New York Times* (1994a).

Subsidies to Develop Alternative Energy Sources

• From the early 1950s until the cancellation of the Clinch River Breeder Reactor Demonstration in 1983, the U.S. government provided major subsidies to the commercialization of nuclear power (Cohen and Noll, 1991).

• The U.S. government created the Synthetic Fuels Corporation in 1980 and subsequently spent billions of dollars in attempts to encourage the commercialization of wood-based, coal-based, and shale-based substitutes for petroleum fuels (Office of Technology Assessment, 1990; Cohen and Noll, 1991; Andrews, 1993).

• Under the Clean Air Act, the U.S. Environmental Protection Agency mandated the use of renewable auto fuels such as ethanol in the production of cleaner-burning forms of gasoline (*New York Times,* 1994b). In addition, ethanol producers benefit from tax exemptions that are estimated to amount to 60 cents per gallon, plus special protective tariffs, loan guarantees, and investment credits (Weiss, 1990b).

Preferential Tax Relief

• Tax preferences have a long history in the United States and take a variety of forms. Tax preferences that directly favor individual firms or industries include exemptions from federal fuel excise taxes for farmers; special depletion allowances extended to producers of sand, gravel, oyster shells, and salt; preferential capital gains tax rates for livestock held more than six months and unharvested crops sold with land; and immediate expensing of development and exploration costs for minerals, oil, and gas. See Pechman (1987) and Department of Treasury (1984).

Box 7.1
Examples of targeted commercial policies, continued

Protection from Foreign Competition

• Preferential treatment of manufacturing and agricultural industries frequently takes the form of import quotas, voluntary export restraint agreements, trigger price mechanisms, and other trade policies that insulate domestic firms from foreign competition. U.S. industries with long histories of import protection include autos, steel, textiles, sugar, dairy products, and beef products. Krugman and Smith (1994), Office of Technology Assessment (1981), and Congressional Budget Office (1986) describe and analyze U.S. trade policy toward manufacturing industries. Hallberg (1992) and Robinson (1989) treat U.S. trade policy toward agricultural products.

Regulatory Exemptions for Small Businesses

• Small businesses are exempted from many regulations that govern the employment relationship, including advance worker notification of layoffs, the filing of affirmative action reports, mandated family and medical leaves, and regulations governing age discrimination, pensions, workplace safety, and civil rights (Brock and Evans, 1986; Brown et al., 1990; Judge, 1994).

Preferences in Government Contract Awards

• Criteria for government contract awards often entail explicit preferences or set-asides for minority-owned and smaller businesses. For example, many government agencies set aside a certain percentage of their bond issues for minority and women-owned brokerage firms (Wayne, 1994). The Federal Communications Commission plans to grant minority-owned businesses and small businesses preferences worth "hundreds of millions of dollars in bidding on new licenses for wireless telephone and data communications" (Andrews, 1994).

Geographically Targeted Tax and Regulatory Relief

• The U.S. federal and most state governments frequently grant special subsidies, tax breaks, and regulatory relief to businesses that create jobs or operate in specially designated geographic areas (Redburn, 1994). Prominent examples of these "enterprise zones" or "empowerment zones" include the Clinton administration's plan to designate impoverished urban neighborhoods for receipt of approximately $300 million in special grants and other federal benefits (Redburn, 1994; Vobejda, 1994).

Alternatively, monopoly power grounded in large fixed costs of production or high entry barriers can lead to inefficiently low levels of output and employment. Although the traditional response from economists to imperfect product market competition has been to promote policies that encourage competition (e.g., antitrust policies), the growing importance of international

trade adds a new dimension to this issue. In an imperfectly competitive industry with relatively few firms worldwide, government subsidies to domestic firms can sometimes enable them to increase their share of worldwide profits.[8]

Another common economic argument for targeting rests on the claim that certain sectors convey positive external benefits on other sectors. For example, improvements in advanced technology products such as semiconductors may lead to productivity improvements in other sectors.[9] If the firms that develop and produce semiconductors cannot appropriate all of the additional economic value that flows from these productivity improvements, they will devote too little employment and capital to the introduction and manufacture of less costly, more powerful semiconductors. Consequently, semiconductor output will be inefficiently low in the absence of a targeted policy intervention. Thus, like product and labor market imperfections, technological spillovers can lead to inefficiently low output and employment in certain sectors, thereby creating a potential efficiency-enhancing role for targeted policies.

Yet another line of argument for targeting particular industries or sectors stems from a desire to help insulate workers from or to cope with the effects of structural change. Workers may find it difficult to fully insure themselves against the costs of job loss induced by greater foreign competition or other sources of structural change. This difficulty provides an economic rationale for government programs that implement risk-sharing arrangements among workers. But the inability of workers to insure adequately against job loss is a weak argument for the preferential policy treatment of declining firms and sectors. Such policies indirectly insulate workers from market forces by directly subsidizing firms. These subsidies distort the allocation of capital and labor resources, and retard the economic adjustment to structural change by propping up failing firms in declining sectors. More efficient risk-sharing policies are likely to involve direct assistance to workers through retraining programs, relocation subsidies, and unemployment compensation.[10]

---

8. Krugman (1986, 1987a, 1987b) more fully articulates and critically evaluates this type of argument for strategic trade policy.

9. Mansfield (1980) and Scherer (1982) provide evidence of productivity growth spillovers across industries. Irwin and Klenow (1994) develop evidence of important productivity spillovers across firms within the semiconductor industry. Whether the spillovers occur across or within industries is not important for the argument at hand.

10. These programs also distort the allocation of resources in the economy, and in evaluating such programs, the costs of the distortions must be weighed against potential risk-sharing benefits. Gruber (1994), for example, develops this point in the context of the unemployment insurance system.

In addition to arguments that stress the potential for greater economic efficiency, international rent capture, and risk-sharing considerations, other arguments for targeted industrial and commercial policies emphasize objectives such as national security, a cleaner environment, a more equal distribution of job opportunities across regions or among racial and ethnic groups, the nurturing of productive work habits among the urban underclass, and the development of an entrepreneurial class of small business owners.

We do not offer a comprehensive evaluation of the various arguments for targeted policies. However, our evidence on the dominant role of idiosyncratic factors in job and productivity growth pertains to the desirability of targeted policies in three respects: (1) difficulties in designing effective targeted policies, (2) difficulties in evaluating targeted policies, and (3) difficulties that the political system encounters in responding to economic losers underwritten by targeted policy programs. We now address these three points in sequence.

7.3.2 Heterogeneous Business Performance and the Efficacy of Targeted Policies

First, the great heterogeneity of plant-level job growth and productivity outcomes suggests that businesses probably exhibit sharply different responses to policy interventions, even within narrowly defined industries or other sectoral groupings. Because businesses are not easily classifiable into sectors with homogeneous behavior, policies that grant preferential treatment to identifiable groups of firms can be poor tools for encouraging or discouraging particular economic activities. For example, when an industry successfully lobbies for import protection in the name of protecting jobs, some firms may not use the resulting increase in cash flow to preserve jobs.

This concern helped shape U.S. trade policy toward the steel industry in the 1980s. In the Fair Trade in Steel Act of 1984, domestic steel-producing interests pressed for highly restrictive import quotas. The United Steelworkers Union successfully lobbied for a provision in the act that required firms to reinvest all net cash flow from steel operations into the steel industry. This provision was motivated by the fear that "protection-induced profits would be used to diversify out of steel as U.S. Steel had with the purchase of Marathon Oil" (Moore, 1994, p. 34).[11]

---

11. The Fair Trade in Steel Act failed to become law, but pressure for its passage provided an important impetus behind the Reagan administration's implementation of a voluntary export restraint program that also required the steel industry to reinvest steel sector profits. See Moore (1994).

Of course, direct targeting of activities rather than firms may circumvent the problem created by heterogeneous firm responses.[12] Even so, policies that target activities require a monitoring effort to ensure that recipient firms actually use subsidies and regulatory relief to expand desired activities or curtail undesired activities. For example, geographically targeted policies often tie subsidies to the employment of local residents. Absent a serious monitoring and enforcement effort, the goal of expanding employment opportunities for local residents is easily evaded.

Second, the dominant role of idiosyncratic factors in job and productivity growth hampers the evaluation of targeted policy interventions for three reasons. First, the large role played by idiosyncratic factors makes it more difficult to discern the impact of policy interventions on the performance of affected firms. Second, the idiosyncratic determinants of business performance may interact with policy interventions in important ways. If the failure or success of targeted policies hinges on interaction with idiosyncratic factors, more data on more firms are required in order to assess the outcomes. Third, to the extent that idiosyncratic factors both interact with policy interventions *and* are difficult to observe and quantify, they more fundamentally undermine the task of policy evaluation. Unlike the first two reasons, this third reason suggests that gathering more data on performance outcomes under targeted policies need not greatly improve our understanding of why particular policies fail or succeed. Absent measures of the key idiosyncratic factors that interact with policy tools, the reasons for heterogeneous outcomes in the wake of targeted policy interventions will remain a mystery.

In short, the idiosyncratic determinants of business performance exacerbate the cost and difficulty of evaluating targeted commercial policies. As a consequence, useless or harmful targeted policies are more likely to persist over time before recognition of their inefficacy sets in.

Our third point turns on observations about political economy. Debates about targeted industrial policy often center on the government's capacity or lack of capacity to identify potential winners. In our view, an even more serious problem with targeted industrial policies involves the government's ability to respond appropriately to economic losers. By their nature, targeted policies engender political constituencies with a special interest in preserving the benefits of preferential tax, subsidy, or regulatory treatment. Once organized,

---

12. For example, marketable emission permits and other market-based devices can be used to reduce pollution while permitting sharply different pollution abatement responses among heterogeneous firms. See Cropper and Oates (1992) for an extensive discussion of market-based environmental policies.

these political constituencies continue to press for preferential treatment regardless of whether the targeted policy continues to promote greater economic efficiency. Thus, targeted policies encourage the formation of special interest groups that, in turn, undermine the application of economic efficiency criteria to future economic policy decisions.

This line of argument is not new,[13] but it acquires greater force from the evidence of heterogeneity in plant-level employment and productivity outcomes. The large magnitude of job creation and destruction, including the important role of births and deaths, suggests that trial and error play a central role in economic growth and in the evolution of businesses and industries. Put differently, large-scale business failure and job destruction are normal, probably essential, elements of a successful market economy. But targeted policies impede the trial-and-error process by inhibiting business failure and job destruction when such outcomes are economically desirable. This book's evidence of large-scale job reallocation underscores the importance of efficient mechanisms that minimize the costs of economic failures. Market mechanisms for dealing with economic failure are likely to operate more efficiently and expeditiously than political mechanisms.[14]

Another important aspect of the political system hampers efficient government responses to economic failures. Like most people, policymakers and bureaucrats evince a reluctance to acknowledge mistakes. Consequently, targeted policy programs tend to persist beyond the point of economic desirability, *and* they are likely to be managed in a way that obscures evidence of policy failure. Once again, this political economy argument is not new, but it acquires added force in light of the dominant role of idiosyncratic determinants of business performance. To minimize job loss and business failure—thereby helping to preserve the image of a successful policy—the least successful businesses in targeted sectors often receive more generous subsidies or other forms of assistance. Absent a strong private-sector profit motive that encourages timely recognition and resolution of failed enterprises, targeted policies may lead governments to deter and delay the job losses and business failures that bring about a more efficient allocation of resources.

---

13. Arguments with a similar flavor arise in the public choice literature; see, e.g., Olson (1982) and Cohen and Noll (1991, esp. chap. 4). According to Cohen and Noll, the "distributive political costs" of program termination played an important role in continued funding for the Clinch River breeder reactor program, the space shuttle program, and the supersonic transport program long after these programs clearly failed to satisfy their original economic objectives.
14. This theme is stressed in Schultze (1993) and Dixit (1986).

7.3.3   Should the Government Pursue Targeted Commercial Policies?

The preceding analysis sets out several reasons to question the desirability of targeted commercial policies. The common thread that links the various strands in our discussion is the dominant role of idiosyncratic determinants of business performance. Some of our arguments rest directly on the importance of idiosyncratic factors, whereas other arguments acquire added force from the importance of idiosyncratic factors. We have not offered a comprehensive assessment of the potential or actual efficacy of targeted industrial and business policies. Instead, we have focused on matters that pertain to the evidence about job creation and destruction activity developed in this book.

Our limited focus neglects problems with targeted commercial policies that are nonetheless central to a full evaluation. Perhaps the most important and recalcitrant problems involve the many challenges in the political arena that confront efforts to implement economically sound policies that target specific sectors or types of firms. We have already mentioned the perverse incentives created by the government's reluctance to acknowledge mistakes and the tendency for targeted policies to engender the formation of special interest groups that undermine the application of economic efficiency criteria. In addition, targeted policy proposals invite political conflicts over the precise structure of subsidies, tax breaks, and preferential regulatory treatment. These conflicts are costly for two reasons. First, they inevitably turn into resource-consuming struggles over the redistribution of society's wealth. Second, the outcomes too often reflect the relative political strengths of the parties to the conflict rather than the economic criteria that shaped the original policy proposal.

In summary, several considerations weigh against the use of targeted industrial and business policies. First, the heterogeneity of firm behavior and our basic ignorance about the sources of this heterogeneity call into question our ability to design policies that lead to more and better jobs. Second, the dominant role of idiosyncratic factors in business performance hampers the evaluation of targeted policies. Third, the political system presents serious obstacles to the successful implementation of targeted policies, even when policy initiatives reflect sound economic analysis. These arguments do not apply with equal force to all targeted policy interventions, but they highlight the many practical barriers to the successful design, implementation, and evaluation of targeted commercial policies.

In our view, these practical problems create a presumption in favor of neutral, untargeted policies. Targeted policies should be pursued only under

compelling circumstances and with clearly articulated and well grounded rationales. When targeted policies are pursued, they should be accompanied by evaluation mechanisms that facilitate prompt recognition and resolution of failed enterprises, and a clear diagnosis of the reasons for failure.

7.4   Preferential Policy Treatment on the Basis of Employer Size

Many important examples of targeted commercial policies involve preferential treatment on the basis of employer size. Box 7.1 lists several regulatory exemptions that favor small businesses. Aside from regulatory exemptions, policy debates over proposed changes in the U.S. tax code typically give prominent play to the actual or purported concerns of small business owners. For example, both President Clinton, in his 1993 State of the Union Address, and House Minority Leader Robert Michel, in his response, appealed to concerns about small business owners.[15] In the 1994 debate over national health insurance, the impact on small businesses of mandatory health insurance was a central and contentious policy issue.[16] In view of such vigorous concern about small businesses, especially about their role in the job creation process, we take up the issue of whether small businesses merit preferential policy treatment.

The alleged job-creating prowess of small business is often advanced as an argument in favor of preferential policy treatment. Chapter 4 shows that the factual claim underlying this argument rests on fallacious and misleading interpretations of the data. We described two statistical fallacies and a common confusion between net and gross job creation that led many previous analysts to overstate the small business contribution to job creation. We also summarized some of the serious problems afflicting the most important source of data in previous studies.

Turning from methodological issues to substantive matters, we examined the connection between employer size and job creation in the U.S. manufacturing sector. We discovered that large firms and plants dominate the creation and destruction of jobs in the manufacturing sector. This finding turns out to have a simple two-part explanation. First, for employers large and small, gross job creation (and destruction) rates are quite high—on the order of 10 percent of employment per year. Second, large firms and plants account for the

---

15. See the excerpts from the speeches by Clinton and Michel reproduced in Davis, Haltiwanger, and Schuh (1993).

16. See, e.g., Blakeley (1994), Thurow (1994), Murray (1994), and Stout (1994).

bulk of the manufacturing jobs base. Because high job creation rates typify employers of all sizes, and because the manufacturing jobs base is dominated by large employers, large employers account for the bulk of job creation (and destruction).

It is true that small businesses create jobs in disproportionate numbers. That is, gross job creation rates are substantially higher for smaller plants and firms. But because gross job destruction rates are also substantially higher for smaller plants and firms, they destroy jobs in disproportionate numbers. We found no strong, systematic relationship between employer size and net job growth rates. Contrary findings in some previous studies partly reflect a bias caused by measurement procedures that suffer from the regression fallacy, as we explained in chapter 4. By replicating the flawed measurement procedures of many previous studies, chapter 4 showed that the regression fallacy introduces a large bias into the calculated relationship between employer size and job growth.[17] Finally, and in contrast to the lack of a clear-cut relationship between employer size and net job growth rates, chapter 4 presented clear evidence that larger employers offer greater job durability.

These findings disagree sharply with the conventional wisdom about job creation and employer size. One source of disagreement lies in differences between the manufacturing and nonmanufacturing sectors of the economy. Unfortunately, data limitations and flawed measurement procedures stand in the way of careful analysis of the connection between employer size and job creation in nonmanufacturing sectors. Given the attention this issue receives, and the misleading nature of the conventional wisdom, we advocate the development of better longitudinal data sets for nonmanufacturing businesses and the application of more appropriate measurement procedures.

Setting aside the questionable factual claims about the job growth performance of small businesses, our previous remarks about the misplaced focus on job creation and problems with targeted commercial policies pertain directly to the issue of preferential treatment for smaller businesses. Especially pertinent are our remarks about job quality and the limitations of simple statistics on job creation and destruction. Regarding job quality, a large body of empirical research documents that, on average, larger employers offer better wages, fringe benefits, working conditions, opportunities for skill enhancement, and

---

17. Studies of Canadian employers by Picot, Baldwin, and Dupuy (1994), of Dutch manufacturing firms by Huigen, Kleijweg, and van Leeuwen (1991), of Australian manufacturing establishments by Borland and Home (1994), and of German manufacturing firms by Wagner (1995) also find that standard measurement procedures exaggerate the relative job growth performance of smaller businesses.

job security.[18] Thus, debates about the regulatory and tax treatment of small businesses should look beyond the mere creation of jobs.

More important, even if small businesses create most new jobs, that fact by itself would not constitute a valid argument for preferential policy treatment. The relevant question is what market failure the preferential policies are expected to address. The small business sector is not obviously undersized because of product or labor market imperfections, nor does it generate obviously important spillovers for other sectors.[19]

These remarks do not deny that smaller businesses play important roles in the economy. For example, many small businesses are also young businesses experimenting with new products, technologies, marketing strategies, and business locations. Because experimentation can yield important innovations, economic policy should facilitate profitable forms of experimentation in business activity. And because experimentation may generate positive economic returns that cannot be fully appropriated by the experimenter, too little experimentation may take place in the absence of government subsidies. But these general observations do not imply that relatively too little experimentation takes place in the small business sector, or that preferential policy treatment of smaller businesses would generate more efficient rates of experimentation or other economic goods such as job creation, productivity growth, and wealth accumulation.

In principle, there may be compelling economic reasons for preferential policy treatment of any economic sector or type of firm. In practice, we are unaware of any economic analysis that convincingly justifies preferential treatment of small businesses. Furthermore, the reasons we set out above for a presumption against targeted commercial policies apply with equal force to the issue of preferential treatment of small businesses. Therefore, it is incumbent upon proponents of preferential policies toward small businesses to explain why we should set aside a general presumption against targeted policies.

We close this section with two further points. We have argued for a presumption in favor of neutral, untargeted commercial policies, including a general presumption against preferential treatment of small businesses. First, even if one accepts our arguments, it does not follow that the appropriate policy response would be a wholesale removal of regulatory exemptions and tax

---

18. Brown, Hamilton, and Medoff (1990) review much of the evidence on the connection between job quality and employer size. Chapter 4 shows that job durability rises with employer size.
19. Some studies find evidence that credit market imperfections disproportionately affect small businesses (e.g., Gertler and Gilchrist, 1994). The nature and implications of these imperfections are active research questions, but they are not closely related to most actual and proposed policies that favor smaller businesses.

breaks for smaller firms. To put it baldly, bad economic policies should not be extended to all firms simply to conform to a benchmark of neutral, untargeted policies. (Indeed, exemptions may mitigate the adverse efficiency consequences of bad economic policies.) In some cases, the appropriate policy response is to grant to all firms the same regulatory exemptions and other preferences currently enjoyed by smaller firms. Second, the costs of implementing and enforcing some government regulations may vary little with firm size, whereas the benefits increase with firm size. Consequently, the costs of regulation may exceed the benefits for sufficiently small firms, possibly justifying a regulatory exemption for small firms on economic efficiency grounds.

7.5 Laws and Policies Governing Worker and Job Flows

Many laws and economic policies purposively influence the magnitude, patterns, and costs of worker and job flows. Some policies or laws bear directly on worker flows, whereas others bear directly on job flows. In either case, because of the close connection between worker flows and job flows, these policies and laws are likely to affect the allocation of both workers and jobs.[20]

As one category of examples, many statutes and much common law governing the employment relationship influence worker flows among jobs. Statutory law now bans discrimination based on age, disability, race, or sex in hiring and firing decisions. Since 1980, key judicial rulings in many states have eroded the employment-at-will doctrine in the common law (Krueger, 1991b). Although these statutory and common law developments may yield important benefits and social goods, they also can inhibit the reallocation of workers among firms, locations, and work activities.

Other policies affect the costs of reallocating jobs and thereby influence the reallocation of workers. For example, the Worker Adjustment and Retraining Notification Act of 1988 requires sixty days' written notice of large-scale layoffs and plant closings. The costs of government mandated employee benefits—to the extent that they are not fully shifted to workers—act as a tax on employment and discourage hiring. Tax schedules in the unemployment insurance system alter the implicit cost of laying off workers. In addition, countless ad hoc policies of state and local governments use special tax breaks and subsidies to influence the location of businesses and jobs (Ferguson, 1993).

The total economic costs of the various policies that restrict or otherwise influence job and worker flows are unknown. Conceivably, some of these poli-

---

20. The introduction and chapter 1 (secs. 1 and 2) spell out the relationship between worker flows and job flows.

cies improve overall economic efficiency. Indeed, whether an unfettered market economy generates efficient rates and patterns of worker and job flows also is unknown. Inefficient wage-setting institutions, imperfect information, and the difficulties of enforcing and verifying contractual performance are potentially important reasons for inefficient job and worker flows.[21] Efforts to address these open questions would benefit enormously from the development of datasets that link workers to employers and follow both over time.

Concerns about anemic job growth in Western European economies underscore the importance of these questions. Relative to the United States, most Western European economies have experienced dismal unemployment and job growth performances since 1975. One prominent hypothesis links the greater flexibility of U.S. labor markets—in particular, milder restrictions on job and worker reallocation—to the more successful U.S. employment performance. Several studies investigate related hypotheses (e.g., Lazear, 1990; Abraham and Houseman, 1993), but data limitations stand in the way of a full and conclusive analysis. Existing studies rely heavily on highly aggregated industry-level data, which hide most of the underlying flows of workers and jobs. As we discuss in chapter 8, prospects for developing richer databases in the United States and other countries hold open the promise of developing a deeper understanding of these issues.

7.6 Worker Retraining, Relocation, and Job-Finding Programs

Recall from chapter 2 that, in an average year, between 12 and 19 percent of workers change jobs or employment status to accommodate the reshuffling of job opportunities across locations. During major recessions in the middle 1970s and early 1980s, the worker reallocation induced by job flows reached a remarkable 16 to 24 percent of employment per year. In this turbulent environment, the ability and incentive of workers to retrain, relocate, and find new jobs are crucial determinants of economic performance and well-being.

Many government programs target workers who lose jobs or have difficulty finding and holding jobs. Examples include the unemployment insurance system, the Job Training Partnership Program, the Job Corps, the Summer Youth Employment and Training Program, the Trade Adjustment Assistance Program, and various state-level "workfare" and "learnfare" programs. These programs provide income maintenance, retraining services, relocation assistance, and job-finding help.

---

21. See Ehrenberg and Jakubson (1988), Lazear (1990), Houseman (1991), Hopenhayn and Rogerson (1993), Davis (1993), and Krueger (1994) for further discussion of these issues.

With respect to these programs, the main policy-relevant empirical finding in this book is the pervasiveness of high job destruction rates. Because almost all industries and sectors exhibit high rates of job destruction, most workers face some risk of job loss. The widespread risk underscores the economic importance of a flexible workforce able to adapt to changes in the location and requirements of available jobs. Workforce flexibility, in turn, rests heavily on an educational system that turns out students with strong basic skills and problem-solving abilities.

Empirical studies of the economic returns to schooling and training find strong complementarity between formal schooling and the return to post-schooling investments (Mincer, 1962). This complementarity suggests that strong primary and secondary schools are especially critical to the development of a flexible workforce that can respond to shifting patterns of opportunity in the labor market. It may also help explain the relatively low rates of return found in most studies of public training programs that target less-skilled and poorly educated workers (Heckman et al., 1994). Complementarity between formal schooling and postschooling training implies that poorly educated workers are among the least well equipped to respond to the ongoing, large-scale job reallocation activity that characterizes the U.S. labor market.

High job destruction rates also raise concerns about public programs that train participants for narrowly focused job tasks. These programs primarily serve less-skilled individuals who have low earning capacities. With this point in mind, recall from chapter 3 that the gross job destruction rate exceeds 13 percent of employment per year in the bottom quintile of the manufacturing plant wage distribution. Although we are unaware of direct evidence, we believe that low wage jobs in other sectors exhibit similarly high rates of destruction. These high destruction rates among the types of jobs open to less-skilled workers reduce the rate of return to job-specific training.

7.7   International Trade, Job Security, and Specific Human Capital Investment

The labor market consequences of international trade occupy a prominent position in many discussions of economic policy. Although the effects of trade developments on the level and structure of wages have received much attention, and rightly so, many commentators also express concerns about the effects on employment levels and job security. These concerns were paramount in the debate over the North American Free Trade Agreement.

Measures such as import quotas, voluntary export restraints, and other trade policy interventions are often advanced in the name of protecting jobs. Our

general discussion of targeted commercial policies applies to these interventions, so we do not repeat it here. Instead, we consider the issue of whether the increasing openness of the U.S. economy threatens to undermine job security, with possibly deleterious consequences for job-specific human capital investment.

Greater international openness exposes American firms and workers to additional sources of disturbances and thus could lead to a more volatile labor market. To the extent that greater openness increases uncertainty about employment possibilities and undermines job security, it reduces the incentive for firms and workers to invest in job-specific skills (Bhagwati and Dehejia, 1993). In this way, greater openness could adversely affect job security and investment in job-specific human capital. On theoretical grounds, however, the relationship between openness and labor market volatility is ambiguous. Although international trade exposes the U.S. economy to disturbances that originate in other countries, it also insulates U.S. producers and workers from the effects of domestic disturbances to product demand. The net effect of openness on job security and labor market volatility is thus an empirical question. As a side point, even if greater openness reduces the incentive to invest in job-specific capital because of greater uncertainty, it can, for the same reason, increase the incentive to invest in general forms of human capital.

Greater openness no doubt undermines job security for some workers in some firms. But it also enhances job security for others and opens up new job opportunities. Here, we consider the overall impact of openness on job security rather than the impact on particular types of firms or workers.

Some of our evidence in chapter 3 addresses this issue in a crude way. We investigated whether industries with greater exposure to foreign competition, through either exports or imports, suffer from higher job destruction rates. We found little evidence of such an effect. Nor did we find evidence of a relationship between job destruction and increases in exposure to foreign competition from one decade to the next. Furthermore, high rates of excess job reallocation characterize virtually every manufacturing industry, regardless of exposure to foreign competition, which suggests that international openness accounts for, at most, a tiny fraction of the large-scale job reallocation activity documented in this book.

Because the evidence in chapter 3 is crude on many counts, a more careful and extensive study might reveal an important connection between international openness and the degree of job security or the extent of job reallocation activity. For example, an abrupt and pronounced increase in international openness might cause a significant transitional rise in gross job

flows that would be difficult to discern with the type of analysis in chapter 3. However, such a one-time, temporary rise in job destruction would not persistently undermine job security and the incentives to invest in job-specific human capital. Thus, in light of our preliminary analysis, we tentatively conclude that greater openness of the U.S. economy is unlikely to undermine overall job security or dampen the incentive to invest in job-specific human capital.

7.8   Aggregate Stabilization Policies

Aggregate stabilization policies seek to promote full employment, steady growth in output, and stable prices. The main tools of aggregate economic stabilization involve monetary policy, tax policy, and government expenditures—or, more simply, monetary and fiscal policy.

The wisdom and efficacy of aggregate stabilization policies are long-standing and unresolved issues. Much of the debate centers on whether the economy is self-correcting in the face of adverse economywide disturbances and, if so, the duration of the correction process. Advocates of activist stabilization policy argue that government intervention can reduce the severity of economic downturns and thereby increase economic welfare. Opponents stress the self-correcting features of the economy, and they further argue that activist policies—although well intentioned—destabilize the economy more often than not. Some opponents of activist stabilization policy argue that aggregate economic fluctuations are not symptomatic of inefficient outcomes and, therefore, that activist policy is irrelevant or harmful. Other opponents argue that mistakes or opportunistic behavior by policymakers are likely to undermine the potential efficiency gains of activist stabilization policy.[22]

Most arguments about stabilization policy take place in the context of highly aggregative economic models populated by representative firms and households. These representative agent models abstract from the heterogeneity of workers and firms, and downplay the reallocation of jobs, workers, capital, and other inputs across locations and activities. In the context of these models, advocates of activist stabilization policy argue that stimulating aggregate demand during an economic downturn speeds the economy's recovery to full employment and rapid output growth. According to this view, a stimulative aggregate demand intervention (e.g., more expansionary monetary policy or a

---

22. Most textbooks on macroeconomics discuss alternative views about aggregate stabilization policy at some length.

reduction in taxes) generates an increase in the demand for the typical firm's output and the typical worker's labor.

The evidence in chapters 2, 5, and 6 on the connection between restructuring activity and business cycles raises several questions about this line of argument and, more fundamentally, about the entire framing of the debate over aggregate stabilization policies. Some examples of these questions follow shortly.

In posing these questions, we deliberately adopt the broad term "restructuring activity," although this book's evidence directly pertains only to worker and job reallocation activity. As we use the term, "restructuring activity" also encompasses the redeployment of physical capital among locations and uses, plus the destruction and creation of information capital embodied in worker-employer matches, creditor-debtor relationships, customer-seller relationships, and the internal organization of business enterprises. Measuring these types of knowledge and organizational capital and their variation over time is difficult, but we suspect that their time variation is important and closely connected to the business cycle. In any case, although the following questions are suggested by our empirical evidence on job and worker flows, our interest in them also reflects the broader significance of cyclical variation in a wider range of restructuring activities.

• If business cycle slumps accelerate the pace of restructuring in the economy, as the evidence in chapters 5 and 6 strongly suggests, do stimulative monetary and fiscal policies delay economic restructuring?

• As a closely related question, to what extent does the apparent impact of stimulative policies simply reflect a delay in restructuring and reallocation activity? Does any such delay sow the seeds for a more severe economic downturn in the future?

• If stimulative policies temporarily delay the pace of economic restructuring, do they thereby alter the economy's longer-term growth prospects? If so, in what direction?

• Are the pace, timing, and pattern of restructuring activity economically efficient? If not, can the efficiency of the restructuring process be improved by aggregate stabilization policies? By some other set of policies?

• Does the efficacy of stimulative policies hinge on whether the economy has already entered a phase of intense restructuring activity? If so, then accurate recognition and forecasting of business cycle developments and timely policy responses become even more important.

• Do the efficacy and desirability of stimulative policies hinge on whether aggregate or allocative disturbances drive a particular business cycle episode? If so, then the accurate and timely diagnosis of the driving forces behind aggregate fluctuations becomes crucial for the determination of appropriate policy responses.

To illustrate the practical importance of some of these questions, we sketch out a speculative interpretation of U.S. macroeconomic performance during the 1970s and early 1980s. During the 1970s, the U.S. economy was buffeted by a series of large, exogenous shocks: the winding down of U.S. involvement in the Vietnam war, a dramatic increase in oil prices, and a rapid growth of international trade. These events seemingly set the stage for high rates of permanent job reallocation and an unusually intense period of restructuring in the U.S. economy. To some extent, an accelerated restructuring took place during the recession of 1974–75, as job reallocation rates rose sharply, but table 2.4 reports that the permanence of the job destruction that occurred between 1974 and 1975 was unusually low. More generally, the table reveals that job destruction persistence rates during the latter half of the 1970s were five to twenty percentage points lower than in the 1980s. Thus, despite being buffeted by large exogenous shocks with seemingly important allocative consequences, plant-level job destruction in the 1970s showed much less permanence than in the 1980s.[23]

Perhaps the relative impermanence of plant-level job destruction in the 1970s was brought about by the highly stimulative monetary policy of the 1976–79 period. Interestingly, when the United States sustained a contractionary monetary policy during the early 1980s to fight inflation, the economy fell into a deep recession characterized by very high gross job destruction rates. The permanence of job destruction also rose during the early 1980s and remained high for the rest of the decade. The evidence on unemployment flows in chapter 6 tells a similar story. Permanent layoffs accounted for 65 percent of the peak-to-trough increase in unemployment during the 1981–82 recession but only 40 percent in the 1974–75 recession. In our view, a key economic and policy question is whether the unusual intensity and permanence of job and worker flows during the early 1980s reflected the consequences of pent-up restructuring activity that had been delayed by stimulative stabilization policies during the second half of the 1970s. Our case study of the steel industry in

---

23. However, plant-level job creation behavior does not show a pattern of greater permanence in the 1980s, at least as measured by the one-year and two-year persistence rates reported in table 2.4.

chapter 5 prompted us to pose essentially the same question for a particular industry.

This brief account of worker and job flow activity during the 1970s and 1980s also points out how the nature and intensity of restructuring activity vary across business cycle episodes. Statistics on both job and worker flows indicate that permanent reallocation activity was more important in the 1981–82 recession than in any period during the 1970s, including the 1974–75 recession. This sort of difference complicates the real-time diagnosis of aggregate economic circumstances, the analysis of economic fluctuations, and the determination of appropriate policy responses under a regime of activist stabilization.

Another issue is the extent to which monetary and fiscal policies drive not just the timing but also the magnitude and pattern of reallocation activity. Monetary policy disproportionately affects credit-sensitive sectors and firms. Taxes and government expenditures can have sharply different effects on different regions, industries, and types of firms. For example, the level and spatial distribution of military expenditures play an important role as driving forces behind regional business cycles (Davis, Loungani, and Mahidhara, 1994). California's relatively sharp cyclical downturn and slow economic recovery during the early 1990s are often linked to defense cutbacks.[24] These observations prompt us to ask how much of job reallocation and its variation over time is induced by the fluctuating "tastes" of economic policymakers. Coupled with detailed information on government expenditures and contract awards, job creation and destruction statistics, broken down by industry, regions, and firms, could be used to evaluate the role of policy shocks as driving forces behind job and worker flows and economic restructuring.

---

24. See, e.g., the report in the *Los Angeles Times* of Dec. 16, 1993, on a study by the UCLA Business Forecasting Project of the role of defense cutbacks.

8

A Postscript on Prospects for
Data Development

In the preceding chapters, we constructed a statistical portrait of job flows and their connection to worker flows. We applied the statistical portrait to inform our thinking about the economy and to develop several points about economic policy. These economic and policy lessons illustrate the usefulness of our statistical portrait, and, taken as a whole, they constitute an argument for developing other longitudinal business-level databases that permit more timely, comprehensive, and detailed measures of job creation and destruction. This chapter discusses possible paths toward that objective. Our most important points fall into four categories:

• **Comprehensive gross job flow statistics:** *Two administrative record databases merit serious consideration as comprehensive sources of gross job flow statistics on manufacturing and nonmanufacturing industries: the Standard Statistical Establishment List (SSEL) maintained by the Bureau of the Census and the 202 dataset maintained by the Bureau of Labor Statistics (BLS).*

• **Virtues of the SSEL and 202:** *The SSEL and 202 data permit gross job flow statistics broken down by employer size, four-digit industry, and detailed geographic area. The SSEL more adequately distinguishes between establishments and enterprises, and it offers the prospect of linking job flows to the employer characteristics measured in other Census Bureau business surveys. The 202 dataset permits more timely statistical releases, and it offers the prospect of linking job flows to the employer characteristics measured in BLS establishment surveys.*

• **Linked job and worker flows:** *The administrative records maintained by state unemployment insurance agencies could be used to construct a national linked employer-worker database. This database would make it possible to measure gross worker and job flows simultaneously and to relate these flows to industry, location, employer size, worker wages, and other characteristics of employers and workers.*

• *Data-sharing arrangements: Cooperative arrangements to share survey and administrative record data on individual businesses would greatly enhance the value of both Census and BLS data as tools for economic research and policy evaluation. Data-sharing arrangements would also lead to improvements in the statistical sampling frames used by each bureau and to greater accuracy in published economic statistics.*

In the ensuing discussion, we limit attention to the potential uses of existing administrative record databases because they offer an inexpensive means of constructing statistics on gross job flows. Within that constraint, our discussion ranges from general remarks about methods for measuring gross flows to specific remarks about the advantages and disadvantages of particular data sources. The specific remarks serve to delineate reasonable objectives for data construction and to highlight some of the issues that must be confronted in developing longitudinal business-level databases.

8.1 The Standard Statistical Establishment List

The Standard Statistical Establishment List (SSEL) merits serious consideration as a comprehensive source of statistics on annual gross job flows. It is the master establishment list for all businesses in the United States with at least one employee. The Bureau of the Census maintains the SSEL using Internal Revenue Service and Social Security Administration administrative records and drawing heavily on information contained in its own annual Company Organization Survey (COS). Currently, the Bureau of the Census uses the SSEL to define the statistical sampling frame for its many economic censuses and surveys of individual businesses.[1] Initial efforts to construct gross job flow statistics from the SSEL have been under way at the Bureau of the Census since 1993.

The SSEL offers important advantages as a potential source of job creation and destruction statistics. First, as with the LRD, establishments (i.e., physical locations) constitute the units of observation. Second, the SSEL is suitable for tracking individual establishments over time in a way that correctly treats mergers, births and deaths, and transfers of ownership and control. These strengths of the SSEL stem in large part from its reliance on the Company Organization Survey.

---

1. The Bureau of the Census (1979) describes the use of the SSEL as a sampling frame for Census surveys.

The COS provides information about the ownership and operational control of production and nonproduction facilities, information that enables the Census Bureau to distinguish between establishments and enterprises.[2] Thus, the SSEL offers the promise of circumventing the spurious linkage problems that potentially compromise efforts to track individual establishments through time, to distinguish between establishments and enterprises, and to measure gross job flows accurately.[3] As our discussion in the technical appendix makes clear, spurious job flows can arise when longitudinal links are incorrectly broken because of simple processing errors or because of changes in ownership, corporate status, business name or address, or taxpayer/employer identification number.

The SSEL contains annual data on employment and payroll plus information on location, industry, and establishment age. The SSEL for any given year becomes available in the subsequent year, so that gross job flow statistics by detailed industry, state, local area, establishment and enterprise size, establishment and enterprise wage level, and establishment age could be made available on a yearly basis with a lag of approximately nine to twelve months. In addition, the SSEL could be linked to the many business censuses and surveys conducted by the Bureau of the Census. In this way, it would be feasible to provide gross job flow statistics broken down by a wealth of other establishment and enterprise characteristics, including sales, investment, input usage, inventories, international trade involvement, and technology usage.

8.2 The Bureau of Labor Statistics 202 Dataset

The Bureau of Labor Statistics (BLS) 202 dataset also merits serious consideration as a comprehensive source of gross job flow statistics for the U.S. economy. It contains quarterly employment and payroll records on all businesses subject to unemployment insurance (UI) laws. The 202 dataset serves as the statistical sampling frame for most BLS establishment surveys (Manser,

---

2. In the SSEL, as in the LRD, an enterprise is either a single establishment owned and operated by a single-unit firm or the set of establishments under the ownership and operational control of the same firm. See Bureau of the Census (1979) for a discussion of how the COS is used to maintain the SSEL.

3. The SSEL contains a variety of establishment and enterprise identifiers (e.g., the Census Bureau identification number, the federal taxpayer identification number, and the permanent plant number [PPN]) that facilitate longitudinal and cross-sectional linkages. Other information in the SSEL, such as company and establishment names, street addresses, detailed industry and location codes, can be used to verify the linkages and enhance their quality. See Bureau of the Census (1979) for a discussion of how the various identifiers in the SSEL are created.

1994). Thus, the 202 dataset closely parallels the SSEL in scope, content, and use as a sample frame. Several researchers have used UI-based data from selected states to create longitudinal files and analyze job flow behavior.[4]

There are two main drawbacks to using UI-based data to measure gross job flows. First, UI reporting units do not correspond precisely to either establishments or enterprises (or any other economic concept of the firm). A UI reporting unit may represent an establishment, an enterprise, a division of an enterprise, one payroll office of an enterprise, or all or some establishments owned by the same firm and located within the same state. In addition, firms can and do change the way in which they report payroll information to UI offices. Because of nonlinearities and the use of experience rating in the UI tax structure, firms may have incentives to change their reporting patterns over time.[5]

A second and related drawback to UI-based data arises from the lack of standardization in reporting practices among states. Although efforts to achieve greater standardization are ongoing, the absence of full standardization is likely to slow progress in clearly identifying establishments and enterprises, in constructing accurate longitudinal linkages, and in developing operational procedures for accurately measuring and reporting gross job flow statistics.

Two important advantages of the BLS 202 dataset, relative to the SSEL, are its greater timeliness and greater frequency. Quarterly employment and wage records become available approximately five months after the close of the quarter (Manser, 1994). Thus, quarterly gross job flow statistics computed from 202 data could be released on a quarterly rather than a yearly basis and with a shorter time lag than statistics calculated from the SSEL.

Another advantage of UI-based data is the possibility of generating monthly statistics on gross job flows, either directly from the 202 data or by linking the monthly BLS 790 data to the 202 data.[6] Thus, in principle UI-based data could be used to generate monthly gross flows on a comprehensive,

---

4. See Leonard (1987), Troske (1993), Lane, Isaac, and Stevens (1993), and Anderson and Meyer (1994).
5. Many previous users of UI-based data have recognized these problems. Some researchers have used information in the UI files to distinguish ownership transfers from births and deaths. Some researchers have also used taxpayer employer identification numbers in an attempt to construct firm-level data from UI records. Unfortunately, the taxpayer employer identification number does not have a precise or stable mapping to an economic concept of the firm. Efforts to address the reporting unit problem with UI data are under way at the BLS; see Armington (1991).
6. The BLS 790 dataset provides monthly employment observations on a sample of establishments covered by the UI system. According to Manser (1994), the BLS 202 also now provides monthly data.

timely basis, broken down by industry and geographic area. For policymakers (e.g., the monetary authorities) and business forecasters who rely heavily on high-frequency, real-time economic indicators, reporting monthly gross job flow statistics with a short lag would be of great interest. Monthly gross job flow data would also be useful in research on business cycles and other topics.

8.3   A National Wage Records Database

Another advantage of UI-based data involves prospects for simultaneously measuring worker and job flows from a longitudinal database that links workers to employers. In addition to the employer records that enter into the BLS 202 dataset, the individual states maintain quarterly earnings records for individuals at UI-covered firms to assess eligibility and compute benefit amounts for UI claimants.[7] These records contain information suitable for following individuals over time and for identifying their employers. A current BLS initiative is considering how these records might be combined into a National Wage Records Database (NWRD) that would be useful for measuring job flows, worker flows, and related concepts.[8]

Unlike the SSEL and the BLS 202 data, the NWRD offers the prospect of comprehensive statistics on job flows *and* worker flows. Because individual workers could be linked to individual employers, this database also offers much greater scope for describing and analyzing the connection between worker and job flows.[9] In addition, a wealth of information in the many BLS employer surveys could be linked to the NWRD and used to shed additional insight on the behavior of worker flows and job flows.[10]

The NWRD would be constructed from the same data collection system as the BLS 202 data. Consequently, it would be subject to the same cross-sectional and longitudinal linkage problems as the 202 data. Relative to its enormous value as a tool for research and policy analysis, however, these shortcomings of a UI-based, longitudinal employer-worker dataset are minor.

---

7. The states also maintain individual-level files that track UI claims and benefit payments.

8. This initiative was the focus of an April 1994 BLS conference held in Washington, D.C.

9. Two sets of researchers have already used the type of data envisioned for the NWRD to simultaneously measure worker and job flows. See Lane, Isaac, and Stevens (1993) and Anderson and Meyer (1994). Both studies expand our knowledge of labor market dynamics, and they demonstrate the feasibility and value of using a UI-based, linked employer-worker database as a research tool.

10. Manser (1994) summarizes the many surveys of labor market behavior carried out by the BLS.

8.4   Possibilities and Practicalities

The preceding discussion makes clear that administrative data already exist at both the Bureau of the Census and the Bureau of Labor Statistics that could be used to measure gross job flows in a timely, comprehensive, and detailed manner. Converting these administrative records into operational longitudinal data files would require considerable effort and resources, but the costs would be small relative to alternative approaches that require major new surveys or other data sources.

The administrative records data at the BLS and Census offer distinct advantages and disadvantages that reflect differences in the history and mission of the two bureaus. Data at the Bureau of the Census offer greater scope for spelling out the connection between job flows and employer characteristics. Data at the BLS offer the prospect of directly linking job flows to worker flows and worker characteristics.

Ideally, data from both bureaus would be combined so as to link job flows to employer characteristics, worker flows, and worker characteristics simultaneously. Although the current institutional structure of the statistical bureaus stands in the way of efforts to pool data resources, we strongly advocate cooperative agreements and mechanisms that facilitate the sharing of survey and administrative record data on individual businesses. Such data-sharing arrangements would greatly enhance the value of both Census and BLS data as tools for economic research and policy evaluation. By providing each bureau with an alternative business universe, data-sharing arrangements would also facilitate the identification of problems with existing statistical sampling frames and, over time, lead to improvements in the accuracy of published statistics.[11]

---

11. Manser (1994, p. 25) also remarks upon the potential benefits of data-sharing arrangements between the Census and BLS.

Technical Appendix

The Longitudinal Research Database (LRD) contains data that permit construction of high-quality job creation and destruction measures for the U.S. manufacturing sector from 1972 to 1988.[1] It includes longitudinal data for more than 160,000 manufacturing plants and their parent firms. These plants comprise a representative sample, so that aggregate LRD statistics are unbiased estimates of the manufacturing universe.

Employment data in the LRD are quarterly and annual, and they distinguish between production workers and nonproduction workers. Information about plant characteristics such as age, size, product specialization, and average worker wage are readily available. Although other sources of U.S. data exist from which job creation and destruction statistics can be calculated, none combines breadth, depth, and statistical integrity as well as the LRD does.

This technical appendix describes in detail the LRD; our methodology for constructing gross job creation, destruction, and related measures; and important issues for potential users of the data. The eight sections are largely self-contained, so that the reader may dip into the text as needed. Generally speaking, the sections appear in reverse order of their importance for data users. We strongly urge all data users to read sections 7 and 8, and we recommend 5 and 6 as well.

Sections 1 through 4 deal with the LRD and details of measurement. These sections are directed toward (1) researchers who use the LRD in other studies, (2) those who wish to compare LRD-based gross job flow statistics to similar measures constructed from other data sources, and (3) those who wish to construct gross job flow statistics. Sections 5 and 6 describe some characteristics

---

1. The LRD continually expands in time-series dimension. Data for 1989–91 became available during the writing of this book, but were not adequately prepared in time to generate gross job flow statistics.

of LRD-based statistics, knowledge of which will be useful to many users of our job creation and destruction measures. Sections 7 and 8 contain essential information for users of these measures.

The eight sections may be summarized in more detail as follows:

1. **Theoretical concepts:** presenting the notation and equations underlying the measures introduced and defined in chapters 1 and 2.

2. **The LRD:** describing the contents of the LRD and the statistical design of the two surveys that produce the data contained in the LRD.

3. **Raw data adjustments:** describing the adjustments made to the raw LRD data before constructing the gross job flow measures.

4. **Measurement methodology:** presenting the methodology used to construct the gross job flow measures.

5. **Statistical precision:** describing the methodology for measuring the standard errors of the aggregate gross job flow data and providing estimates of those errors.

6. **Published versus sample data:** analyzing the difference between the aggregate LRD statistics and the published statistics in the Census of Manufactures and Annual Survey of Manufactures.

7. **Sector definitions:** containing detailed descriptions of all the sectoral classifications for which the gross job flow data are available.

8. **Data usage:** describing the gross job flow data files (available on diskette) and how to use them; also providing guidance on important issues and limitations associated with using the data.

The appendix concludes with instructions for obtaining the gross job flows data from the Center for Economic Studies of the U.S. Bureau of the Census.

A.1   Theoretical Concepts

Before presenting theoretical concepts, we establish a few notational conventions. Variables have as many as three subscripts: the letter e denotes the establishment or plant; the letter s denotes the sector to which the establishment belongs, such as industry or region; and the letter t denotes the time period.[2] Capital letters E and S refer to a set of establishments or sectors, respectively.

---

2. If the sector classification is multidimensional, then the subscript s represents the most disaggregated sector, e.g., industry by region. When it is necessary to distinguish among multiple sectors, another subscript is added. For annual data t refers to year. For quarterly data, t refers to year and (q) denotes quarter.

In referring to employment, job creation, job destruction, and related measures, we use uppercase letters to denote levels, and we use lowercase letters to denote rates (i.e., levels normalized by a measure of size). The symbol Δ denotes the first-difference operator, such as $\Delta X_t = X_t - X_{t-1}$.

A.1.1 Gross Job Creation, Destruction, and Reallocation

When employment at a plant increases, the increase is called job creation; when employment at a plant decreases, the decrease is called job destruction. Gross job creation is the sum of all new jobs at expanding and newly born plants; gross job destruction is the sum of all lost jobs at contracting and dying plants. Formally, gross job creation in sector s at time t is

$$C_{st} = \sum_{e \in S^+} \Delta X_{est}, \tag{1}$$

and gross job destruction is

$$D_{st} = \sum_{e \in S^-} |\Delta X_{est}|, \tag{2}$$

where X denotes employment, and the superscripts $+$ and $-$ indicate the subset of plants in the sector that expand and contract, respectively.[3]

Job creation and destruction can be expressed as rates by dividing by a measure of sector size. Plant size, Z_{est}, is the average of employment in periods t and $t - 1$:

$$Z_{est} = 0.5(X_{est} + X_{es,t-1}), \tag{3}$$

and the corresponding plant-level employment growth rate is

$$g_{est} = \Delta X_{est} / Z_{est}. \tag{4}$$

Sectoral rates of gross job creation and destruction are size-weighted sums of plant-level growth rates:

$$c_{st} = \frac{C_{st}}{Z_{st}} = \sum_{e \in S^+} \left(\frac{Z_{est}}{Z_{st}} \right) g_{est} \tag{5}$$

---

3. The C and D notation corresponds to the *POS* and *NEG* notation used in other research by the authors. See Davis and Haltiwanger (1990, 1992) and Davis, Haltiwanger, and Schuh (1990).

and

$$d_{st} = \frac{D_{st}}{Z_{st}} = \sum_{e \in S^-} \left(\frac{Z_{est}}{Z_{st}} \right) |g_{est}| . \tag{6}$$

Unlike the conventional growth rate measure, G, which divides employment change by lagged employment and ranges from -1.0 to $+\infty$, our growth rate measure, g, ranges from -2.0 to $+2.0$ and portrays expansion and contraction symmetrically. Thus, for example, plant startups and shutdowns have growth rates of $+2.0$ and -2.0 rather than $+\infty$ and -1.0. The two growth rate measures are monotonically related according to the identity

$$G \equiv 2g/(2 - g) , \tag{7}$$

and numerical values of the two growth rate measures are approximately equal for rates that are small in absolute value.

The gross job reallocation rate equals the sum of the creation and destruction rates:

$$r_{st} = c_{st} + d_{st} . \tag{8}$$

The level, R, is defined analogously. These job reallocation measures have several useful interpretations. First, $R_t = Z_t \times r_t$ equals the gross change from $t - 1$ to t in the number of employment positions at establishments. Second, R is an upper bound on the number of workers who must switch jobs or employment status to accommodate the redistribution of employment positions across plants, as discussed more fully in chapter 1. Third, r equals the size-weighted mean of the absolute value of establishment-level growth rates. Accordingly, it can be interpreted as a statistical measure of dispersion in establishment-level employment growth rates.

A.1.2   Net Job Creation

Gross job creation and destruction are related to the net change in employment, or net job creation, by the simple formula

$$net_{st} = c_{st} - d_{st} = \left(\frac{\Delta X_{st}}{Z_{st}} \right) . \tag{9}$$

In other words, gross job creation and destruction decompose the aggregate net employment change, ΔX_{st}, into one component associated with growing plants and a second component associated with shrinking plants.

Net job creation also equals the size-weighted sum of plant growth rates, which by substituting equations 5 and 6 into equation 9 is

$$net_{st} = \sum_{e \in S} \left(\frac{Z_{est}}{Z_{st}} \right) g_{est} .$$

(10)

The measure *net* is frequently analyzed when studying labor market behavior because it is typically the only measure of job change available. But *net* conceals important heterogeneity and asymmetry in creation and destruction rates, as shown throughout this book.

At the plant level, however, equations 1 and 2 (*C* and *D*) are measures of *net* job creation, just as equation 10 is net at the sectoral level. The reason is that plant-level employment change does not include the total number of jobs created and destroyed within the plant between sampling dates. Since the LRD does not identify individual jobs at a plant, some newly created and newly destroyed jobs may not show up as plant-level employment changes. For example, a plant may destroy ten assembler jobs and create ten robotics technician jobs, so that total employment does not change. In this respect, *C* and *D* understate the true levels of gross job creation and destruction.

A.1.3   Persistence of Job Creation and Destruction

We define the persistence of job creation (destruction) in period t as the fraction of jobs created (destroyed) in period t that continue to exist (not exist) through period $t + j$ at the same establishments. To be precise, consider the following counting rule for an expanding or new establishment at time t: (1) if $X_{es,t+j} \geq X_{es,t}$, then all of the new jobs at e in period t are said to be present in $t + j$; (2) if $X_{es,t+j} \leq X_{es,t-1}$, then none of the new jobs at e in period t are present in $t + j$; (3) if $X_{es,t+j} \in [X_{es,t-1}, X_{est}]$, then $(X_{es,t+j} - X_{es,t-1})$ of the new jobs at e in t are present in $t + j$.

In accordance with this rule, let $\delta_{est}(j)$ be the number of jobs newly created at establishment e in period t that are present in period $t + j$, and let $P^c_{est}(j) = min\{\delta_{est}(1), \delta_{est}(2), \ldots, \delta_{est}(j)\}$. In words, $P^c_{est}(j)$ equals the number of jobs newly created at establishment e in period t that remain present in all periods from $t + 1$ through $t + j$. Summing $P^c_{est}(j)$ over all new and expanding establishments at time t, and dividing by gross job creation at t, yields our measure of the j-period persistence rate for jobs created at t:

$$p^c_{st}(j) = \sum_{e \in S^+_t} \frac{P^c_{est}(j)}{C_{st}} .$$

(11)

Using analogous definitions and notation, the j-period persistence rate for jobs destroyed at t is given by

$$p_{st}^d(j) = \sum_{e \in S_t^-} \frac{P_{est}^d(j)}{D_{st}}. \tag{12}$$

A.2 The Longitudinal Research Database (LRD)

The LRD contains historical data from two Census Bureau economic surveys of the manufacturing sector: the Census of Manufactures (CM), conducted quinquenially in years ending in 2 and 7 (e.g., 1982, 1987), and the Annual Survey of Manufactures (ASM). Both collect calendar year and some quarterly economic data from manufacturing plants, and they identify plants' corporate affiliations.

However, there are two important differences between the surveys. First, Census conducts the CM for the universe of plants, but conducts the ASM only for a probability-based sample of plants. Sample weights for the ASM permit estimation of the CM levels in noncensus years. Second, the scope of data collected in the two surveys differs; each survey collects some data items that the other does not. The scope of the employment data is the same in both surveys.

A.2.1 Longitudinality

The LRD links plant-level data from the CM and the ASM over the period 1963 through 1988. It includes CM data for 1963, 1967, 1972, 1977, 1982, and 1987, and ASM data from 1972 through 1988.[4] This study constructs quarterly and annual job creation and destruction measures from ASM data.[5] The annual portion of the LRD contains about 1 million observations for more than 160,000 plants. Table A.1 lists the subset of CM and ASM variables in the LRD used to construct the gross job creation and destruction data.[6]

Two variables play key roles in linking plants and companies over time. The first, the permanent plant number (*PPN*), is the one that allows the LRD

---

4. The first CM contained in the LRD was conducted in 1963 rather than 1962.
5. Dunne, Roberts, and Samuelson (1989a) contains quinquennial measures of gross job creation and destruction. Although the five-year CM rates of creation and destruction are smaller, their time-series and cross-section properties are largely consistent with those of the annual and quarterly measures.
6. More complete details of the LRD contents appear in McGuckin and Pascoe (1988).

Table A.1
Variables in the Longitudinal Research Database Used to Construct Job Creation and Destruction Data

Variable	Description
AR	Administrative record (CM only)
BAE	Building assets (end of year)
CC	Coverage code
CF	Cost of fuels
COU	County
EE	Cost of purchased electricity
ET	Establishment type (CM only)
ID	Census identification number
IND	Four-digit industry (1987 SIC basis, CM only)
MAE	Machinery assets (end of year)
OE	Other employment
OIND	Original four-digit industry (current-year SIC basis, 1972 or 1987)
OW	Other worker wages
PH	Production worker hours
PH1	Production worker hours, Q1
PH2	Production worker hours, Q2
PH3	Production worker hours, Q3
PH4	Production worker hours, Q4
PPN	Permanent plant number
PPSR	Primary product specialization ratio
PW	Production worker employment
PW1	Production worker employment, Q1
PW2	Production worker employment, Q2
PW3	Production worker employment, Q3
PW4	Production worker employment, Q4
REG	Census region
SMSA	Standard metropolitan statistical area
ST	State
SW	Total salaries and wages (WW + OW)
TE	Total employment (PW + OE)
TVS	Total value of shipments
WT	Sample weight (ASM only)
WW	Production worker wages

Note: Data are from the *Census of Manufactures* (CM) and *Annual Survey of Manufactures* (ASM). All variables are annual unless otherwise noted. Quarters are denoted by a ''Q'' followed by a number 1-4 (for example, Q1).

to be longitudinal. The *PPN* is a ten-digit number that Census assigns to a plant and physical location, and it remains the same throughout the life of the plant.[7] Therefore, although the CM and ASM are often conceived of as cross-sectional surveys, longitudinal data for the plants in these surveys can be constructed by using the *PPN* number to link plant-level data across consecutive surveys. The second key variable is the Census identification number (*ID*), a ten-digit number that identifies the enterprise, or parent company, that owns the plant. (The first six digits of the *ID* identify the parent company, and the last four digits, the plant itself.) If a plant is sold by its parent company to another company, for example, the *PPN* remains the same but the *ID* changes.

A company, or enterprise, in the LRD is defined as follows: "The enterprise is the entire economic unit consisting of one or more establishments under common ownership or control. It may vary in composition from a single legal entity (e.g., corporation, partnership, individual proprietorship) with only one establishment to the most aggregative level of business organization, as a complex family of legal entities (and their constituent establishments) under common ownership or control." Common ownership or control in multiunit companies is determined from the Census Bureau's annual Company Organization Survey. For more details about definitions of plants (establishments) and companies (enterprises), see Bureau of the Census (1979, esp. p. 12).

A.2.2 ASM Sampling and Panels

An important characteristic of the ASM for the longitudinal properties of the LRD is the rotating panel of plants in the survey. An ASM panel contains a sample of plants drawn from the universe of plants identified by the CM (excluding certain small plants). ASM sample plants represent about one-seventh to one-fifth of all manufacturing plants and three-fourths of total manufactur-

---

7. In practice, though, many plants' *PPN*s changed across time, for two reasons. First, prior to 1987 there were more than 48,000 occurrences of incorrect *PPN* changes. Second, in 1987 Census changed the manner in which it issued (numbered) *PPN*s and began issuing new *PPN*s that were already in use prior to 1987. This numbering change forced the vast majority of *PPN*s to require reassignment each year throughout the LRD sample period (typically two-thirds or more). Tim Dunne, Cyr Linonis, and Jim Monahan of the Center for Economic Studies conducted a massive multiyear project to reassign *PPN*s throughout the LRD, which reestablished accurate plant-level linkages and preserved the longitudinality of the LRD.

The gross job creation and destruction data reported in this volume were constructed from the newly linked LRD data. However, the data constructed from the incorrectly linked LRD data did not differ dramatically—in particular, they contained the same four common characteristics described in chapter 2.

ing employment. Large plants, usually those with 250 or more employees, are selected with certainty for all ASM panels. Plants with 5 to 249 employees are selected randomly, with selection probabilities inversely related to size. (Details of the sampling procedure appear in section A.5.) These randomly selected plants are called noncertainty plants.[8] A new ASM panel begins two years after the CM from which it was drawn and lasts five years. Random sampling and federal regulations limiting the burden of survey response by small plants cause the composition of plants to change between ASM panels.

Two significant changes in the ASM sample selection procedure occurred during the period covered by the LRD. The first pertained to the definition of the sampling unit. Before 1979, the parent company served as the sampling unit. If Census selected a company (using probabilities derived from company size), then all plants belonging to that company entered the ASM panel. Since 1979, however, the plant has been the sampling unit. Only the plants selected (using probabilities derived from plant size) enter the panel, regardless of the status of other plants in the company. Census switched to the plant-based sampling scheme because it requires fewer plants to achieve the same estimation efficiency.

The second major sampling change altered the nature of the sample weights. Since 1963, Census has excused certain small, single-unit plants (i.e., the company has only one plant) from completing the CM in order to reduce respondent burden. These plants, known as administrative records (AR), represent about one-third of the manufacturing universe of approximately 350,000 plants and about 4 to 7 percent of manufacturing employment.[9] From 1972 through 1978, the sample weights generated for the noncertainty, non-AR plants accounted for the presence of AR plants in the economy. Beginning in 1979, however, the sample weights no longer accounted for the presence of AR plants, so it became necessary to estimate, or impute, AR plant data independently. This independently imputed estimate is discussed in sections A.5 and A.6.

---

8. Prior to 1979, the plant's company was used to determine certain inclusion in the ASM panel. A company was a certainty if (1) any plant in the company had 250 or more total employees (called a TE certainty); or (2) after removing (1), the sample variance within the five-digit product class was too large and it was necessary to add more companies (called an analytical certainty). Beginning in 1979, a plant was a certainty if (1) it was a TE certainty; or (2) it belonged to a company with $500 million or more in total value of shipments (called a company certainty); or (3) after removing (1) and (2), it was deemed an analytical certainty; or (4) it did not satisfy (1)–(3) in the CM but it did satisfy one of them at some time during the ASM panel.

9. In 1972, all single-unit plants with fewer than ten total employees were AR plants; in 1977, 1982, and 1987 the cutoff depended on payroll levels and varied across industries, but it implied a cutoff of about five TE in most industries.

A.2.3   Sample Frame Maintenance

To offset exit from the ASM panel and to account for plant entry into the universe, the Census Bureau adds two types of plants to the panel each year. One type is new plants started by multiplant companies. These births are identified by the Company Organization Survey. A second type is single-unit plant births identified from Social Security Administration listings of new employer identification numbers. The precise treatment of plant births, and the rules governing their inclusion in an ongoing panel, vary over time.[10]

Prior to 1979, a third type of plant also could enter an ongoing ASM panel as a consequence of a corporate acquisition. Recall that in this period, all plants belonging to an ASM company appeared in the panel. Consequently, if an ASM company acquired a plant from a non-ASM company, the plant would be added to the panel. Plant additions due to mergers and acquisitions are unnecessary for sample frame maintenance, and they actually led the LRD data to slightly overestimate total manufacturing employment in the later years of the 1974 panel (see section A.6).

The LRD is well suited to accurate measurement of plant startups and shutdowns during the life of a panel. The database contains information, such as the PPN, ID, and coverage code (CC), that permits accurate distinction of startups and shutdowns from spurious plant entry and exit from the panel. The CC variable, described in detail in section A.4, provides information regarding why the plant did or did not appear in current or contiguous years.[11]

Some timing difficulties arise, however, regarding births and shutdowns. Most births appear in the ASM panel for the first time in the year following

---

10. Births in multi-unit companies before 1979 entered the ASM panel if the company belonged to the panel, and the birth received the company sample weight. In 1979 and 1980, these multi-unit births received a sample weight using the same process as noncertainty plants, and were sampled randomly. Since 1981 all multi-unit births have entered the panel with certainty (sample weight one). Before 1979, single-unit births with 100 or more TE entered with certainty (sample weight equals one) and all others were sampled randomly using the sample weights described in the text. From 1979 to 1988, single-unit births with 35 or more TE entered with certainty, and all others were added to the imputed data associated with the AR plants—unless a plant grew large enough during the panel to mandate certain inclusion. Beginning in 1989, all single-unit births with five or more TE entered with certainty (sample weight one).

11. One example of spurious entry and exit that troubles other longitudinal data bases is the change in the EI number. The EI number, which is sometimes used to link business units in creating a longitudinal data base, may change over time for noneconomic reasons such as changes in plant ownership, names of plants or firms, and firms' tax-filing status. In practice, the Census Bureau finds that about one-third of all new EI numbers are true births and therefore eligible for entry into the ASM panel.

the actual birth year. For annual data (constructed from March *TE*), the extent of timing mismeasurement is minimal because births that occur after March 12 are properly timed with respect to March employment figures. For quarterly data, however, both births and shutdowns are subject to a mistiming of as much as several months. Fortunately, this type of measurement error can be corrected or greatly mitigated by using the quarterly birth and shutdown retiming methodology described in section A.4.

A.3 Adjusting the Raw Data

Some of the key LRD variables are not fully satisfactory for the purpose of measuring gross job creation and destruction. Four types of problems arise. First, the definition of annual employment in the raw LRD data combines time-averaged and point-in-time data. Second, first-quarter employment data reflect employment in the third, rather than second, month of the quarter. Third, some essential variables, such as the sample weight, have missing values that must be imputed. Fourth, the quarterly employment data contain systematic mismeasurement due to data entry and processing errors in certain quarters. This section describes how we addressed each problem before measuring gross job creation and destruction.

A.3.1 Annual Employment Data

The annual *PW* employment figure in the LRD equals the simple average of quarterly values:

$$PW_{est} = \left(\frac{1}{4}\right) \sum_{q=1}^{4} PW(q)_{est}, \tag{13}$$

where q indexes quarters and t indexes years. The $PW(q)$ variables represent the number of production workers employed during the payroll period including March 12, May 12, August 12, and November 12. Annual *TE* in the raw LRD is then measured as

$$TE_{est} = PW_{est} + OE_{est}, \tag{14}$$

where *OE* is the number of other employees on the payroll in the pay period that includes March 12.

To avoid this mixture of annual average and March data, we converted the LRD *TE* figure to a March *TE* value, using the formula

$$TE_{est}^m = \max[(TE_{est} - PW_{est}), 0] + PW(1)_{est}, \tag{15}$$

where the superscript m stands for March.[12] All subsequent references to *TE* in this appendix and all references to *TE* in the main body of the text refer to the March total employment figure, unless otherwise noted.

A.3.2 Quarterly Employment Data

The quarterly $PW(1)$ variable must be adjusted because it measures production worker employment at a different point in the first quarter (third month) than do the other $PW(q)$ variables (second month). To adjust for the uneven sampling intervals, we use the following random reassignment formula for first-quarter employment:

$$PW(1)_{est}^f = \begin{cases} PW(1)_{est} & \text{if } 0.00 \le \Phi_{est} \le 0.75 \\ PW(4)_{es,t-1} & \text{if } 0.75 < \Phi_{est} \le 1.00 \end{cases} \tag{16}$$

where superscript f denotes February and Φ_{est} is a uniformly distributed random variable. Equation 16 randomly changes 25 percent of all plants' $PW(1)$ data to the previous quarter's value and leaves the remaining 75 percent unchanged. This adjustment potentially alters the seasonal pattern in creation and destruction rates, a matter we return to in section A.8.

At the aggregate level, this plant-level random reassignment formula is equivalent to the linear combination of first- and fourth-quarter employment, $PW(1)_t^f = \left(\frac{3}{4}\right) PW(1)_t + \left(\frac{1}{4}\right) PW(4)_{t-1}$, where the weights reflect the four-month interval between November and March. Linear interpolation is inappropriate at the plant level because it distorts the timing of startups and shutdowns. Henceforth, all occurrences of PW refer to the adjusted data so we suppress the f superscript for brevity.

---

12. We use this formula for two reasons. First, *TE* and *PW* are more likely to be reported data, whereas *OE* is more likely to be imputed data. Second, since *OE* may be derived from equation 14, the max(.) formula prevents measured *OE* from being negative, which could otherwise occur as the result of measurement errors in the raw LRD figures for *TE* or *PW*.

A.3.3   Missing Values and Processing Errors

ASM sample weight (WT) values are missing in the census years 1972 and 1977. For plants that appear in any year of the panel containing the census year, we replaced the missing WT with the plant's sample weight in the nearest succeeding panel year (if available) or the nearest preceding year.[13] For plants that do not appear elsewhere in the panel, we set WT equal to the average sample weight (in the nearest census year) among other plants of similar employment size and the same two-digit SIC industry.[14] In 1982, 1984, and 1985, we reassigned about 6 percent of the WT values, using the same procedure, because of miscoded PPN identifiers in the files containing WT values.

In the LRD raw data files, some $PW(q)$ observations were incorrectly set to 0 by processing errors. In 1977, $PW(1) = 0$ for all plants, but implementing equation 13 yields the correct values. In 1984 and 1985, $PW(2) = 0$ for approximately 23 percent and 14 percent of all ASM plants, respectively. In this case equation 13 is not helpful, because Census constructed PW after the $PW(2)$ values were set to 0. Instead, for 1984 and 1985 we set most $PW(2) = 0$ cases equal to $PW(1)$ or $PW(3)$ of the same year in a manner that retained the relative sizes of second- and third-quarter job creation and destruction rates among plants that did not experience $PW(2) = 0$. We conducted the reassignment procedure at the four-digit SIC industry level.

Let PZP (positive-zero-positive) represent the average fraction of TE normally associated with plants that have the $PW(q)$ time-series pattern— $PW(1) > 0, PW(2) = 0$, and $PW(3) > 0$—in the first three quarters of 1979 to 1983 and 1986.[15] This fraction is about 0.05 percent of all plants. For the fraction PZP of plants in 1984 and 1985 experiencing the positive-zero-positive $PW(q)$ pattern, $PW(2)$ is left at 0. For the remaining fraction $(1 - PZP)$ of plants in 1984 and 1985 with the positive-zero-positive pattern, $PW(2)$ is reassigned according to the rules described below.

---

13. In practice, a plant's sample weight seldom changes during the lifetime of a panel. Ownership changes are the main reason for changes in WT during the life of an ongoing panel. Prior to 1979, LRD sampling units were companies rather than plants, so that WT depended on company, not plant, characteristics. In this period, plants that changed corporate affiliation received the new company's WT.

14. This WT assignment procedure is more appropriate for the period after 1978, when Census selected the ASM panel on a plant basis rather than on a company basis.

15. Although data for 1987 and 1988 appear in the same panel, they were not used because the SIC industry basis changed in 1987 (see section A.8).

For plants not experiencing the *PZP* pattern, define the percentage of second-quarter plus third-quarter creation occurring in the third quarter of 1984 and 1985 as

$$cwt(3)_{it} = \frac{c(3)_{it}}{c(2)_{it} + c(3)_{it}} \tag{17}$$

for $t=\{1984, 1985\}$. We call the quantity in equation 17 the creation weight for industry i, and we define the destruction weight $dwt(3)_{it}$ analogously. For a fraction $(1 - PZP)$ of plants that experienced the positive-zero-positive pattern, we reassigned $PW(2)$ in the following way: For expanding plants $(PW(3) > PW(1))$, we set fraction $cwt(3)_{it}$ of $PW(2)$ equal to $PW(1)$ and fraction $(1\text{-}cwt(3)_{it})$ of $PW(2)$ equal to $PW(3)$. Likewise, for contracting plants $(PW(3) < PW(1))$, we set fraction $dwt(3)_{it}$ of $PW(2)$ equal to $PW(1)$ and fraction $(1\text{-}dwt(3)_{it})$ of $PW(2)$ equal to $PW(3)$.

A.4 Measurement Methodology

After adjusting the raw data as described above, it is possible to calculate job creation and destruction measures. However, three additional measurement issues must be handled carefully in order to preserve the quality of the measures defined by equations 1 and 2. First, it is necessary to distinguish between accurately measured plant-level employment changes and those due to data processing errors and panel rotation. Second, panel rotation precludes the measurement of employment changes in the first period of each panel for a large fraction of the noncertainty plants. Third, the employment changes associated with quarterly births (first-time startups) and shutdowns require retiming.

A.4.1 Measurement Mechanics

Measurement of plant-level employment change, ΔX_{est}, occurs in three stages. The first stage involves matching the plant-level data by *PPN* across all time periods. The second stage involves separating plants into groups defined by current-period employment behavior. The third stage involves calculating employment changes separately for each group of plants, subject to additional conditions. The second and third stages, which are necessary to distinguish valid employment changes from invalid ones, are repeated for each time period. We use information on past, current, and future employment as well as

Table A.2
Definitions of Coverage Codes Used to Filter Out Spurious Startups and Shutdowns

Code	Definition
·	Missing value
0	No change in operator or operations
11	Plant is out of business
13	Plant is inactive but still owned, expected to resume activity
21	Plant is believed to be a newly opened operation
23	Previously idle plant resumed activity
28	Old plant from ASM company structure change (single-versus multi-unit)
30	Plant erroneously deleted from processing, now being restored
31	New plant only because of physical location change from original county
38	Unmatched to prior-year plant without explanation
39	Reserved for Census Industry Division use
40	Plant under construction but not in operation
50	Plant previously included in the ASM in error
51	Plant has changed physical location
53	Multi-unit ownership change requires linkage but no successor plant found
59	Out-of-business birth (plant opened and closed in same year)
70–83	Birth added from Social Security Administration records (year-specific)

Census coding information to construct tests for the validity of employment changes.

Once the plant-level data are longitudinally linked by PPN, it is necessary to determine whether the observed ΔX_{est} is valid. To do so, plants are separated according to whether they are continuing plants ($TE_{t-1} > 0$ and $TE_t > 0$), startup candidates ($TE_{t-1} = 0$ and $TE_t > 0$), or shutdown candidates ($TE_{t-1} > 0$ and $TE_t = 0$). Measured ΔX_{est} for continuing plants always equals actual ΔX_{est} by assumption. However, the potential for measurement error related to panel structure and data processing requires further examination of startup and shutdown candidates.[16]

We require startup and shutdown candidates to satisfy additional conditions, so that spurious startups and shutdowns are filtered out of measured ΔX_{est}. Two types of information play key roles in the filtering process. The coverage code, CC, indicates whether and how plant operations have changed since the previous year.[17] Table A.2 lists the definitions of the coverage codes used in

---

16. It is possible that ΔX_{est} for continuing plants contains measurement error that is unrelated to the difficulties affecting candidate startups and shutdowns. If such measurement error were important, however, it would be reasonable to expect much smaller job creation and destruction persistence rates than we actually observe.

17. Unfortunately, the breadth of CC data declined over the LRD sample period, which increases the difficulty of identifying valid panel entry and exit over time. In particular, $CC = 0$, which indicates no change in operation, becomes increasingly prevalent over time.

Table A.3
**Conditions Indicating that Employment Changes Represent Valid
Startups and Shutdowns**

Startups	Shutdowns
$TE_{t-1} = 0$ and $TE_t > 0$ and one of the following:	$TE_{t-1} > 0$ and $TE_t = 0$ and one of the following:
• $CC_t = 0$	• ($CC_t = \cdot$ and $CC_{t+1} \neq 30$ and $CC_{t+1} \neq 38$ and [$CC_{t-1} \neq 10$ or 12 or 14 or 16 or 17 or 19 or 24 or 26 or 28 or 29 or 44 or 50 or 53 or 54 or 58 or 90])
• $CC_t = 21$	
• $CC_t = 23$	• ($CC_t = 0$ and $CC_{t+1} \neq 30$ and $CC_{t+1} \neq 38$)
• $CC_t = 31$	• $CC_t = 11$
• ($TE_{t-2} = 0$ and $CC_t = 38$)	• $CC_t = 13$
• $CC_t = 40$	• $CC_t = 21$
• $CC_t = 59$	• $CC_t = 23$
• $70 \leq CC_t \leq 83$	• $CC_t = 39$
	• $CC_t = 40$
	• $CC_t = 51$
	• $CC_t = 59$
	• $70 \leq CC_t \leq 83$

the employment change filters. The other variable used in the filtering process is TE in periods other than t. The employment change filters for startups and shutdowns are conceptually similar but the details differ. The guiding principle in both cases is that candidates must provide convincing evidence that they are a startup or a shutdown. This conservative measurement principle probably causes the magnitude of job creation and destruction to be understated.[18]

Startup candidates include three types of plants: (1) first-time plant openings, that is, births; (2) reopened plants; and (3) misclassified startups. Items (1) and (2) reflect true job creation, whereas item (3) does not. The most important example of potentially misclassified startups involves panel rotation. The first period of a new ASM panel contains thousands of continuing plants that were not sampled in the previous panel. For such plants, we set $\Delta X_{est} = 0$ in the first period of each panel. Table A.3 lists the additional

---

18. The employment change filters apply to annual data and the first quarter of the quarterly data.

Table A.4
**Special Conditions Indicating That Employment Changes
Represent Valid Startups**

Period	Years	Condition
Second LRD Year	1973	DROP: "$TE_{t-2} = 0$" from the $CC_t = 38$ condition
Last LRD Year	1988	None
First Panel Years	1974, 1979, 1984	DROP: "$CC_t = 0$" ADD: "$TE_{t-2} = 0$" independently
Last Panel Years	1973, 1978, 1983, 1988	None
Census Years	1972, 1977, 1982, 1987	ADD: "$(ET_t \neq 1$ or $CC_{t+1} \neq$ t+1) and $(ET_t \neq 1$ or $CC_t \neq 28)$ and $(ET_t \neq 1$ or $CC_t \neq 50)$ and $(ET_t \neq 1$ or $CC_t \neq 53)$ and $(ET_t \neq 1$ or $CC_{t-1} \neq 50)$ and $(ET_t \neq 1$ or $CC_{t-1} \neq 53)$"

conditions that filter out misclassified startups.[19] If a startup candidate satisfies one of these conditions, ΔX_{est} is treated as valid; otherwise ΔX_{est} is set to 0.[20] For example, the condition "$TE_{t-2} = 0$ and $CC = 38$" identifies the subset of plants with $CC = 38$ that are likely to be true startups, as opposed to the subset for which the previous year's observation is simply missing.

The precise list of conditions for identifying valid startups (and shutdowns) varies over time due to special circumstances in the LRD, such as ASM panel rotation, CM-ASM differences, and other considerations. Table A.4 contains the special conditions that apply in particular years. Most of the special conditions are self-explanatory.[21]

Shutdown candidates likewise include three types of plants: (1) permanent shutdowns, that is, deaths; (2) temporary or indefinite shutdowns; and (3) misclassified shutdowns. Tables A.3 and A.5 list the conditions that filter out

---

19. The births added from Social Security Administration records (CC 70-83) are identified from new employer identification (EI) numbers. Since EI numbers can change for existing firms, not all new EI numbers reflect true births. The Census Bureau screens the new EI numbers for new manufacturing plants.

20. In tables A.3 through A.5 the condition $TE = 0$ also includes missing TE, which occurs when a plant is not in the panel.

21. In census years, the plants belonging to the current ASM panel are distinguished by having $ET = 0$. To protect against miscoding in this variable, however, certain plants with $ET = 1$ are treated as valid startups.

Table A.5
**Special Conditions Indicating That Employment Changes
Represent Valid Shutdowns**

Period	Years	Condition
Second LRD Year	1973	ADD: "$ET_{t-1} \neq 1$" TO: "$CC_t =.$ and $CC_{t+1} \neq 30$ and $CC_{t+1} \neq 38$"
Last LRD Year	1988	DROP: "and $CC_{t+1} \neq 30$ and $CC_{t+1} \neq 38$" See also Last Panel years
First Panel Years	1974, 1979, 1984	REPLACE: "$CC_t \neq .$ and $CC_{t+1} \neq 30$ and $CC_{t+1} \neq 38$" WITH: "$CC_t =.$ and $TE_{t-2} \geq 250$ and $TE_{t-3} \leq 0$"
Last Panel Years	1978, 1983, 1988	ADD: "and $[(ET_{t-1} \neq 1$ and $ET_{t-1} \neq 4)$ or $TE_{t-4} > 0$ or $TE_{t-3} > 0$ or $TE_{t-2} > 0]$" ADD: "$ET_{t-1} \neq 1$" TO: "$CC_t =.$ and $CC_{t+1} \neq 30$ and $CC_{t+1} \neq 38$"
Census Years	1972, 1977, 1982, 1987	None

misclassified shutdowns. If a shutdown candidate satisfies one of these conditions, ΔX_{est} is treated as valid; otherwise ΔX_{est} is set to 0.

A.4.2 Imputation in the First Periods of ASM Panels

The employment change filters described in the previous subsection deliver high-quality estimates of job creation and destruction rates in all LRD periods except the first period of each ASM panel. In the latter (i.e., first year for annual data, first quarter for quarterly data), the percentage of plants that can be linked to the prior year falls dramatically, because thousands of noncertainty plants are rotated into the panel. Only about one-third of sampled plants appear in consecutive panels, and most of these are large certainty plants. Consequently, job creation and destruction of noncertainty plants in first panel periods must be imputed.

We use a simple regression-based imputation procedure to estimate job creation and destruction rates in first panel periods. The imputation model assumes that after controlling for the total manufacturing employment growth rate, there exists a time-invariant relationship between the creation rate of continuing plants that do not cross panels (noncertainty plants) and the creation rate of continuing plants that do cross panels (certainty plants). We fit such

models sector by sector, and we use analogous models for the job destruction of continuing plants and for the job creation and destruction associated with births and deaths. Predicted values from the regression models deliver imputed creation and destruction figures for the plants that do not cross panels. Sectoral job creation and destruction figures in the first period of each panel are then computed as a weighted sum of the actual rate among certainty plants and the imputed rate for noncertainty plants.

The regression model is modified for sectors in which no or very few plants cross panels. This situation occurs in sectors that are defined to encompass only smaller plants or very young plants, and, occasionally, in highly disaggregated sectors. In such cases, the regression imputation models relate the job creation and destruction of noncertainty plants to creation and destruction among all certainty plants.

A.4.3   Retiming Quarterly Births and Shutdowns

Quarterly births and shutdowns in the LRD are disproportionately (and inaccurately) concentrated in the first quarter of each year. Many of the births and shutdowns recorded in the first quarter actually occurred during the previous year. This mistiming problem arises because the ASM mail survey takes place before all births and deaths are accurately identified. In view of this problem, it is necessary to smooth the spurious seasonal increase in first-quarter job creation and destruction by retiming most of the births and shutdowns to a previous quarter.

Births are potentially mistimed in the quarterly LRD records because the ASM survey for year $t - 1$ is mailed early in year t, before Census receives information about year $t - 1$ births. Information about births arrives in midyear from the Standard Statistical Establishment List (SSEL) and from the Company Organization Survey. Consequently, many year $t - 1$ births are first surveyed in year $t + 1$, at which time information for year t is collected.[22]

For shutdowns that occur in year $t - 1$, the LRD correctly records $PW(1)_t = 0$. If the shutdown occurs in the first quarter of year $t - 1$, the LRD correctly records $PW(1)_{t-1} = 0$ on the basis of March payroll records that are available for all plants in the processing of the ASM. Similarly comprehensive payroll records are not available for the remaining quarters of the year. Thus, the quarterly employment values for $PW(q)_{t-1}, q = \{2, 3, 4\}$ are often

---

22. This problem is more prevalent for multi-unit plants. For single-unit plants, at least two quarters of data on startups are usually available by the time the ASM mail survey takes place.

incorrectly set to positive values for plants that shut down in the second, third, or fourth quarter of $t - 1$. Because Census analysts may not have timely verification that a shutdown occurred, they may set $PW(q)_{t-1}$ ($q = \{2, 3, 4\}$) to either the last available nonzero value or to an imputed value. As a consequence, the quarterly time series for employment inaccurately bunches shutdowns into the first quarter of the year following actual shutdown.

Our retiming procedures for births and shutdowns are similar. They randomly redistribute the first-quarter births and shutdowns in year-t over the year-t first quarter and several previous quarters (three for shutdowns, four for births). Our procedures impose the same quarterly job creation and destruction patterns for retimed births and deaths as the quarterly patterns exhibited by continuing plants. We allow the quarterly retiming weights to vary by four-digit SIC and by year simultaneously.

We construct creation retiming weights for industry i from observations on continuing plants in the industry by using the formula

$$crwt_{i,t-q} = \frac{c^c_{i,t-q}}{(0.5 * c^c_{it}) + c^c_{i,t-1} + c^c_{i,t-2} + c^c_{i,t-3} + (0.5 * c^c_{i,t-4})} \tag{18}$$

for $q = \{0, 1, 2, 3, 4\}$, where a c superscript indicates continuing plants. Similarly, we construct destruction retiming weights from observations on continuing plants by using the formula

$$drwt_{i,t-q} = \frac{d^c_{i,t-q}}{d^c_{it} + d^c_{i,t-1} + d^c_{i,t-2} + d^c_{i,t-3}} \tag{19}$$

for $q = \{0, 1, 2, 3\}$. The denominator for the creation retiming weights uses half of current and half of lagged first-quarter creation because of the imperfect overlap between ASM quarters and calendar years. Recall that the ASM first-quarter employment change measures the change from November 12 to February 12. Therefore, the mistimed births include ones that occurred between January 1 and February 12 (half of $PW(1)_{t-1}$) and between November 12 and December 31 (half of $PW(1)_t$). Destruction retiming weights, however, use only current first-quarter destruction, because only second-through fourth-quarter shutdowns in year $t - 1$ are mistimed. The retiming weights represent the fraction of the previous year's job creation and destruction occurring in quarter q, and they sum to 1.

The retiming weights determine the fraction of employment in births and shutdowns to move to earlier quarters. Letting Φ_{eit} denote a uniformly dis-

tributed random variable, births recorded in the first quarter of year t are re-timed according to the rule

If $0 \leq \Phi_{eit} < crwt_{i,t-4}$, then $PW_{t-j} = PW_t$, for $j = \{1, 2, 3, 4\}$

If $crwt_{i,t-4} \leq \Phi_{eit} < \sum_{j=3}^{4} crwt_{i,t-j}$, then $PW_{t-j} = PW_t$, for $j = \{1, 2, 3\}$

If $\sum_{j=3}^{4} crwt_{i,t-j} \leq \Phi_{eit} < \sum_{j=2}^{4} crwt_{i,t-j}$, then $PW_{t-j} = PW_t$, for $j = \{1, 2\}$ \hfill (20)

If $\sum_{j=2}^{4} crwt_{i,t-j} \leq \Phi_{eit} < \sum_{j=1}^{4} crwt_{i,t-j}$, then $PW_{t-j} = PW_t$, for $j = \{1\}$

If $\sum_{j=1}^{4} crwt_{i,t-j} \leq \Phi_{eit} \leq 1$, then PW_t is unchanged.

Likewise, shutdowns recorded in the first quarter of year t are retimed according to the rule

If $0 \leq \Phi_{eit} < drwt_{i,t-3}$, then $PW_{t-j} = PW_t$, for $j = \{1, 2, 3\}$

If $drwt_{i,t-3} \leq \Phi_{eit} < \sum_{j=2}^{3} drwt_{i,t-j}$, then $PW_{t-j} = PW_t$, for $j = \{1, 2\}$

If $\sum_{j=2}^{3} drwt_{i,t-j} \leq \Phi_{eit} < \sum_{j=1}^{3} drwt_{i,t-j}$, then $PW_{t-1} = PW_t$, for $j = \{1\}$ \hfill (21)

If $\sum_{j=1}^{3} drwt_{i,t-j} \leq \Phi_{eit} \leq 1$, then PW_t is unchanged.

Because the retiming procedure described by (18)–(21) relies on the year-$t + 1$ LRD to fully allocate quarterly births and deaths in year t, we cannot implement the procedure in the last year of the sample. Thus, our quarterly time series understate the job creation due to births and the job destruction due to deaths in 1988.

A.5 Statistical Precision

This section reports standard errors for the LRD-based estimates of gross job creation and destruction rates. The standard errors provide information about the precision with which our job creation and destruction figures measure the true job creation and destruction rates in the U.S. manufacturing universe.[23]

The universe value for employment, say, is simply the sum over all plant-level employment observations in the Census of Manufactures. We represent this sum as

$$X_t = \sum_{e \in E} X_{est}, \tag{22}$$

where E denotes the set containing the universe of plants. When CM data are unavailable, one can estimate the universe employment level from a randomly selected sample of the plants in E. Using weights derived from the sample selection probabilities, one can compute a linear unbiased estimate of the universe employment value and the variance of the sampling error for this estimate, as we explain below.

In selecting an ASM panel from the CM, the Census Bureau defines independent sampling units (plants) and uses a probability-proportional-to-size (PPS) method to assign sampling probabilities to each noncertainty plant.[24] A linear unbiased estimate of the universe employment level in equation (22) can be computed from ASM sample data as

$$\widehat{X}_t = \sum_{e \in E^A} W_{est} X_{est}, \tag{23}$$

where E^A denotes the set of plants in the ASM panel, and where W_{est} denotes the sample weight. This sample weight equals the reciprocal of the sampling probability, so that a sampling probability of 0.25, for example, implies a sample weight of 4.0.

In principle, a separate selection probability could be assigned for each data item in the LRD, but in practice a common size measure based on the value of shipments (VS) within a five-digit product class determines the sample weight

---

23. The technical description of sampling procedures in this section is only a summary of the salient issues. See Ogus and Clark (1971) and Waite and Cole (1980) for more details.

24. Recall that certainty plants are typically large plants with at least 250 employees. (See section A.2 of the technical appendix.) These certainty plants receive a sampling probability of 1.0 and do not contribute to the standard error calculations. The certainty plants can be thought of as a separate subuniverse.

for all LRD data items.[25] An advantage of this PPS sampling procedure is that certain probabilities can be arbitrarily assigned—for instance, a probability of 1 (certain inclusion) for large plants.

It is helpful to rewrite the estimate of the universe employment level as

$$\widehat{X}_t = \sum_{e \in E^A} W_{est} X_{est} = \sum_{e \in E} W_{est} X_{est} I_{est}, \tag{24}$$

where I_{est} is a random indicator variable that equals 1 with the sample selection probability $(1/W_{est})$, and 0 with probability $1 - (1/W_{est})$. The sampling variance of $\widehat{X}_t$ equals the variance of equation (24),

$$\sigma^2(\widehat{X}_t) = \sum_{e \in E} X_{est}^2 W_{est}^2 \sigma^2(I_{est}) = \sum_{e \in E} (W_{est} - 1) X_{est}^2. \tag{25}$$

To obtain an unbiased estimate of this sampling variance, one calculates the weighted variance of the employment values for the ASM plants,

$$s^2(\widehat{X}_t) = \sum_{e \in E^A} W_{est}(W_{est} - 1) X_{est}^2. \tag{26}$$

The square root of $s^2(\widehat{X}_t)$—that is, the standard error of $\widehat{X}_t$—informs us about the precision of the LRD-based estimate of manufacturing employment.

Equation (26) pertains to employment levels rather than the employment changes that underlie the gross job creation and destruction figures reported in this book. However, because the sample weights do not change during the life of an ongoing panel, the analysis leading to (26) carries over directly to the LRD-based estimates of employment changes for all but the first period of each panel.[26] Hence, the estimated variance of the sampling error for the estimated employment change is given by

$$s^2(\Delta \widehat{X}) = \sum_{e \in E^A} W_{est}(W_{est} - 1)(\Delta X_{est})^2. \tag{27}$$

---

25. In designing the 1994 ASM panel, the Census Bureau plans to implement a new procedure called the Chromy algorithm. The algorithm assigns selection probabilities that simultaneously satisfy variance constraints within product class, industry, and two-digit-SIC-by-state classifications. See Zayatz and Sigman (1993) for details. Product class is a more disaggregated version of the SIC industrial classification scheme based on product types.

26. As explained in section A.2 of the technical appendix, plant-level sample weights can change within the panel in the pre-1979 period. This matter is a minor concern in the present context, and we ignore it.

Table A.6
Relative Standard Errors of Annual Employment (TE), Job Creation (C), and Job Destruction (D) in Total Manufacturing

Data	1973	1974	1975	1976	1977	1978	1979	1980	1981	1982	1983	1984	1985	1986	1987	1988
TE	0.2	0.3	0.3	0.3	0.3	0.3	0.3	0.4	0.4	0.4	0.4	0.3	0.3	0.3	0.3	0.3
C	0.5	0.8	1.0	0.7	0.8	0.7	1.1	1.1	1.3	1.6	1.9	0.5	0.8	0.9	1.1	0.9
D	0.8	0.8	0.7	0.8	1.1	0.9	0.8	0.8	0.9	0.9	0.9	1.4	1.0	0.7	0.8	1.0

Note: Standard errors are for data levels, expressed as percentages of the level.

It follows that the estimated variance of the sampling error is

$$s^2(\widehat{C}) = \sum_{e \in E^A} W_{est}(W_{est} - 1)[\max(\Delta X_{est}, 0)]^2 \tag{28}$$

for job creation, and

$$s^2(\widehat{D}) = \sum_{e \in E^A} W_{est}(W_{est} - 1)[\max(-\Delta X_{est}, 0)]^2 \tag{29}$$

for job destruction, where the max(.) functions select for plant-level creation (C_{est}) or destruction (D_{est}).

Table A.6 reports relative standard errors for LRD-based estimates of employment (TE) and the levels of gross job creation (C) and destruction (D) in the manufacturing sector.[27] The relative standard error equals $s(\widehat{X})/\widehat{X}$ for employment, $s(\widehat{C})/\widehat{C}$ for gross job creation, and $s(\widehat{D})/\widehat{D}$ for gross job destruction. According to the table, the standard error of the employment estimate is less than 0.5 percent of employment in all years. The standard errors of the job creation and destruction estimates are about 1 percent of the corresponding levels. Since the job creation and destruction rates are in the neighborhood of 10 percent of employment per year, the table A.6 entries imply that the standard errors of the gross job flow estimates are on the order of 0.1 percent of employment. In short, our estimated job creation and destruction rates for the total manufacturing sector are subject to tiny sampling errors.

Of course, the standard errors of the estimated creation and destruction rates are usually larger for disaggregated sectors. Inspection of table A.6 suggests that relative standard errors for creation and destruction are roughly three times larger than relative standard errors for employment. Published ASM

---

27. Strictly speaking, panel rotation means that the formulas given by (28) and (29) are not applicable to the first year of each panel—1974, 1979, and 1984.

statistics for 1985 indicate relative employment standard errors for two-digit SIC manufacturing industries in the neighborhood of 3 percent or smaller. Relative employment standard errors for states fall mostly in the range of 1–3 percent and exceed 5 percent for only five states. Thus, the 3 : 1 rule of thumb suggests that relative job flow standard errors are in the range of 3–9 percent for most two-digit SIC industries and most states. This rule of thumb would be highly misleading for sectoral classifications based on size or variables highly correlated with size (e.g., age). For example, relative standard errors for categories restricted to plants with at least 250 employees are 0, because such plants are sampled with probability 1. Relative standard errors for categories dominated by smaller plants are higher than suggested by the 3 : 1 rule of thumb.

A.6 Published versus Sample Data

Employment statistics generated by aggregating the ASM portion of the LRD data do not correspond exactly to published ASM/CM statistics for two reasons. First, in census years the published statistics are obtained from the CM universe rather than the LRD (weighted ASM) sample. Second, in noncensus years the published statistics include adjustments to the ASM sample data contained in the LRD. These adjustments, which are related to sampling error and imputation, produce more accurate estimates than can be obtained from the LRD alone.

As a related matter, changes over time in the relationships among the CM, ASM, and LRD data lead to important differences in the employment growth rates generated by these three data sources. In census years, it is likely that the published growth rate is biased upward, and that the LRD growth rate is more accurate. But in the first year of each ASM panel, it is likely that the LRD growth rate is biased upward, and that the published ASM growth rate is more accurate. In practice, because our imputation procedure for estimating gross job flows in the first period of each panel relies upon the job flow behavior of certainty plants (see section 4.2), we effectively sidestep the potential first-period problem created by ASM panel rotation.

In short, this section describes the relationship between published statistics and statistics implied by simple aggregation of the ASM sample data.[28] It explains why the levels and growth rates differ. The most serious problem

---

28. This material provides an updated and revised version of material in Davis, Haltiwanger, and Schuh (1990) .

identified in the sample-based estimate of employment growth does not apply to our gross job flow measures.

A.6.1 Published Data

There are two related types of published manufacturing employment data. In census years, the published CM data are the sums of data from all plants in the universe, as in equation (22). In noncensus years, the published ASM data contain three components: (1) the LRD-based estimate from the current ASM panel, that is, equation (23); (2) a sampling error adjustment; and (3) a small-plant imputation adjustment for administrative record (*AR*) plants.

Formally, published ASM employment is

$$X_{st}^p = X_{st}^l + X_{st}^f + X_{st}^i,$$ \hfill (30)

where superscript p denotes published ASM data, l denotes sample LRD (weighted ASM) data, f denotes fixed-base difference (sampling error) adjustment, and i denotes imputed small-plant data. The two nonsample components are small relative to the sample LRD in terms of levels (roughly 5 percent combined), but they vary over the course of an ASM panel and can significantly affect the growth rates of the published data. Prior to 1979, $X_{st}^i = 0$ in every year, because the sample weights accounted for the *AR* data.[29]

A.6.1.1   *Fixed-Base Difference*
The fixed-base difference (FBD) represents an adjustment to equation (23), the sample LRD data, that corrects for sampling error. The FBD at the beginning of a panel, called FBD1, is

$$X_{st}^f = \sum_{e \in E_{s,t-2}} X_{es,t-2}^l - \sum_{e \in E_{s,t-2}^A} W_{es,t-2} X_{es,t-2}^l$$ \hfill (31)

for the period t representing the first year of a panel, where E_{st} and E_{st}^A denote the set of plants in the CM and ASM surveys. Equation (31) can also be expressed as the difference between equations (22) and (23) in the census year that the panel was drawn, $(X_{s,t-2} - \widehat{X}_{s,t-2})$. FBD1 can be set arbitrarily close to 0 by adjusting the ASM panel size and composition; in fact,

---

29. Equation 30 and subsequent equations in this section are written in terms of sectoral aggregates because the nonsampling components are constructed at a disaggregated level. The total manufacturing published data are simply the unweighted sum across the S sectors.

minimizing FBD1 is an important criterion for determining sample selection probabilities.

FBD1 is constant throughout the ASM panel. In the fourth panel year, the published CM data are used rather than the ASM panel data, so that the FBD1 adjustment is unnecessary. In the fifth and final panel year, Census uses the new universe of plants obtained from the CM in the fourth panel year to recalculate the FBD. This new FBD, called FBD2, is a more accurate estimate of current sampling error because it accounts for new plants not initially included in the panel and for deterioration in the representativeness of the (fixed) sampling weights caused by large changes in plant size. FBD2 is computed as

$$X^f_{s,t+4} = \sum_{e \in E_{s,t+3}} X^l_{es,t+3} - \sum_{e \in E^A_{s,t+3}} W_{es,t+3} X^l_{es,t+3} , \qquad (32)$$

where the sampling weights $W_{es,t+3}$ are set equal to $W_{es,t-2}$, except for births added to the panel after $t - 2$.

A.6.1.2 Small Plant Impute Block

Since 1979, Census has imputed most data items for small plants outside the ASM panel by using payroll and employment information in the Standard Statistical Establishment List (SSEL). This information derives from administrative records compiled by the Social Security Administration and the Internal Revenue Service. These small plants, which include administrative record (AR) plants and small births, are collectively called the impute block (IB). For each IB plant, Census receives March TE and quarterly payroll (PAY) data, which it uses to impute most data items for those plants.[30] The imputations are carried out at the level of sectors defined in terms of industry, state, and metropolitan statistical area.

For each such sector s in year t, the imputed value for a data item X_{st} is set according to the formula

$$X_{st} = \left[\frac{\sum_{e \in E^A_{st}} X_{est}}{\sum_{e \in E^A_{st}} PAY_{est}} \right] \left[\sum_{e \in E^{IB}_{st}} PAY_{est} \right] . \qquad (33)$$

---

30. The only exception to this procedure for ASM data is the imputation of exports. See appendix C of Bureau of the Census (1991).

That is, the IB data item is set equal to the ratio of X to payroll in the ASM, multiplied by payroll for IB plants. Census uses a similar procedure to impute data items that are unreported by ASM plants.

A.6.2   Comparisons of Levels and Growth Rates

This section compares four annual TE time series: (1) the published ASM/CM data (TE^p); (2) the sample LRD (weighted ASM) data (TE^l); (3) the Bureau of Labor Statistics (BLS) Employment and Earnings data; and (4) the Census County Business Patterns (CBP) data. Because the published ASM/CM data do not include March TE, defined by equation (15), we estimate it with the equation

$$TE_t^{pm} = TE_t^p \left(\frac{TE_t^{lm}}{TE_t^l} \right) . \tag{34}$$

That is, published March TE equals published annual TE, adjusted for the ratio of March to annual TE in the LRD. The CBP TE data are available only in March, and the BLS TE data are the March estimate from the monthly establishment survey data. The BLS data contain employees of auxiliary manufacturing establishments, which are owned by manufacturing enterprises but are not directly involved in production. Auxiliary establishment employment is about 1 million, or roughly 5 percent of total manufacturing employment. Although published ASM/CM data and the CBP data report auxiliary establishment employment separately, such data are not available for the sample LRD data. For this reason, the analysis below excludes auxiliary employment except for the BLS data.

Although the levels and growth rates of all four TE estimates follow the same basic time-series pattern, as shown in figures A.1 and A.2, five important differences stand out. First, the difference between ASM/CM and LRD data levels is much larger after 1979 because of the impute block. The effect of the impute block on the growth rate, however, is less evident. Second, the relationship between the ASM/CM and LRD data varies within panels. Beginning in 1979, the difference between the levels of these data increasingly diverges each year within a panel. Third, the ASM/CM and LRD growth rates differ sharply in census years (1977, 1982, and 1987) because the ASM/CM data include many plants not added to the ASM panel during its first three years. These plants are primarily small births and plants previously classified in nonmanufacturing industries. Fourth, the ASM/CM and LRD growth rates

Figure A.1
Total Manufacturing Employment: Annual, 1972 to 1988

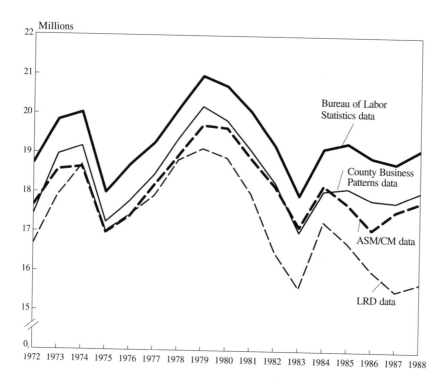

differ sharply in first panel years (1974, 1979, and 1984) because the LRD data suddenly close the gap between published and sample data levels when a new panel begins. Fifth, the ASM/CM data track the CBP and BLS data better than do the LRD data.[31]

31. The general correspondence among level and growth rate estimates breaks down as disaggregation across time and sector increases. At the quarterly frequency, the correlation between ASM/CM and BLS growth rates for production worker (*PW*) data is high except in 1985 and 1986 where a couple of quarters have unusually large, unexplained differences (not pictured). It is unclear whether the differences can be attributed to one data source or the other, but the concerned reader may wish to investigate the issue further. For more disaggregated sectoral classifications, the correlation between ASM/CM and BLS *TE* data is weaker—increasingly so as the degree of sectoral disaggregation increases. This phenomenon is particularly evident in sectors dominated by smaller plants, perhaps because the BLS data do not originate from a survey conducted with a probability sample.

Figure A.2
**Total Manufacturing Employment Growth Rates:
Annual, 1972 to 1988**

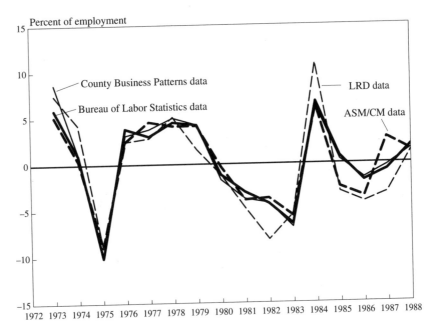

A.6.3   Decomposition of Published Data

To better understand the difference between the ASM/CM and LRD data, it is useful to decompose the difference into two parts.[32] We obtained unpublished four-digit SIC industry-level *TE* data for FBD1 and FBD2 for 1982–84 and 1987–88.[33] Because the FBD is mostly constant during a panel, these data provide estimates for the entire period 1979–88. Given the published, sample, and FBD data, it is possible to derive the IB adjustment, denoted $\widetilde{IB}$, for the entire 1979–88 period by using equation (30).

The difference between the ASM/CM and LRD data,

$$DTE = TE^p - TE^l = FBD + \widetilde{IB}, \tag{35}$$

32. In this section, all *TE* data are annual, as defined in equation 14, because the nonsample data are only available in that format.
33. In principle, it is possible to use the LRD data to recreate FBD1 and FBD2 using equations 31 and 32, and derive the IB beginning in 1979 from equation 30.

Figure A.3
**Analysis of the Difference (DTE) Between Published
ASM/CM Total Employment Data and Sample LRD
Total Employment Data: Annual, 1979 to 1988**

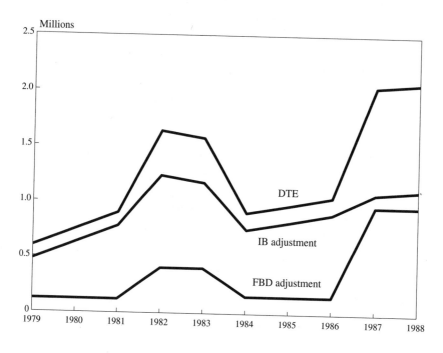

Note: IB is the adjustment corresponding to the impute block of small plants excluded from the
ASM; FBD is the adjustment corresponding to the fixed-base-difference (sampling error).

varies considerably over the life of a panel. Figure A.3 plots *DTE* and its components from 1979 to 1988. In the first three years of each panel (1979–81 and 1984–86), *DTE* grows relatively slowly. In the fourth panel (census) years, 1982 and 1987, *DTE* nearly doubles, increasing 82 and 95 percent, respectively. The difference remains large in the fifth panel years, 1983 and 1988, then falls substantially as a new panel begins (1984), because the IB adjustment is smaller.

The decomposition of *DTE* into FBD and IB components depicted in figure A.3 provides a better understanding of the time-series behavior of *DTE*. Initially, the FBD adjustment in each panel is very small, about 100,000 to 150,000, but the recalculated FBD jumps to slightly more than 400,000 in

1982 and nearly 1 million in 1987.[34] This large revision to the FBD is the result of obtaining updated and more accurate information about small-plant employment from the CM data. In contrast, the IB adjustment is larger and grows steadily during the panel. The initial value of $\widetilde{IB}$ is about 500,000 in the first panel and 750,000 in the second panel, and these values increase markedly during the panels.

A.6.4   A Hypothetical Panel

A summary of the relationship between the ASM/CM and LRD data appears in figure A.4, which depicts the stylized development of a hypothetical ASM panel. The figure illustrates and summarizes the relationships among the levels and growth rates of published and sample employment data.

In terms of employment levels, the sample LRD data are never superior to the published ASM/CM data. The two estimates are closest in the first panel year, but the sample LRD data deviate from the published data by the FBD and (since 1979) the IB. As the panel progresses, the sample LRD employment level increasingly deviates from the published ASM/CM data (exhibited by the different slopes) because the IB grows rapidly, and because the suitability of the sample weights deteriorates. The sudden increase in the published employment level in census years reflects a recalculation of the fixed-base difference. This adjustment to the ASM/CM employment level in census years reflects developments that occurred over several previous years.

In terms of employment growth rates, the ASM/CM and LRD data are very similar except in the first and fourth years of the panel. The LRD rate is more accurate in the fourth panel year; in the first panel year the ASM/CM rate is more accurate. The selection of a new panel with new sample weights and the recalculation of FBD1 and IB in the first panel year lead to an inaccurate LRD-based employment growth rate in the first panel year. The ASM/CM data are relatively unaffected by the panel rotation. In the fourth panel year, the ASM/CM data change sharply for the reasons discussed previously, producing a less accurate growth rate measure. The LRD data are relatively unaffected by this phenomenon. Although both ASM/CM and LRD measures of the employment growth rate suffer some inaccuracies, the first-panel-year problem with the LRD measure appears more serious than the census-year problem with the ASM/CM measure.

---

34. Strictly speaking, there is no FBD adjustment in census years, because the Bureau simply publishes the CM data. Figure A.3 shows the decomposition of the difference between the ASM estimate and the CM total in Census years.

Figure A.4
**Hypothetical Development of Total Employment During
an ASM Panel**

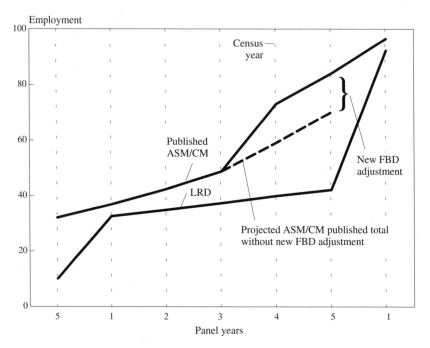

Note: The employment data in the Longitudinal Research Database (LRD) differ from those published
in the Annual Survey of Manufactures (ASM) and the quinquennial Census of Manufactures (CM)
because of adjustments made for sampling error and imputation. An adjustment (FBD) is made in the
fifth and final year of a sample panel, based on the new universe of plants obtained from the Census of
Manufactures in the previous year.

A.6.5   Adjustments to Job Flows Data

In principle, it would be desirable to adjust our job creation and destruction
statistics so that the implied net employment change is consistent with published ASM/CM statistics. Unfortunately, certain practical problems stand in
the way of straightforward and satisfactory adjustment procedures.

One possible adjustment method is to treat the *DTE* figures as employment
changes for pseudo plants (one for each sector) and to add the pseudo-plant
employment change to the LRD-based job creation or destruction figure.[35]

───────────────

35. The pseudo-plant procedure understates actual job creation and destruction associated with
nonsample plants, because it equals the net employment change among IB plants in the sector.

Davis, Haltiwanger, and Schuh (1990) explored this method and judged it inadequate because of large *DTE* changes in census and first-panel years. In other years the procedure works well, but the magnitude and timing of the adjustments have little effect on the magnitude and timing of the LRD-based job creation and destruction statistics.

A second possible method is to use information from the LRD about the relationships between net and gross job flows among small plants with characteristics similar to plants in the impute block. This relationship, as summarized by regression models similar to the ones described in section A.4.2, could be used to impute gross job creation and destruction for the nonsample portion from the net employment change of the nonsample portion. Further, an adjustment could be made in the census years and the first year of each panel to spread the observed discrete changes appropriately over the course of the panel.

Ultimately, however, these kinds of adjustment techniques are limited by the absence of actual FBD and IB data for many sectors and for early years of the LRD. In the absence of such data, it is necessary to infer *DTE* data from the LRD and published ASM/CM statistics. The published statistics are not available for many of the sectors for which we provide job creation and destruction statistics.

A.7   Sector Definitions

This section describes sectoral classifications for the job creation and destruction statistics. These sectors fall into three general categories: industry, geography, and plant characteristics. Job creation and destruction statistics are available for each one-dimensional sector described below and for some two-dimensional sectors. Researchers can construct more aggregated sectors by using the procedure described in section A.8.

A.7.1   Industry

The Standard Industrial Classification (SIC) system developed by the Office of Management and Budget defines industrial sectors. The SIC system divides manufacturing into three increasingly disaggregated levels of industries: two-digit, three-digit, and four-digit. For convenience, table A.7 reproduces the 20 two-digit SIC industry groups. There are about 450 four-digit SIC industries. See Executive Office of the President, Office of Management and Budget (1972, 1987) for details about the structure of the SIC system.

Table A.7
Two-digit Standard Industrial Classification (SIC) Industries

SIC code	Nondurable Goods Industries	SIC code	Durable Goods Industries
20	Food and Kindred Products	24	Lumber and Wood Products
21	Tobacco Manufactures	25	Furniture and Fixtures
22	Textile Mill Products	32	Stone, Clay and Glass Products
23	Apparel and Other Textile Products	33	Primary Metal Industries
26	Paper and Allied Products	34	Fabricated Metal Products
27	Printing and Publishing	35	Machinery, Except Electrical
28	Chemicals and Allied Products	36	Electrical Machinery
29	Petroleum and Coal Products	37	Transportation Equipment
30	Rubber and Plastics Products	38	Instruments and Related Products
31	Leather and Leather Products	39	Other Durable Goods

The SIC system experienced three changes during the annual LRD time period, 1972–88. Two of the changes were minor, involving only a small number of four-digit industry redefinitions in 1977 and 1982. Table A.8 contains the discontinuous industries that we combined to account for these changes. The third change was substantial, a complete redefinition of many industries in 1987. Due to the complexity of the SIC system, the nature of product changes that led to the 1987 SIC revision, and the structure of the ASM sampling procedure, it is difficult to construct a concordance between the 1972 and 1987 SIC systems. We make no attempt to do so here. Consequently, our industry-level data use the 1972 SIC (*OIND*) for the years 1972 to 1986 and the 1987 SIC (*IND*) for 1987 and 1988.

A number of four-digit SIC industries were miscoded during data entry in the period 1972–86. A typical miscoding is the assignment of a plant to an industry that does not exist in the SIC system. Using product code data and industry codes in other years for the same plant, we replaced the incorrect codes. Table A.8 lists the miscoded industries and the industry reassignments we used.[36]

---

36. We thank Tim Dunne for providing this correspondence.

Table A.8
Four-digit Standard Industrial Classification (SIC) Reassignments, 1972 to 1986

Old Industry	New Industry
Discontinuous Industries	
2794	2793
3672	3671
3673	3671
Miscoded Industries	
2015	2016
2031	2091
2042	2048
2071	2065
2072	2066
2093	2076
2094	2077
2317	3317
2433	2439
2443	2449
2689	2649
3323	3325
3391	3399
3392	3399
3461	3466
3472	3743
3481	3496
3578	3579
3614	3674
3642	3646
3716	3713
3722	3724
3729	3728
3741	3743
3791	2451

A.7.2 Geography

Geographic classifications are available at two levels of disaggregation: region and state. Table A.9 lists the four geographic divisions and nine regions defined by the Census Bureau, as well as the states in each region (abbreviated by U.S. Postal Service state codes). The data diskette includes a file called STCODES that links the Census numeric state codes (11–95) to the state names.

Data users should be aware of one measurement error related to geographic data. For a number of years, the data for Hawaii (95) and Rhode Island (15)

Table A.9
Census Geographic Classifications: Divisions, Regions, and States

Region	States
Northeast Division	
(1) New England	CT, ME, MA, NH, RI, VT
(2) Middle Atlantic	NJ, NY, PA
Midwest Division	
(3) East North Central	IL, IN, MI, OH, WI
(4) West North Central	IA, KS, MN, MO, NE, ND, SD
South Division	
(5) South Atlantic	DC, DE, FL, GA, MD, NC, SC, VA, WV
(6) East South Central	AL, KY, MS, TN
(7) West South Central	AR, LA, OK, TX
West Division	
(8) Mountain	AZ, CO, ID, MT, NM, UT, WY
(9) Pacific	AK, CA, HI, NV, OR, WA

appear to have been inadvertently combined in the LRD data under the Rhode Island code. Unfortunately, at the time this book was published, it was not possible to correct this problem accurately for all years. Consequently, the state-level data exclude these two states for all years. The regional data, however, include plants affected by this problem and hence are contaminated by this measurement error. We expect revised gross job flow data by geographic units to be available in the future.

A.7.3 Plant Characteristics

A.7.3.1 Size
Size-class data are available for four classification schemes: current plant size, average plant size, firm size, and plant ownership type. The first three classification schemes use the total employment (*TE*) ranges listed in table A.10. Plant ownership type is a crude measure of size that classifies plants according to whether they belong to a company that owns only one plant or multiple plants in the current year.

Table A.10
Plant and Firm Employment Size Classes

| Size | Total Employment | |
	Plants	Firms
1	0–19	0–19
2	20–49	20–49
3	50–99	50–99
4	100–249	100–249
5	250–499	250–499
6	500–999	500–999
7	1,000–2,499	1,000–2,499
8	2,500–4,999	2,500–4,999
9	5,000+	5,000–9,999
10		10,000–24,999
11		25,000–49,999
12		50,000+

Current size, Z_{et}, is defined in equation (3) as the average of current and lagged employment. Average plant size is the size-weighted time-series average of observed employment values,

$$\overline{Z}_e = \sum_{t=1963}^{1987} \left(\frac{TE_{et}}{\sum_{\tau=1963}^{1987} TE_{e\tau}} \right) TE_{et} . \tag{36}$$

Only years in which we observe $TE_{et} > 0$ contribute to the average. Average plant size provides a proxy for long-run capacity.

Firm size is the time-series average over census years of the TE values for all plants belonging to the company. Letting TE_{ft} denote manufacturing employment at firm f in census year t, the firm size measure is computed as

$$\overline{Z}_f = \sum_{t=1963}^{1987} \left(\frac{TE_{ft}}{\sum_{\tau=1963}^{1987} TE_{f\tau}} \right) TE_{ft} , \tag{37}$$

where the summations are over census years only.

A.7.3.2   Age
ASM panel rotation precludes detailed, time-invariant categories for plant age. Panel rotation limits our ability to determine the exact year in which a plant is born (first-time startup), because the first year in which a plant appears in the LRD is not necessarily its year of birth. Furthermore, prior to 1972, only 1963 and 1967 census data are available to determine birth year. In view

Table A.11
Simple Plant Age Classes, 1972 to 1988

LRD Year	Plant Age in Years		
	Young	Middle-Aged	Mature
1972	–	1–8	9+
1973	0–1	2–9	10+
1974	0–1	2–10	11+
1975	0–2	3–11	12+
1976	0–1	2–8	9+
1977	0–1	2–9	10+
1978	0–1	2–10	11+
1979	0–1	2–11	12+
1980	0–2	3–12	13+
1981	0–1	2–8	9+
1982	0–1	2–9	10+
1983	0–1	2–10	11+
1984	0–1	2–11	12+
1985	0–2	3–12	13+
1986	0–1	2–8	9+
1987	0–1	2–9	10+
1988	0–1	2–10	11+

of these considerations, we provide job flow statistics for two different plant age classifications: a crude classification with three categories available in all years, and a detailed classification with eight categories available only in the last year of each panel.

Table A.11 shows the definitions for the crude plant age categories—young, middle-aged, and mature. The boundaries between age categories vary systematically over the course of a panel. The boundary between young and middle-aged plants is relatively stable, but the boundary between middle-aged and mature plants varies considerably. Fortunately, job creation and destruction rates are similar for eight-year-old and twelve-year-old plants. In contrast, sharp differences exist between the job creation and destruction rates of two-year-old and five-year-old plants. These patterns in the data motivated our choice of the three-way age classification.

Nevertheless, users should be aware that the data for the young class are markedly different in the three years where it includes two-year-old plants, because these plants create and destroy jobs less intensively than one-year-old plants. It may be prudent to combine the two younger classes for time-series work or to treat the three special years differently. Time-series average data for young plants should probably be calculated by excluding the three special years.

Table A.12
Product Specialization Classes

Class	Primary Product Specialization Ratio (Percent of output)
Highly Diversified	0 — 53
Moderately Diversified	54 — 73
Moderately Specialized	74 — 92
Highly Specialized	93 — 99
Completely Specialized	100

In the last year of each ASM panel (1978, 1983, and 1988), we can construct detailed plant age categories because four previous years of continuous data are available. The detailed age categories are: births, 1, 2, 3, 4–5, 6–10, 11–14, and more than 15 years.

A.7.3.3 Product Specialization
The primary product specialization ratio variable (*PPSR*) measures the extent to which a plant specializes in producing its chief product. *PPSR* equals the share of a plant's total shipments value (*TVS*) accounted for by shipments in its primary five-digit product class. Table A.12 shows the product specialization categories, which range from completely specialized (*PPSR* = 100 percent) to highly diversified (*PPSR* of about 50 percent or less). We chose cutoffs for the diversified plants by computing employment-weighted quartiles of *PPSR* among the plants that do not specialize in a single five-digit product class, using the pooled 1972–88 LRD data.

A.7.3.4 Real Average Hourly Wage
For each plant, we construct the mean hourly production worker real wage as

$$AHW_{et} = \frac{WW_{et}}{PH_{et} \times PGNP_t}, \tag{38}$$

where *WW* denotes the production worker wage bill, *PH* denotes production worker hours, and *PGNP* denotes the GDP implicit price deflator for personal consumption expenditures (base year of 1982). Table A.13 defines five plant wage categories. We chose the category boundaries by computing quintiles of the employment-weighted distribution of real hourly production worker wages for each year of the LRD, and then averaging over years.

Table A.13
Real Average Hourly Wage Classes

Class	Average Hourly Wage (1982 dollars)
Very Low	0.00 — 5.80
Moderately Low	5.80 — 7.60
Average	7.60 — 9.60
Moderately High	9.60 — 12.30
Very High	12.30+

Table A.14
Import Penetration Ratio Classes

Class	Import Penetration Ratio (Percentage of imports plus output)
Very Low	0.0 — 0.8
Moderately Low	0.8 — 3.3
Average	3.3 — 6.8
Moderately High	6.8 — 13.1
Very High	13.1+

A.7.3.5 *International Trade Exposure*

We use the National Bureau of Economic Research (NBER) Immigration, Trade, and Labor Markets Data File to construct measures of exposure to international trade. The data file contains four-digit SIC industry-level data from the departments of Commerce and Labor from 1958 to 1986. See Abowd (1990) and references therein for detailed documentation.

One measure of trade exposure is the import penetration ratio given by

$$IPR_{it} = \frac{IMPORTS_{it}}{(OUTPUT_{it} + IMPORTS_{it})}, \tag{39}$$

where the subscript i denotes four-digit industry and $IMPORTS$ is the customs (current-dollar) value of imports. The denominator approximates domestic industry sales. Table A.14 defines import penetration categories, which we chose based on quintiles of the shipments-weighted distribution of the pooled 1972–86 industry-level data for IPR.

A second measure of trade exposure is the export share given by

$$EXPSHARE_{it} = \frac{EXPORTS_{it}}{OUTPUT_{it}}, \tag{40}$$

Table A.15
Export Share Classes

Class	Export Share (Percentage of output)
Very Low	0.0 — 1.3
Moderately Low	1.3 — 3.1
Average	3.1 — 5.8
Moderately High	5.8 — 12.5
Very High	12.5+

where *EXPORTS* is the free alongside ship (current-dollar) value of exports. Table A.15 defines export share categories, which we chose based on quintiles of the shipments-weighted distribution of the pooled 1972–86 industry-level data for *EXPSHARE*.

A.7.3.6   Capital Intensity

LRD data on building and machinery asset values underlie our measure of plant-level capital intensity (*KLR*) and our capital intensity categories. The plant-level capital intensity measure is given by

$$KLR_{et} = \frac{BAE_{et} + MAE_{et}}{\overline{Z}_e}, \tag{41}$$

where the numerator equals the book value of structures plus equipment, and the denominator equals the average plant size measure defined in equation (36).

The *KLR* asset measure is difficult to compare among plants because the purchase price of capital varies over time and place, the quality of capital varies, and the book value treatment of depreciation is highly imperfect. To mitigate these problems, we first group plants by birth cohort based on first appearance in the Census of Manufactures. For each year in the LRD, we then compute deciles for the employment-weighted distribution of *KLR* for each birth cohort. Next, we compute employment-weighted mean job creation and destruction rates by decile for each cohort-year cell and average across cohorts in each decile to obtain annual job creation and destruction statistics by capital intensity class. Table A.16 reports the capital intensity classes and the employment-weighted mean ranges for *KLR* in current dollars computed over all cohorts and years.

Table A.16
Capital Intensity Classes

Class	Capital Intensity (Millions of dollars per worker)
Least	0.00 — 3.02
Ninth	3.02 — 6.20
Eighth	6.20 — 9.30
Seventh	9.30 — 12.67
Sixth	12.67 — 16.49
Fifth	16.49 — 20.96
Fourth	20.96 — 26.91
Third	26.91 — 36.75
Second	36.75 — 60.09
Most	60.09 +

Table A.17
Energy Intensity Classes

Class	Energy Expenditures (Percentage of shipments)
Least	0.0 — 0.4
Ninth	0.4 — 0.6
Eighth	0.6 — 0.8
Seventh	0.8 — 1.0
Sixth	1.0 — 1.3
Fifth	1.3 — 1.6
Fourth	1.6 — 2.1
Third	2.1 — 2.9
Second	2.9 — 5.3
Most	5.3+

A.7.3.7 Energy Intensity

Fuel and electricity cost data in the LRD permit construction of plant-level energy intensity measures. For each plant, we measure energy intensity as

$$ENERGY_{et} = \frac{CF_{et} + EE_{et}}{TVS_{et}}, \tag{42}$$

where the numerator equals the cost of purchased fuels plus purchased electricity, and the denominator equals total shipments. Energy expenditures are measured in current dollars. Table A.17 defines ten energy intensity categories in terms of deciles for the employment-weighted distribution of $ENERGY$ in each LRD year. The energy intensity ranges listed in the table reflect time-series averages of yearly deciles.

A.7.4   Two-Dimensional Sectoral Classifications

In addition to the one-dimensional sectoral classifications, gross job flow statistics are available for a limited number of two-dimensional classifications. Available two-dimensional sectoral classifications include two-digit SIC by Census region. Data availability for two-dimensional classifications may expand in the future. Interested data users should check with the Census Bureau periodically for updates. See the end of this appendix for details on obtaining the data.

A.8   Using the Data

This section describes the contents of the computer diskette containing the gross job flows data files and the most important issues associated with using the data. Among these issues are aggregation of sectoral data, conversion from rates to levels, seasonality, industry changes, and analysis of startups and shutdowns.

A.8.1   The Data Diskette

The data diskette containing the gross job creation, destruction, and related statistics includes several files. All data files are stored in variable-length DOS ASCII format with .DAT filename extensions. Documentation files appear with .DOC filename extensions. All annual data files have the one-letter filename prefix R (for release), and all quarterly data files have the two-letter prefix RZ. The next two to four characters refer to the sectoral classifications listed in table A.18. Finally, files with the two-letter suffix BD contain separate statistics for startups and shutdowns and for continuing plants, in addition to data for all plants. Files without the suffix contain data only for all plants in the sector.

Each data file is organized in a similar manner, shown in Table A.19. The only difference between the annual and quarterly data files is that the latter contain the variable *QTR*, which denotes the quarters 1–4. The only difference between BD and non-BD files is the disaggregation between continuing and noncontinuing plants.

One important matter that affects the structure of some files is disclosure. Title XIII of the U.S. Code prohibits disclosure of the identity of individuals and organizations that provide data to the Census Bureau. Consequently, data are not available for sectors that do not contain sufficient coverage of plants to ensure confidentiality of identity. There are no disclosure violations for

Table A.18
Sectoral Classification Codes in the Data Diskette

Code	Sectoral Classification
I2	Two-digit SIC industry
I4	Four-digit SIC industry
RG	Census region
ST	State
S1	Current size
S2	Average size
S3	Firm size
A1	Simple age class
A2	Detailed age class
PT	Plant type
PS	Product specialization
WG	Real wage
IM	Import-competing
EX	Export-competing
CI	Capital intensity
EI	Energy intensity

Table A.19
Contents of Data Files

Column	Variable	Definition
1	XXXX	Sectoral classification variable(s) — see Table A.18
2	YEAR	Year
3	QTR	Quarter ("RZ" files only)
4	POS	Rate of gross job creation, all plants
5	POSB	Rate of gross job creation, startups ("BD" files)
6	POSC	Rate of gross job creation, continuing plants ("BD" files)
7	NEG	Rate of gross job destruction, all plants
8	NEGD	Rate of gross job destruction, shutdowns ("BD" files)
9	NEGC	Rate of gross job destruction, continuing plants ("BD" files)
10	EMPSH	Employment share of the sector, Z_{st}/Z_t

any single-sector classification of the gross job flows data. However, there are a few violations for certain single-sector startup and shutdown breakdowns. Table A.20 lists the startup and shutdown categories that were combined (in all years) to avoid disclosure violations.

A.8.2   Levels of Gross Job Creation and Destruction

Gross job creation and destruction levels are not included in the data diskette for two reasons. First, the employment change filters described in section A.4, which are required to account for ASM panel rotation and processing

Table A.20
**Startup and Shutdown Sectors Combined to Avoid
Disclosure Violations**

Data Classes	Sectors Combined
Two-digit SIC Industry	Food (20), Tobacco (21)
Current Plant Size	250+ employees (sizes 5–9)
Average Plant Size	0–49 employees (sizes 1–2)
Average Plant Size	1,000+ employees (sizes 7–9)
Firm Size	25,000+ employees (sizes 11–12)
Detailed Age, 1988	Ages 2–3

errors, cause the sample of plants contributing to creation or destruction to vary over time. This variation leads to large variation in the levels, but not necessarily rates, of creation and destruction. Second, the sampling error and imputation adjustments described in section A.6 cause the LRD employment data to understate levels, but not rates, relative to the published data.

Data users can construct suitable estimates of gross job creation and destruction levels by combining weighted LRD job flow rates with published employment data. For the level of job creation in a base year, use the formula

$$C_{st} = c_{st} z_{st} X_t^*, \tag{43}$$

where $z_{st} = (Z_{st}/Z_t)$ is the sector s share of manufacturing employment, and X_t^* is an unbiased estimate of total manufacturing employment in the base year.[37] The level of gross job destruction can be constructed in an analogous manner. Given levels of employment, creation, and destruction in a base year, levels in other years can be derived from the creation and destruction rates using an appropriate adjustment for the nonstandard growth rates we use in this study. Any of the four series discussed in section A.6—ASM/CM, LRD, BLS, and CBP—may be used for X_t^* in equation (43).[38] For the convenience of users, the data diskette provides annual total manufacturing employment for each candidate from 1972 to 1988 in a file called XSTARTM.DAT. This file contains five variables: YEAR, ASM, LRD, BLS, and CBP.

---

37. To adjust for the nonstandard measure of size used in this study, Z_{st} and Z_t should be computed as the simple average of employment in periods t and $t-1$. See section A.1.1. The data diskette contains the appropriately constructed z_{st} values based on LRD data; alternatively, the data user can construct appropriate values from some other data source.

38. Since our job creation and destruction rates are constructed from data that exclude auxiliary employment, the BLS data may be the least appropriate. Data users electing to use the CBP data may wish to exclude auxiliary employment.

A.8.3   Alternative Aggregate Data Classifications

Data users may wish to aggregate over sectors provided in the data diskette. Since the gross job flow data are rates, rather than levels, they cannot simply be summed or averaged across sectors. This section describes how alternative aggregate classifications can be obtained from the sectoral rates available.

A.8.3.1   Full-Sector Aggregation

Data for the aggregate sector of a complete group of subsectors can be obtained by weighting all of the sectoral rates with the employment share variable provided in each data file. To obtain the total manufacturing *rate* of job creation from any group of subsectors, for example, use the formula

$$c_t = \sum_{s \in S} z_{st} c_{st} .$$ (44)

For multisectoral classes, such as industry-region, the total manufacturing rate is the weighted sum of rates in all sectors. Likewise, any particular sectoral rate, such as industry, is the weighted sum of rates in the other sectors, such as region. For example, the industry creation rate is

$$c_{it} = \sum_{r \in R} z_{irt} c_{irt} ,$$ (45)

where subscripts i and r denote industry and region, and R denotes the set of all regions.

Aggregation over different sectoral classification schemes will not produce exactly the same aggregate job flow rates for three reasons: The first reason is rounding error, although this error should be quite small. The second reason is missing values in the data files for some classification variables (e.g., product specialization). The third reason arises from the imputed values of creation and destruction rates in first panel periods (1974, 1979, and 1984). The reported total manufacturing rates in first panel years are based on aggregating the four-digit SIC industry data. Total manufacturing rates computed by aggregating over other sectoral classifications, such as geography or plant size, need not produce the same aggregate rate in first panel periods because of differences among sectors in the regression imputation model. However, for sectoral classifications in which there are aggregative hierarchies, such as industry (four-digit, two-digit, one-digit) or geography (state,

region, division, U.S.), aggregation at different levels will produce consistent results.

A.8.3.2 Partial-Sector Aggregation

Data users may also want to construct subsectors that are partial aggregates of more disaggregated sectors. For example, one could create sectors for small plants ($TE < 500$) and large plants ($500 \geq TE$) from the more disaggregated size class data (classes 1 through 9). In this case, the employment shares, z_{st}, must be normalized by the new sectors' total employment share, so that they represent the more aggregated size sectors (small and large). For example, gross job creation for small (S) plants is

$$c_{St} = \sum_{s=1}^{5} \left(\frac{z_{st}}{z_{St}} \right) c_{st} \tag{46}$$

and for large (L) plants is

$$c_{Lt} = \sum_{s=6}^{9} \left(\frac{z_{st}}{z_{Lt}} \right) c_{st}, \tag{47}$$

where $z_{St} = \sum_{s=1}^{5} z_{st}$ and $z_{Lt} = \sum_{s=6}^{9} z_{st}$.

A.8.4 Quarter Definitions and Seasonality

The adjustment described in equation (16) changes the timing of aggregate $PW(1)$ from March to February. This adjustment may inadvertently affect the true seasonal pattern in the data. Consequently, the seasonal pattern of the job creation and destruction data may not correctly match the seasonal pattern of other quarterly data that use February data as the first-quarter observation. Data users should be cautious of this potential mismatch and, where possible, use the procedure described in this section to construct other data in a similar manner.[39]

The difficulty arises because of the plant-level adjustment and the possibility of variation in monthly seasonal patterns. Recall that for one-fourth of

---

39. The retiming of startups and shutdowns also may affect the seasonal pattern of the quarterly data. If the accuracy of the retiming procedure varies across time, perhaps due to changes in Census procedures to identify these plants, then the retimed data may exhibit different seasonal patterns across time. Since there appears to be some evidence of time-varying seasonality in the second half of the LRD sample period, data users should carefully consider seasonality when using the quarterly data.

Table A.21
Seasonal Factors for the Monthly Growth Rate of Production-Worker Employment in Total Manufacturing

Month	Coefficient	t-statistic	p-value
Jan	−0.0007	−0.36	0.72
Feb	0.0038	2.05	0.04
Mar	0.0020	1.07	0.29
Apr	0.0034	1.84	0.07
May	0.0108	5.81	0.00
Jun	−0.0179	−9.64	0.00
Jul	0.0155	8.33	0.00
Aug	0.0112	6.03	0.00
Sep	−0.0053	−2.82	0.01
Oct	−0.0036	−1.95	0.05
Nov	−0.0071	−3.84	0.00
Dec	−0.0136	−7.09	0.00
R-squared		0.625	
Std. error		0.008	

Note: Results are from an ordinary least squares regression of the log of monthly total employment on 12 seasonal dummy variables. The employment data are from the Bureau of Labor Statistics Employment and Earnings Survey.

all plants, we reset $PW(1)_{est}$ to $PW(4)_{es,t-1}$. Therefore, if the seasonal component of actual February employment differs from that of November and March employment, the procedure fails to incorporate the proper seasonality. Consider the following simple example. Suppose January employment is seasonally high, February employment seasonally low, and all other months have no seasonal component. Then actual midquarter $PW(1)$ (February) contains a seasonal decline, but measured quarterly, $PW(1)$ (March or November) will not contain the decline.

Table A.21 shows the seasonal factors for the monthly growth rate of total manufacturing production worker employment in the BLS employment, hours, and earnings data. The factors are the coefficients from an OLS seasonal dummy regression over the period 1972:1 to 1988:12. The February seasonal is about +0.004, the March seasonal is insignificantly different from 0, and the November seasonal is about −0.007. To the extent that the LRD and BLS data have similar seasonal factors, it appears that the discrete plant-level reassignment of $PW1$ leads to a seasonal understatement of the $PW1$ growth rate.[40]

---

40. The seasonal regression for the period 1947:1 to 1992:4, however, shows that the November seasonal is significantly negative, but the February and March seasonals are both insignificantly different from zero.

When comparing the quarterly job creation and destruction data with other quarterly data, users should attempt to construct the other data in a consistent manner. In particular, we recommend that users obtain the other data on a monthly basis, and then construct the first-quarter data by taking the linear combination of November (0.25 weight) and March (0.75 weight) data. If possible, the other monthly data should be collected during the payroll period covering the twelfth day of the month.

A.8.5   Change in the SIC Industry Definition

The Standard Industrial Classification (SIC) system changed dramatically in 1987. As a consequence, the industry-level time-series data provided on the diskette reflect different classification systems for 1972–86 and 1987–88. (See Section A.7.) Users who wish to obtain or construct a concordance between the two classification systems should consult analysts at the Census Bureau, Bureau of Economic Analysis, or Bureau of Labor Statistics.

A.8.6   Analysis of Startups and Shutdowns

Although gross job creation and destruction estimates are available for plant startups and shutdowns at both annual and quarterly frequencies for many classifications, analyses of the relationships between the creation and destruction estimates of startups and shutdowns and those of continuing plants should be conducted only with the annual data. The reason is clear from the startup and shutdown retiming technique described in section A.4. The fractions used to determine how much startup and shutdown creation and destruction to re-allocate to other quarters were constructed from the creation and destruction data for continuing plants. Therefore, although the quarterly time series for startup creation and shutdown destruction are probably reliable for analysis of the cyclical behavior of startups and shutdowns, their respective contributions to total creation and destruction are derived. The relative contributions of startups and shutdowns in the annual data reflect direct observations and are not subject to this problem.

A.9   How to Obtain the Data

The complete set of annual and quarterly gross job creation, destruction, and related data for U.S. manufacturing, 1972–88, is available from the Center for Economic Studies of the U.S. Bureau of the Census. Data at the total manufacturing level and the sectoral classifications listed in table A.18 are available. A

README file is available upon request from the Center for Economic Studies describing the available data, including possible updates (see below for contact number). The README file also contains documentation on the format of the datafiles (all datafiles are ASCII) and other documentation. The procedures for obtaining the data are as follows:

1. Annual and quarterly data for 1972–88 are available for purchase separately. The price for the annual data is $50.00; the price for the quarterly data is $50.00 also.

2. Data can be purchased by mail or by calling the Center for Economic Studies.

3. To purchase by mail, send a check or money order to: GROSS JOB FLOWS DATA, Center for Economic Studies, U.S. Bureau of the Census, Room 2621-3, Washington, DC 20233. Please make the check payable to "Census/Commerce." Be sure to specify the data requested (annual, quarterly, or both). The standard order will be processed using $3\frac{1}{2}$ inch, high density diskettes. If this is not acceptable, then contact the Center for Economic Studies to make other arrangements.

4. To purchase by phone, call the Center for Economic Studies (301) 457-1830. Refer to CES Gross Flows. The data diskettes can be purchased using a MasterCard or VISA credit card.

At the time of publication of this book, only the data for 1972–88 were available. However, an update of the data through 1993 is planned for release some time in 1996. The updated data will be available at the total manufacturing level and by 2-digit and 4-digit industry. For those who purchase the 1972–88 data prior to the release of the updated data, the updated data will be available for purchase at the discounted price of $25.00 each for the annual or quarterly data. A user may make arrangements for purchasing the updated data at the time of purchasing the 1972–88 data, and the updated data will be sent to the user as soon as it becomes available.

References

Abowd, John. 1990. "The NBER Immigration, Trade, and Labor Market Data Files." *NBER Working Paper* no. 3351. Cambridge, MA: NBER.

Abowd, John, and Arnold Zellner. 1985. "Estimating Gross Labor Force Flows." *Journal of Economic and Business Statistics* 3, no. 3: 254–83.

Abraham, Katherine, and Lawrence Katz. 1986. "Cyclical Unemployment: Sectoral Shifts or Aggregate Disturbances?" *Journal of Political Economy* 94, no, 3: 507–22.

Abraham, Katherine G., and Susan N. Houseman. 1993. *Job Security in America: Lessons from Germany.* Washington, D.C.: Brookings Institution.

Acs, Zoltan, and David Audretsch. 1988. "Innovation in Large and Small Firms: An Empirical Analysis." *American Economic Review* 78, no. 4: 678–90.

Addison, John, and Pedro Portugal. 1989. "Job Displacement, Relative Wage Changes, and the Duration of Unemployment." *Journal of Labor Economics* 7, no. 3: 281–302.

Aghion, Philippe, and Olivier Blanchard. 1994. "On the Speed of Transition in Central Europe." *NBER Working Paper* no. 4736. Cambridge, MA: NBER.

Akerlof, George, Andrew Rose, and Janet Yellen. 1988. "Job Switching and Job Satisfaction in the U.S. Labor Market." *Brookings Papers on Economic Activity* (1988:2): 495–582. Washington, D.C.: Brookings Institution.

Albaek, Karsten, and Bent E. Sorensen. 1995. "Worker Flows and Job Flows in Danish Manufacturing, 1980–91." Unpublished working paper.

Aldrich, Howard, Arne Kallenberg, Peter Marsden, and James Cassell. 1988. "In Pursuit of Evidence: Five Sampling Procedures for Locating New Businesses." Paper prepared for 1988 Babson College Entrepreneurship Conference.

Anderson, Patricia M., and Bruce D. Meyer. 1994. "The Nature and Extent of Turnover." Brookings Papers on Economic Activity: Microeconomics. Washington, D.C.: Brookings Institution.

Andolfatto, David. 1992. "On the Nature of Employment Fluctuations in a Search Economy." Working paper, University of Waterloo, Canada (May).

Andolfatto, David. 1993. "Business Cycles and Labor Market Search." University of Waterloo, Canada. Unpublished paper.

Andrews, Edmund L. 1993. "Clinton's Technology Plan Would Redirect Billions from Military Research." *New York Times,* February 24, A14.

_____. 1994. "F.C.C. Plan for License Diversity: Wireless Auction to Feature Set-Asides." *New York Times,* June 23, C1.

Armington, Catherine. 1991. "Firm Linkage of the 1989 Universe Data Base." Final Report on Department of Labor Contract no. J-9-J-9-0091. Washington, D.C.: Department of Labor.

Armington, Catherine, and Marjorie Odle. 1982a. "Small Business—How Many Jobs?" *Brookings Review* (Winter). Washington, D.C.: Brookings Institution.

_____. 1982b. "Sources of Employment Growth, 1978–80." Washington, D.C.: Brookings Institution. Unpublished report.

Atkeson, Andrew, and Patrick Kehoe. 1992. "Industry Evolution and Transition: The Role of Informational Capital." Working paper, University of Chicago.

Attanasio, Orazio, and Steven J. Davis. 1994. "Relative Wage Movements and the Distribution of Consumption." University of Chicago manuscript.

Baily, Martin Neil, Eric J. Bartelsman, and John Haltiwanger. 1994. "Downsizing and Productivity Growth: Myth or Reality?" *NBER Working Paper* no. 4741. Cambridge, MA: NBER.

Bak, Per, Kan Chen, Jose Scheinkman, and Michael Woodford. 1992. "Aggregate Fluctuations from Independent Sectoral Shocks: Self-Organized Criticality in a Model of Production and Inventory Dynamics." Santa Fe Institute. Working paper.

Baldwin, John, Timothy Dunne, and John Haltiwanger. 1994. "A Comparison of Job Creation and Job Destruction in Canada and the United States." NBER Working Paper no. 4726. Cambridge, MA: NBER.

Banerjee, Abhijit. 1992. "A Simple Model of Herd Behavior." *Quarterly Journal of Economics* 107: 797–818.

Barnett, Donald F., and Robert W. Crandall. 1986. *Up from the Ashes: The Rise of the Steel Minimill in the United States.* Washington, D.C.: Brookings Institution.

Becker, Gary S. 1975. *Human Capital.* 2nd ed. Chicago: University of Chicago Press.

Berman, Eli, John Bound, and Zvi Griliches. 1993. "Changes in the Demand for Skilled Labor within U.S. Manufacturing Industries: Evidence from the Annual Survey of Manufacturing." *NBER Working Paper* no. 4255. Cambridge, MA: NBER.

Bertola, Giuseppe, and Ricardo J. Caballero. 1990. "Kinked Adjustment Costs and Aggregate Dynamics." In *NBER Macroeconomics Annual.* Ed. Olivier Blanchard and Stanley Fischer. Cambridge, Mass.: MIT Press for NBER.

Bhagwati, Jagdish, and Vivek Dehejia. 1993. "Implications of Trade Theory for Wages of the Unskilled." Paper presented at the American Enterpise Institute, Washington, D.C., September 10.

Bikhchandani, Sushil, David Hirschleifer, and Ivo Welch. 1992. "A Theory of Fads, Fashion, Custom, and Cultural Change as Informational Cascades." *Journal of Political Economy* 100: 992–1026.

Birch, David L. 1979. *The Job Generation Process.* Cambridge, Mass.: MIT Program on Neighborhood and Regional Change.

———. 1987. *Job Creation in America: How Our Smallest Companies Put the Most People to Work.* New York: Free Press.

Birch, David, and Susan MacCracken. 1983. "The Small Business Share of Job Creation: Lessons Learned from the Use of a Longitudinal File." Cambridge, Mass.: MIT Program on Neighborhood and Regional Change. Unpublished report.

Birley, Susan. 1984. "Finding the New Firm." *Proceedings of the Academy of Management Meetings* 47:64–68.

Black, Fischer. 1982. "General Equilibrium and Business Cycles." *NBER Working Paper* no. 920. Repr. in Fischer Black, *Business Cycles and Equilibrium.* New York: Basil Blackwell.

Blackburn, M. L., D. E. Bloom, and R. B. Freeman. 1990. "The Declining Economic Position of Less-Skilled American Males." In *A Future of Lousy Jobs?* Ed. G. Burtless. Washington, D.C.: Brookings Institution.

Blakeley, Ann. 1994. Testimony before the Senate Finance Committee, March 17. *Federal Document Clearing House Congressional Testimony.* Washington, D.C.: U.S. Government Printing Office.

Blanchard, Olivier. 1993. "Consumption and the Recession of 1990–1991." *AEA Papers and Proceedings* 83, no. 2: 270–74.

Blanchard, Olivier, and Peter Diamond. 1989. "The Beveridge Curve." *Brookings Papers on Economic Activity* (1989:1): 1–60. Washington, D.C.: Brookings Institution.

———. 1990. "The Cyclical Behavior of Gross Flows of Workers in the U.S." *Brookings Papers on Economic Activity* (1990:2): 85–155. Washington, D.C.: Brookings Institution.

Blanchflower, David G., and Simon Burgess. 1993. "Job Creation and Job Destruction in Britain: 1980–1990." Working paper.

Boeri, Tito. 1994. "Is Job Turnover Countercyclical?" Paris Organization for Economic Cooperation and Development.

Boeri, Tito, and Ulrich Cramer. 1992. "Employment Growth, Incumbents and Entrants: Evidence from Germany." *International Journal of Industrial Organization* 10, no. 4: 545–65.

Borland, Jeff. 1994. "Job Creation and Destruction in Australia." University of Melbourne (March). Working paper.

Borland, Jeff, and Richard Home. 1994. "Establishment-Level Employment in Manufacturing Industry: Is Small Really Beautiful?" *Australian Bulletin of Labor* 20121: 110–28 (June 1994).

Bound, John, and George Johnson. 1992. "Changes in the Structure of Wages During the 1980s: An Evaluation of Alternative Explanations." *American Economic Review* 82, no. 3: 371–92.

Bradsher, Keith. 1994. "U.S. to Aid Industry in Computer Battle with the Japanese." *New York Times,* April 27, A1.

Brainard, S. Lael, and David M. Cutler. 1993. "Sectoral Shifts and Cyclical Unemployment Reconsidered." *Quarterly Journal of Economics* 108, no. 1: 219–43.

Bresnahan, Timothy F., and Valerie A. Ramey. 1993. "Segment Shifts and Capacity Utilization in the U.S. Automobile Industry." *University of California, San Diego, Discussion Paper* 93-08 (February).

Broersma, Lourens, and Pieter Gautier. 1995. "Job Creation and Destruction in the Netherlands." Tinbergen Institute Discussion Paper 95-16. Free University of Amsterdam.

Bronars, Stephen. 1990. "Employment and Hours Variation over the Business Cycle." Washington, D.C.: Bureau of Labor Statistics. Working paper.

Brock, William A., and David S. Evans. 1986. *The Economics of Small Business: Their Role and Regulation in the U.S. Economy.* New York: Holmes and Meier.

Brown, Charles, Judith Connor, Steven Heeringa, and John Jackson. 1990. "Studying (Small) Businesses with the Michigan Employment Security Commission Longitudinal Data Base." *Small Business Economics* 2, no. 4: 261–77.

Brown, Charles, James Hamilton, and James Medoff. 1990. *Employers Large and Small.* Cambridge, Mass.: Harvard University Press.

Brown, Charles, and James Medoff. 1989. "The Employer Size Wage Effect." *Journal of Political Economy* 97, no. 5: 1027–59.

Burda, Michael, and Charles Wyplosz. 1994. "Gross Worker and Job Flows in Europe." *European Economic Review* 38, no. 6: 1287–1315.

Bureau of the Census. 1979. "The Standard Statistical Establishment Program." *Bureau of the Census Technical Paper* no. 44 (January). Report prepared by the Economic Surveys Division.

————. 1986. *Statistical Abstract of the United States.* Washington, D.C.: U.S. Department of Commerce.

————. 1987. *Enterprise Statistics.* Washington, D.C.: U.S. Department of Commerce.

————. 1988. *County Business Patterns.* Washington, D.C.: U.S. Department of Commerce.

————. 1991. *Exports from Manufacturing Establishments: 1987.* Industry Division Analytical Report Series. Washington, D.C.: U.S. Department of Commerce.

Business Wire. 1994. "NAFPD Poised to Participate in U.S. Government's National Flat Panel Initiative." (May): 3.

Caballero, Ricardo. 1992. "A Fallacy of Composition." *American Economic Review* 82, no. 5: 1279–92.

Caballero, Ricardo, Eduardo Engel, and John Haltiwanger. 1994. "Aggregate Employment Dynamics: Building from Microeconomic Evidence." Cambridge, Mass.: MIT. Unpublished.

Caballero, Ricardo, and Mohamad Hammour. 1993. "On the Timing, Pace, and Efficiency of Creative Destruction." Prepared for the workshop on Labour Market Dynamics and Aggregate Fluctuations, Paris, September 9–11.

————. 1994a. "The Cleansing Effects of Recessions." *American Economic Review* December 1994, vol. 84, no. 5, pp. 1350–1368.

————. 1994b. "On the Timing and Efficiency of Creative Destruction." *NBER Working Paper* no. 4768. Cambridge, MA: NBER.

Campbell, Jeffrey R. 1994. "Technical Change, Diffusion, and Productivity." Evanston, Ill.: Northwestern University. Working paper.

Caplin, Andrew, and John Leahy. 1993a. "Mass Layoffs and Unemployment." Columbia University (December).

Caplin, Andrew, and John Leahy. 1993b. "Sectoral Shocks, Learning, and Aggregate Fluctuations." *Review of Economic Studies 60:* 777–94.

Caplin, Andrew, and John Leahy. 1993c. "Business as Usual, Market Crashes, and Wisdom after the Fact." *American Economic Review* June 1994, vol. 84, no. 3, pp. 548–565.

Carrington, William J. 1993. "Wage Losses for Displaced Workers." *Journal of Human Resources* 28, no. 3: 435–62.

Chamley, Christophe, and Douglas Gale. 1994. "Information Revelation and Strategic Delay in a Model of Investment." *Econometrica* 62, no. 5: 1065–85.

Chari, V.V., and Hugo Hopenhayn. 1991. "Vintage Human Capital, Growth, and the Diffusion of New Technology." *Journal of Political Economy* 99, no. 6: 1142–65.

Cochrane, John. 1993. "Shocks." University of Chicago. NBER Working Paper no. 4698. Cambridge, MA: NBER.

Cohen, Linda R., and Roger C. Noll. 1991. *The Technology Pork Barrel.* Washington, D.C.: Brookings Institution. With Jeffrey S. Banks, Susan A. Edelman, and William M. Pegram.

Congressional Budget Office. 1986. *Has Trade Protection Revitalized Domestic Industries?* Washington, D.C.: Congressional Budget Office.

Contini, Bruno, Andrea Gavosto, Riccardo Revelli, and Paolo Sestito. 1994. "Job Creation and Detruction in Italy." Rome: Bank of Italy. Working paper.

Contini, Bruno, and Riccardo Revelli. 1992. "Gross Flows vs. Net Flows: What Is There to Be Learned." Paper prepared for ICER Workshop on Labor Market Dynamics, Turin, September 4–5.

Cooper, Russell, and John Haltiwanger. 1993. "The Aggregate Implications of Machine Replacement: Theory and Evidence." *American Economic Review* 83, no. 3: 360–82.

Cropper, Maureen L., and Wallace E. Oates. 1992. "Environmental Economics: A Survey." *Journal of Economic Literature* 30(2), June, pp. 675–740.

Cutler, David M., and Lawrence F. Katz. 1991. "Macroeconomic Performance and the Disadvantaged." *Brookings Papers on Economic Activity* (1991:2): 1–74. Washington, D.C.: Brookings Institution.

Darby, Michael, John Haltiwanger, and Mark Plant. 1985. "Unemployment Rate Dynamics and Persistent Unemployment under Rational Expectations." *American Economic Review* 75, no. 4: 614–37.

———. 1986. "The Ins and Outs of Unemployment: The Ins Win." *NBER Working Paper* no. 1997. Cambridge, MA: NBER.

Davis, Steven J. 1985. "Allocative Disturbances, Aggregate Disturbance, and Unemployment Fluctuations." Ph.D. thesis, Brown University.

———. 1987. "Fluctuations in the Pace of Labor Reallocation." *Carnegie-Rochester Conference Series on Public Policy* 27: 335–402.

———. 1990. "Size Distribution Statistics from County Business Patterns Data." University of Chicago. Processed.

———. 1992. "Cross-Country Patterns of Change in Relative Wages." *NBER Macroeconomics Annual* 5: 239–92.

————. 1993. "The Quality Distribution of Jobs in Search Equilibrium." Processed. Working paper.

Davis, Steven J., and John Haltiwanger. 1990. "Gross Job Creation and Destruction: Microeconomic Evidence and Macroeconomic Implications." *NBER Macroeconomics Annual* 5: 123–68.

————. 1991. "Wage Dispersion between and within U.S. Manufacturing Plants, 1963–86." *Brookings Papers on Economic Activity: Microeconomics* 115–200.

————. 1992. "Gross Job Creation, Gross Job Destruction, and Employment Reallocation." *Quarterly Journal of Economics* 107, no. 3: 819–63.

————. 1993. "Employer Size and the Wage Structure in U.S. Manufacturing." University of Chicago. Processed.

————. 1994a. "Measuring Gross Worker and Job Flows." Prepared for the NBER/CRIW Conference on Labor Statistics Measurement Issues, Washington, D.C., December 15–16.

————. 1994b. "Driving Forces and Employment Fluctuations: New Evidence and Alternative Explanations." Processed.

Davis, Steve, John Haltiwanger, and Scott Schuh. 1990. "Published versus Sample Statistics from the ASM: Implications for the LRD." *Proceedings of the American Statistical Association, Business and Economics Statistics Section,* 52–61.

————. 1993. "Small Business and Job Creation: Dissecting the Myth and Reassessing the Facts." *NBER Working Paper* no. 4492. Cambridge, MA: NBER.

Davis, Steven J., Prakash Loungani, and Ramamohan Mahidhara. 1994. "Regional Unemployment Cycles." Unpublished paper.

Devine, Theresa, and Nicholas Kiefer. 1991. *Empirical Labor Economics: The Search Approach.* New York: Oxford University Press.

Diamond, Peter. 1981. "Mobility Costs, Frictional Unemployment, and Efficiency." *Journal of Political Economy* 89: 798–812.

Dixit, Avinash K. 1986. "Trade Policy: An Agenda for Research." In Paul Krugman, editor, *Strategic Trade Policy and New International Economics.* Cambridge, MA: MIT Press, pp. 283–304.

Dixit, Avinash K., and Robert S. Pindyck. 1994. *Investment under Uncertainty.* Princeton: Princeton University Press.

Dunne, Timothy, and Mark Roberts. 1989. "The Duration of Employment Opportunities in U.S. Manufacturing." Pennsylvania State University. Working paper.

Dunne, Timothy, Mark Roberts, and Larry Samuelson. 1989a. "The Growth and Failure of U.S. Manufacturing Plants." *Quarterly Journal of Economics* 104, no. 4: 671–98.

————. 1989b. "Plant Turnover and Gross Employment Flows in the U.S. Manufacturing Sector." *Journal of Labor Economics* 7, no. 1: 48–71.

Eberly, Janice C. 1994. "Adjustment of Consumers' Durable Stocks: Evidence from Automobile Purchases." *Journal of Political Economy* 102, no. 3: 403–36.

Ehrenberg, Ronald G., and George H. Jakubson. 1988. *Advance Notice Provisions in Plant Closing Legislation.* Kalamazoo, Mich.: W. E. Upjohn Institute for Employment Research.

Ericson, Richard, and Ariel Pakes. 1989. "An Alternative Theory of Firm and Industry Dynamics." Yale University. Working paper.

Ettner, Susan L. 1994. "Is Working Good for You? Evidence on the Endogeneity of Mental and Physical Health to Female Employment." Harvard University Medical School, Department of Health Care Policy.

Evans, David. 1987a. "Tests of Alternative Theories of Firm Growth." *Journal of Political Economy* 95, no. 4: 657–74.

———. 1987b. "The Relationship between Firm Growth, Size and Age: Estimates for 100 Manufacturing Industries." *Journal of Industrial Economics* 35, no. 4: 567–81.

Executive Office of the President, Council of Economic Advisers. 1991. "FY 1992 Economic Statistics Initiative: Improving the Quality of Economics Statistics." February 14 press release.

———. 1993. *Economic Report of the President.* Washington, D.C.: U.S. Government Printing Office.

Executive Office of the President, Office of Management and Budget. 1972. *Standard Industrial Classification Manual.* Washington, D.C.: U.S. Government Printing Office.

———. 1987. *Standard Industrial Classification Manual.* Washington, D.C.: U.S. Government Printing Office.

Ezzy, D. 1993. "Unemployment and Mental Health: A Critical Review." *Social Science Medicine* 37, no. 1: 41–52.

Farber, Henry S. 1993. "The Incidence and Costs of Job Loss: 1982–1991." Working Paper 309. Princeton: Princeton University, Industrial Relations Section.

Feldstein, Martin S. 1975. "The Importance of Temporary Layoffs: An Empirical Analysis." *Brookings Papers on Economic Activity* (1975:3): 725–44. Washington, D.C.: Brookings Institution.

Ferguson, Tim W. 1993. "Locales Still Shopping for a Corporate Catch." *Wall Street Journal,* July 6, A13.

Flamm, Kenneth. 1993. "Semiconductor Dependency and Strategic Trade Policy." *Brookings Papers on Economic Activity, Microeconomics* (1993:1), 249–333. Washington, D.C.: Brookings Institution.

Forcier, M. W. 1988. "Unemployment and Alcohol Abuse: A Review." *Journal of Occupational Medicine* 30, no. 3: 246–51.

Friedman, Milton. 1992. "Do Old Fallacies Ever Die?" *Journal of Economic Literature* 30, no. 4: 2129–32.

Gaston, Robert J. 1989. "The Scale of Informal Capital Markets." *Small Business Economics* 1, no. 3: 223–30.

Gautier, Pieter, and Lourens Broersma. 1993. "The Timing of Labor Reallocation and the Business Cycle." Amsterdam: Tinbergen Institute. Processed.

Gavosto, Andrea, and Paolo Sestito. 1993. "Turnover Costs in Italy: Some Preliminary Evidence." *Statistica* 53, no. 3: 1–23.

Gertler, Mark, and Simon Gilchrist. 1994. "Monetary Policy, Business Cycles, and the Behavior of Small Manufacturing Firms." *Quarterly Journal of Economics* 109, no. 2: 309–40.

Gibbons, Robert, and Lawrence F. Katz. 1991. "Layoffs and Lemons." *Journal of Labor Economics* 9, no. 4: 351–80.

Gray, Wayne B. 1989. "Productivity Database." Processed.

Greenwood, Jeremy, Glenn M. MacDonald, and Guang-Jia Zhang. 1994. "The Cyclical Behavior of Job Creation and Destruction: A Sectoral Model." Institute for Empirical Macroeconomics Discussion Paper no. 88. Minneapolis: Federal Reserve Bank.

Grossman, Gene M., and Elhanan Helpman. 1991. *Innovation and Growth in the Global Economy.* Cambridge: MIT Press.

Gruber, Jonathan. 1994. "The Consumption Smoothing Benefits of Unemployment Insurance." NBER Working Paper no. 4750. Cambridge, MA: NBER.

Hall, Bronwyn. 1987. "The Relationship between Firm Size and Firm Growth in the U.S. Manufacturing Sector." *Journal of Industrial Economics* 35, no. 4: 583–606.

Hall, Robert E. 1979. "A Theory of the Natural Unemployment Rate and the Duration of Employment." *Journal of Monetary Economics* 5: 159–169.

———. (1982) "The Importance of Lifetime Jobs in the U.S. Economy." *American Economic Review* 72, no. 4: 716–24.

———. 1991. "Labor Demand, Labor Supply, and Employment Volatility." *NBER Macroeconomics Annual* 6: 17–47.

———. 1993. "Macro Theory and the Recession of 1990–1991." *AEA Papers and Proceedings* 83, no. 2: 275–79.

Hallberg, M. C. 1992. *Policy for American Agriculture: Choices and Consequences.* Ames: Iowa State University Press.

Hamermesh, Daniel S. 1987. "The Costs of Worker Displacement." *Quarterly Journal of Economics* 102, no. 1: 51–75.

———. 1989. "What Do We Know about Worker Displacement in the U.S.?" *Industrial Relations* 28, no. 1: 51–59.

Hamilton, James D. 1988. "A Neoclassical Model of Unemployment and the Business Cycle." *Journal of Political Economy* 96, no. 3: 593–617.

Hansen, Gary D., and Edward C. Prescott. 1993. "Did Technology Shocks Cause the 1990–1991 Recession?" *AEA Papers and Proceedings* 83, no. 2: 280–86.

Hansen, John A. 1992. "Innovation, Firm Size, and Firm Age." *Small Business Economics* 4, no. 1: 37–44.

Heckman, James J., Rebecca L. Roselius, and Jeffrey A. Smith. 1994. "U.S. Education and Training Policy: A Re-evaluation of the Underlying Assumptions behind the 'New Consensus.'" In *Labor Markets, Employment Policy and Job Creation.* Ed. Lewis Solmon and Alec Levenson. Boulder, Colo.: Westview Press.

Holzer, Harry. 1988. "Search Method Used by Unemployed Youth." *Journal of Labor Economics* 6: 1–20.

Hopenhayn, Hugo. 1992. "Entry, Exit, and Firm Dynamics in Long Run Equilibrium." *Econometrica* 60, no. 5: 1127–50.

Hopenhayn, Hugo, and Richard Rogerson. 1993. "Job Turnover and Policy Evaluation: A General Equilibrium Analysis." *Journal of Political Economy* 101, no. 5: 915–38.

Horvath, Michael, T. K. 1994. "Circularity and Cyclicality: Aggregate Fluctuations from Independent Sectoral Shocks." Evanston, Ill.: Northwestern University. Processed.

Hosios, Arthur J. 1994. "Unemployment and Vacancies with Sectoral Shifts." *American Economic Review* 84, no. 1: 124–44.

Houseman, Susan N. 1991. *Industrial Restructuring with Job Security: The Case of European Steel.* Cambridge, Mass.: Harvard University Press.

Howland, Marie. 1988. *Plant Closings and Worker Displacements: The Regional Issues.* Kalamazoo, Mich.: W. E. Upjohn Institute for Employment Research.

Huigen, R. D., A. J. M. Kleijweg, and G. van Leeuwen. 1991. "The Relationship between Firm Size and Firm Growth in Dutch Manufacturing Estimated on Panel Data." The Hague: Netherlands Central Bureau of Statistics.

Irwin, Douglas A., and Peter J. Klenow. 1994. "Learning-by-Doing Spillovers in the Semiconductor Industry." *Journal of Political Economy* no. 6, vol. 102, Dec. 1994, pp. 1200–27.

Jacobson, Louis S., Robert J. Lalonde, and Daniel G. Sullivan. 1993. "Earnings Losses of Displaced Workers." *American Economic Review* 83, no. 4: 685–709.

Jovanovic, Boyan. 1979. "Job Matching and the Theory of Turnover." *Journal of Political Economy* 87: 972–90.

———. 1982. "Selection and the Evolution of Industry." *Econometrica* 50, no. 3: 649–70.

Jovanovic, Boyan, and Glenn M. MacDonald. 1994. "Competitive Diffusion." *Journal of Political Economy* 102, no. 1: 24–52.

Jovanovic, Boyan, and Robert Moffitt. 1990. "An Estimate of a Sectoral Model of Labor Mobility." *Journal of Political Economy* 98, no. 4: 827–52.

Jovanovic, Boyan, and Rafael Rob. 1989. "The Growth and Diffusion of Knowledge." *Review of Economic Studies* 56: 569–82.

Judge, Clark S. 1994. "Thresholds of Pain." *Wall Street Journal,* August 10, A10.

Juhn, Chinhui. 1992. "Decline of Male Labor Market Participation: The Role of Declining Labor Market Opportunities." *Quarterly Journal of Economics* 107, no. 1: 79–121.

Juhn, Chinhui, Kevin M. Murphy, and Brooks Pierce. 1993. "Wage Inequality and the Rise in the Return to Skill." *Journal of Political Economy* 101, no. 3: 410–42.

Juhn, Chinhui, Kevin M. Murphy, and Robert H. Topel. 1991. "Why Has the Natural Rate of Unemployment Increased over Time?" *Brookings Papers on Economic Activity* (1991:2), 75–142. Washington, D.C.: Brookings Institution.

Kashyap, Anil, and Jeremy Stein, 1992. "Monetary Policy and Bank Lending." University of Chicago. NBER working paper no. 4317, Cambridge, MA: NBER.

Katz, Lawrence F., and Bruce D. Meyer. 1990. "Unemployment Insurance, Recall Expectations, and Unemployment Outcomes." *Quarterly Journal of Economics* 105, no. 4: 973–1002.

Katz, Lawrence F., and Kevin M. Murphy. 1992. "Changes in Relative Wages, 1963–1987: Supply and Demand Factors." *Quarterly Journal of Economics* 107, no. 1: 35–78.

Katz, Lawrence F., and Lawrence G. Summers. 1989. "Industry Rents: Evidence and Implications." *Brookings Papers on Economic Activity* spec. iss., 209–75. Washington, D.C.: Brookings Institution.

Kinsley, Michael. 1993. "At the Shrine of Small Business." *Washington Post,* August 8, A29.

Klette, Tor Jakob, and Astrid Mathiassen. 1994. "Job Creation, Job Destruction and Plant Turnover in Norwegian Manufacturing, 1976–86." Oslo: Statistics Norway. Working paper.

Kletzer, Lori G. 1989. "Returns to Seniority after Permanent Job Loss." *American Economic Review* 79, no. 3: 536–43.

Krueger, Alan B. 1991a. "How Computers Have Changed the Wage Structure: Evidence from Microdata, 1984–89." *NBER Working Paper* no. 3858. Cambridge, MA: NBER.

———. 1991b. "The Evolution of Unjust-Dismissal Legislation in the United States." *Industrial and Labor Relations Review* 44, no. 4: 644–60.

———. 1994. "Observations on Employment-Based Government Mandates, with Particular Reference to Health Insurance." In *Labor Markets, Employment Policy and Job Creation.* Ed. Lewis Solmon and Alec Levenson. Boulder, Colo.: Westview Press.

Krugman, Paul. 1987a. "Is Free Trade Passe?" *Journal of Economic Perspectives* 1, no. 2: 131–44.

———. 1987b. "Strategic Sectors and International Competition." In *U.S. Trade Policies in a Changing World Economy.* Ed. Robert M. Stern. Cambridge, MA: MIT Press.

———, ed. (1986) *Strategic Trade Policy and the New International Economics.* Cambridge, MA: MIT Press.

Krugman, Paul, and Alasdair Smith, eds. 1994. *Empirical Studies of Strategic Trade Policy.* Chicago: University of Chicago Press for NBER.

Kuhn, Peter, and Ian Wooton. 1991. "Immigration, International Trade, and the Labor Market." In *Immigration, Trade, and the Labor Market.* Ed. John M. Abowd and Richard B. Freeman. Chicago: University of Chicago Press.

Lagarde, S., E. Maurin, and C. Torelli. 1994. "Job Reallocation between and within Plants: Some Evidence from French Micro Data on the Period 1984–92." Paris: INSEE, Direction Statistique Démographique et Sociale. Working paper.

Lambson, Val E. 1991. "Industry Evolution with Sunk Costs and Uncertain Market Conditions." *International Journal of Industrial Organization* 9, no. 2: 171–96.

Lane, Julia, Alan Isaac, and David Stevens. 1993. "How Do Firms Treat Workers? Worker Turnover at the Firm Level." Processed. Working paper.

Lawrence, Robert Z., and Matthew J. Slaughter. 1993. "Trade and U.S. Wages: Great Sucking Sound or Small Hiccup?" Paper presented at Brookings Institution, Washington, D.C., June 11.

Lazear, Edward P. 1990. "Job Security and Unemployment." In *Advances in the Theory and Measurement of Unemployment.* Ed. Yoram Weiss and Gideon Fishelson. New York: St. Martin's Press.

Leonard, Jonathan S. 1986. "On the Size Distribution of Employment and Establishments." *NBER Working Paper* no. 1951. Cambridge, MA: NBER.

———. 1987. "In the Wrong Place at the Wrong Time: The Extent of Frictional and Structural Unemployment." In *Unemployment & the Structure of Labor Markets.* Ed. Kevin Lang and J. Leonard. New York: Basil Blackwell.

Leonard, Jonathan S., and Jeffrey S. Zax. 1993. "The Stability of Jobs in the Public Sector." Paper presented at the NBER Labor Studies Program Meeting, Cambridge, Mass.

Levy, Frank, and Richard J. Murnane. 1992. "U.S. Earnings Levels and Earnings Inequality: A Review of Recent Trends and Proposed Explanations." *Journal of Economic Literature* 30, no. 3: 1333–81.

Lilien, David. 1980. "The Cyclical Pattern of Temporary Layoffs in United States Manufacturing." *Review of Economics and Statistics* 62, no. 1: 24–31.

———. 1982. "Sectoral Shifts and Cyclical Unemployment." *Journal of Political Economy* 90, no. 4: 777–93.

Loungani, Prakash. 1986. "Oil Price Shocks and the Dispersion Hypothesis." *Review of Economics and Statistics* vol. 68(3): 536–39.

Loungani, Prakash, Mark Rush, and William Tave. 1990. "Stock Market Dispersion and Unemployment." *Journal of Monetary Economics* 25, no. 3: 367–88.

Lucas, Robert E., Jr. 1977a. "Understanding Business Cycles." *Journal of Monetary Economics* supp. ser. 5: 7–29.

———. 1977b. "On the Size Distribution of Business Firms." *Bell Journal of Economics* 9: 508–23.

Lucas, Robert E., Jr., and Edward Prescott. 1974. "Equilibrium Search and Unemployment." *Journal of Economic Theory* 7: 188–209.

Manser, Marilyn E. 1994. "Existing Labor Market Data: Current and Potential Research Uses." Bureau of Labor Statistics. Working paper.

Mansfield, Edwin. 1980. "Basic Research and Productivity Increase in Manufacturing." *American Economic Review* 70: 863–73.

Mansfield, Edwin, Mark Schwartz, and Samuel Wagner. 1981. "Imitation Costs and Patents." *Economic Journal* 91: 907–18.

Marshall, Jonathan. 1993. "Dispelling a Small Business Myth." *San Francisco Chronicle,* March 29, D1.

McGuckin, Robert, and George A. Pascoe Jr. 1988. "The Longitudinal Research Database: Status and Research Possibilities." *Survey of Current Business* 68, no. 11: 30–37.

Mincer, Jacob. 1962. "On the Job Training: Costs, Returns, and Some Implications." *Journal of Political Economy* 70, supp.: 50–79.

Mincer, Jacob, and Boyan Jovanovic. 1981. "Labor Mobility and Wages." In *Studies in Labor Markets.* Ed. Sherwin Rosen. Chicago: University of Chicago Press.

Montgomery, James. 1991. "Social Networks and Labor-Market Outcomes: Towards an Economic Analysis." *American Economic Review* 81: 1408–18.

Moore, Michael O. 1994. "Steel Protection in the 1980s: The Waning Influence of Big Steel." *NBER Working Paper* no. 4760. Cambridge, MA: NBER.

Mork, Knut A. 1989. "Oil and the Macroeconomy When Prices Go Up and Down: An Extension of Hamilton's Results." *Journal of Political Economy* 97, no. 3: 740–44.

Mortensen, Dale T. 1982. "The Matching Process as a Non-Cooperative Bargaining Game." In *The Economics of Information and Uncertainty*. Ed. J. McCall. Chicago: University of Chicago Press.

———. 1992. "The Cyclical Behavior of Job and Worker Flows." Evanston, Ill.: Northwestern University. Working paper.

Mortensen, Dale T., and Christopher A. Pissarides. 1992. "The Cyclical Behavior of Job Creation and Job Destruction." Evanston, Ill.: Northwestern University. Working paper.

———. 1994. "Job Creation and Destruction in the Theory of Unemployment." *Review of Economic Studies* 61, no. 3: 397–416.

Mortensen, Dale, and Tara Vishwanath. 1994. "Personal Contacts and Earnings: It Is Who You Know." *Labour Economics*.

Murphy, Kevin, and Robert Topel. 1987. "The Evolution of Unemployment in the United States: 1968–1985." *NBER Macroeconomics Annual*. Cambridge, MA: MIT Press.

Murphy, Kevin M., and Finis Welch. 1992. "The Structure of Wages." *Quarterly Journal of Economics* 107, no. 1: 285–326.

———. 1993. "Occupational Change and the Demand for Skill, 1940–1990." *American Economic Review* 83, no. 2: 122–26.

Murray, Alan. 1994. "The Outlook: Mom, Apple Pie and Small Business." *Wall Street Journal*, August 15, A1.

Nasbeth, Lars, and George Ray, eds. 1974. *The Diffusion of New Industrial Processes: An International Study*. Cambridge: Cambridge University Press.

New York Times. 1994a. "U.S. Outlines Subsidy Plan." April 29, D4.

———. 1994b. "This Clean Air Looks Dirty." July 8, A26. Editorial.

Nocke, Volker R. 1994. "Gross Job Creation and Gross Job Destruction: An Empirical Study with French Data." University of Bonn. Processed. Working paper.

Office of Technology Assessment. 1981. *U.S. Industrial Competitiveness: A Comparison of Steel, Electronics, and Automobiles*. Washington, D.C.: U.S. Government Printing Office.

———. 1990. *Making Things Better: Competing in Manufacturing*. Washington, D.C.: U.S. Government Printing Office.

Ogus, Jack L., and Donald F. Clark. 1971. "The Annual Survey of Manufactures: A Report on Methodology." *U.S. Bureau of the Census Technical Paper* no. 24. Washington, D.C.: U.S. Government Printing Office.

Oi, Walter. 1962. "Labor as a Quasi-Fixed Factor." *Journal of Political Economy* 70, no. 6: 538–55.

Olson, Mancur. 1982. *The Rise and Decline of Nations: Economic Growth, Stagflations, and Social Rigidities*. New Haven: Yale University Press.

Organization for Economic Co-operation and Development. 1987. *Employment Outlook* (September).

———. 1994. *Employment Outlook* (July).

Pakes, Ariel, and Richard Ericson. 1990. "Empirical Implication of Alternative Models of Firm Dynamics." Yale University. Working paper.

Pakes, Ariel, and Mark Schankerman. 1984. "The Rate of Obsolescence of Patents, Research Gestation Lags, and the Private Rate of Return to Research Resources." In *R&D, Patents, and Productivity*. Ed. Zvi Griliches. Chicago: University of Chicago Press for NBER.

Parsons, Donald O. 1986. "The Employment Relationship: Job Attachment, Work Effort, and the Nature of Contracts." In *Handbook of Labor Economics*. vol. 2. Ed. Orley C. Ashenfelter and Richard Layard. New York: North-Holland.

Pechman, Joseph. 1987. "Tax Reform: Theory & Practice." *Journal of Economic Perspectives* 1(1), Summer, p. 11–28.

Perry, George L., and Charles L. Schultze. 1993. "Was This Recession Different? Are They All Different?" *Brookings Papers on Economic Activity* (1993:1): 145–95. Washington, D.C.: Brookings Institution.

Picot, G., J. Baldwin, and R. Dupuy. 1994. "Have Small Firms Created a Disproportionate Share of New Jobs in Canada? A Reassessment of the Facts." Processed. Working paper.

Pissarides, Christopher. 1990. *Equilibrium Unemployment Theory*. Oxford: Basil Blackwell.

Platt, S. 1984. "Unemployment and Suicidal Behavior: A Review of the Literature." *Social Science Medicine 19*, no. 2: 93–115.

Podgursky, Michael, and Paul Swaim. 1987. "Job Displacement and Earnings Loss: Evidence from the Displaced Worker Survey." *Industrial and Labor Relations Review* 41, no. 1: 17–19.

Poterba, James, and Lawrence Summers. 1986. "Reporting Errors and Labor Market Dynamics." *Econometrica* 54, no. 6: 1319–38.

Prescott, Edward C., and John H. Boyd. 1986. "Dynamic Coalitions, Growth and the Firm." In *Contractual Arrangements for Intertemporal Trade*. Ed. Edward C. Prescott and Neil Wallace. Minneapolis: University of Minnesota Press.

Quah, Danny. 1992. "Galton's Fallacy and Tests of the Convergence Hypothesis." *London School of Economics Discussion Paper* EM/93/265 (June).

Redburn, Tom. 1994. "21 Enterprise Zones Created, Including 4 in New York City." *New York Times,* July 28, B4.

Regev, Haim. 1990. Unpublished tabulations from Central Statistical Bureau, of Israel.

Rhee, Yung Whee, Bruce Ross-Larson, and Garry Pursell. 1984. *Korea's Competitive Edge: Managing the Entry into World Markets*. Baltimore: Johns Hopkins University Press for the World Bank.

Richards, Evelyn. 1991. "Consortia and Competitiveness: Reviews Mixed; with Sematech up for Renewal, Ventures' Success Is Debated." *Washington Post,* December 15, H1.

Roberts, Kevin, and Martin L. Weitzman. 1981. "Funding Criteria for Research, Development, and Exploration Projects." *Econometrica* 49: 1261–88.

Roberts, Mark J. 1994. "Employment Flows and Producer Turnover in Three Developing Countries." In *Industrial Evolution in Developing Countries: Micro Patterns of Turnover, Productivity and Market Structure.* Ed. Mark J. Roberts and James R. Tybout. Oxford, England: Oxford University Press. Forthcoming.

Robinson, Kenneth L. 1989. *Farm and Food Policies and Their Consequences.* Englewood Cliffs, N.J.: Prentice-Hall.

Rogers, Everett M. 1983. *Diffusion of Innovations.* 3rd ed. New York: Free Press.

Rosen, Sherwin. 1972. "Learning by Experience as Joint Production." *Quarterly Journal of Economics* 86: 366–82.

Ruhm, Christopher. 1991. "Are Workers Permanently Scarred by Job Displacements?" *American Economic Review* 81, no. 1: 319–23.

Scherer, Frederic M. 1982. "Inter-Industry Technology Flows and Productivity Growth." *Review of Economics and Statistics* 64: 627–34.

Schultze, Charles. 1983. "Industrial Policy: A dissent." *The Brookings Review,* Fall, vol. 2, no. 1: pp. 3–12. Washington, D.C.: Brookings Institution.

Small Business Administration. 1983, 1987, 1988, 1991. *The State of Small Business: A Report of the President.* Washington, D.C.: U.S. Government Printing Office.

Staiger, Doug. 1990. "The Effect of Connections on the Wages and Mobility of Young Workers." MIT. Processed. Working paper.

Stout, Hilary. 1994. "In Health-Care Debate, Small Business Benefits at the Expense of Big." *Wall Street Journal,* July 21, A1.

Thurow, Lester. 1994. "Clinton's Payroll Tax." *Boston Globe,* March 1, p. 38.

Topel, Robert. 1990. "Specific Capital and Unemployment: Measuring the Costs and Consequences of Job Loss." *Carnegie-Rochester Series on Public Policy* 33: 181–214.

Troske, Kenneth. 1993. "The Dynamic Adjustment Process of Firm Entry and Exit in Manufacturing and Finance, Insurance and Real Estate." Processed. Working paper.

Tyson, Laura D'Andrea. 1992. *Who's Bashing Whom?: Trade Conflict in High-Technology Industries.* Washington, D.C.: Institute for International Economics.

U.S. Congress, General Accounting Office. Unpublished tabulations from the Government Accounting Office.

U.S. Dept. of Treasury. *Tax Reform for Simplicity, Fairness and Economic Growth.* 3 vols., 1984.

Vobejda, Barbara. 1994. "Gore Unveils Antipoverty Stategy; Three Departments Plan to Work Together to Revitalize Communities." *Washington Post,* January 1, A3.

Wagner, Joachim. 1994. "Job Duration, Firm Size, and Firm Age: Evidence from German Firm Panel Data." Prepared for the Third Global Workshop on Small Business Economics at the Tinbergen Institute, Rotterdam, August 26–27.

———. 1995. "Firm Size and Job Creation in Germany." University of Lüneburg, Institute of Economics. Working paper.

Waite, P. J., and S. J. Cole. 1980. "Selection of a New Sample Plan for the Annual Survey of Manufactures." American Statistical Association, *Proceedings of the Social Statistics Section* 307–11.

Walker, David A. 1989. "Financing the Small Firm." *Small Business Economics* 1, no. 4: 285–96.

Wayne, Leslie. 1994. "Big Firms Take Business Slated for Minorities." *New York Times,* August 11, A1.

Weiss, Andrew. 1990a. *Efficiency Wages: Models of Unemployment, Layoffs, and Wage Dispersion.* Princeton: Princeton University Press.

Weiss, Michael J. 1990b. "The High-Octane Ethanol Lobby." *New York Times,* April 1, sec. 6, pt. 2, 19.

Wessel, David, and Buck Brown. 1988. "The Hyping of Small-Firm Job Growth." *Wall Street Journal,* November 8, sec. 2, p. 1, col. 3.

Wilson, William Julius. 1987. *The Truly Disadvantaged: The Inner City, the Underclass, and Public Policy.* Chicago: University of Chicago Press.

Yashiv, Eran. 1994. "Explaining the Time Path of Unemployment: The Differential Role of Growth, Business Cycles, Search Intensity, and Labor Supply Factors." Stern School of Business Working Paper EC-94-25. New York University.

Zayas, Edison R. 1978. Testimony in *Small Business and Job Creation,* hearings before the Subcommittee on Antitrust, Consumers, and Employment of the Committee on Small Business. 95th Cong., 2nd sess., September 25 and 26. Washington, D.C.: U.S. Government Printing Office.

Zayatz, Laura, and Richard Sigman. 1993. "Feasibility Study of the Use of Chromy's Algorithm in Poisson-Sample Selection for the Annual Survey of Manufactures." In Bureau of the Census, *ESMD Report Series ESMD-9305* (August).

Index